From
HEGEL
to
MADONNA

SUNY Series in Postmodern Culture
Joseph Natoli, Editor

From
HEGEL
to
MADONNA
—————————— *Towards a General Economy*
of "Commodity Fetishism"

Robert Miklitsch

State University of New York Press

Cover art, "Time for Bed," is reproduced by permission of Eric Fischl.

Photograph of Andy Warhol's *100 Cans* is reproduced by permission of the Albright-Knox Art Gallery, Buffalo, New York.

Two photographs of the Rolling Stones' *Sticky Fingers* album cover are reproduced by permission of Virgin Records, Beverly Hills, California.

Photograph of Marcel Duchamp's *Fountain* is reproduced by permission of the Philadelphia Museum of Art.

Published by
State University of New York Press, Albany

For information, address the State University of New York Press, State University Plaza, Albany, NY 12246

Marketing by Fran Keneston
Production by Bernadine Dawes

Library of Congress Cataloging-in-Publication Data

Miklitsch, Robert, 1953–
    From Hegel to Madonna : towards a general economy of "commodity fetishism" / Robert Miklitsch.
        p.   cm. — (SUNY series in postmodern culture)
    Includes bibliographical references and index.
    ISBN 0-7914-3539-3 (alk. paper). — ISBN 0-7914-3540-7 (pbk. : alk. paper)
        1. Popular culture—History—20th century.   2. Body, Human—Social aspects—History—20th century.   3. Body, Human (Philosophy)
    4. Commodity fetishism.   5. Consumers' preferences—Philosophy.
    6. Dialectic.   I. Title.   II. Series.
    CB430.M55   1998
    306'.09—dc21   97-32814
                                                              CIP

1 2 3 4 5 6 7 8 9 10

Contents

Imagination

In some worlds it is always summer.

In one such world it is dusk,
and the sky is the color blue
the sea is in our dreams.

After driving from dawn to dusk
the line in the road unwinds
like a spool of white ribbon.

Eyes smoking, you feel as if
you have been driving for days
and too tired to sleep, you realize

the gas needle is almost on empty.
Everything, nothing, looks familiar
but when you close your eyes

your destination materializes
before you like a painting
you saw once as a child:

set in the middle of nowhere
a gas station leaks fluorescent light.
The attendant, a middle-aged man

whose head is bald as a baby's,
stands before three identical pumps.
Across the highway, the trees

turn from spruce-green to aqua-
marine. The man, who seems to be all
alone in the world, is not afraid

of the dark. After night falls
he will still have his lighthouse,
his Mobil sign lit like a tabernacle:

a flying horse with flames for wings.

—Robert Miklitsch

What chance has Vulcan against Roberts &
Co., Jupiter against the lightning-rod and
Hermes against the Crédit Mobilier?

—Karl Marx, *Grundrisse*

Even a nonaffirmative culture will be burdened
with mutability and necessity: dancing on the
volcano, laughter in sorrow, flirtation with
death.

—Herbert Marcuse, "The Affirmative
Character of Culture"

Credits

I am tempted to fashion a baroque allegory of the sort Walter Benjamin favored, a "fairy tale" vivid as a Technicolor dream where all the people who have played a role, however large or small, in the production of this book are the characters, each one kissed briefly back to life like Sleeping Beauty herself. Instead, I hope I will be excused if I simply mark the following debts.

At Ohio University, the English faculty—in particular, my chairs over the last six years or so, Betty Pytlik and the late John Hollow—have provided me with an amiable atmosphere within which to work, while a number of students, especially those in my cultural studies seminars, have pushed me as only students can to rethink my sometimes dogmatic positions. Thanks, in addition, to Janis Holm for being my "guardian angel" on more than one occasion, Dean McWilliams for his expertise in all things Gallic and Parisian, Joyce Barlow Dodd for sharing her knowledge of graphic design with me, Corey Andrews and David Rankin for helping me with the proofreading, and John Marsden for dutifully compiling the bibliography.

Among those who took time to comment on some part of this work at one point or another, including the various readers at SUNY Press, I will spare all of them the guilt by association that comes with being cited in this space. Thanks, however, to David Downing and James Sosnoski for an opportunity, early on, to present papers on affirmation at, respectively, the MLA and the Project for Affirmation in Critical Theory (PACT); Paul Smith for allowing me to talk about Warhol and Adorno at the annual MLG Summer Institute at Carnegie Mellon and George Mason University respectively; Diana Fuss and my fellow participants in the seminar on "The Frontiers of Psychoanalysis" at the 1995 School of Criticism and Theory for jumpstarting my thinking about, among other things, fetishism; Abdul R. JanMohamed and Donna Przybylowicz for very graciously working with me on an earlier version of that part of Part Two which appeared as "The Commodity-Body-Sign" in *Cultural Critique* (Spring 1996).

At SUNY Press, thanks to Joseph Natoli for recommending my manuscript for the Postmodern Series there; Carola Sautter for shepherding it through the editorial process; James Peltz for keeping me up to speed on its progress in the latter stages; Gordon Hartig for the scrupulous copyediting; and, last but by no means least, Bernadine Dawes for her adept assistance on the production end. Thanks as well to Nancy Basmagian at the Ohio University Press for literally working overtime to assemble the Index.

For art-reproduction permissions, thanks to Lil Gary at Virgin Records for the *Sticky Fingers* cover; Kathleen Ryan at the Philadelphia Museum of Art for the Duchamp; Daisy Stroud at my "hood" museum, the Albright-Knox Art Gallery, for the Warhol; and special thanks to Ron Warren at the Mary Boone Gallery for the Fischl.

With respect to intellectual debts (of which there are, of course, too many to name), I would like to take this opportunity to cite the most seminal and, I think, obvious influence on my work: Fredric Jameson.

As for my everyday life here in Athens, thanks to Ken and Devorah Daley for generally being an all-around fun couple and, in particular, David Lazar for not only reminding me, Mister Low, about the "high" in "high culture" but for being his usual super-witty and amusing self. More widely, I owe debts to my mother for instilling in me a love of poetry and *le mot juste*, my father for teaching me about swing (see, for a sample, Anthony Mann's *Glenn Miller Story*—a family favorite), and my brother and sisters—Cathy, Dave, Tre, Fran, and Rose—who have kept me going more than they know over the years. Special thanks to Fran X 3, artist extraordinaire, for designing the cover and laboring beyond the call of duty—as only a super sister can—on my behalf.

Finally (cause I promised to remember her when I got to this point), thanks to Teresa "Noonie" Gaudet for being her inimitable self. Play it again, Joe: "It's Different for Girls."

As for my future, back-to-the-future Siouxsie lookalike, see you as planned—rendezvouz of rendezvouz—at the stroke of midnight, in the year 2000, at the Hong Kong Garden.

List of Abbreviations

The following abbreviations are employed in the body of the text and in the notes:

ACC   = Marcuse, "Affirmative Character of Culture"
AG   = Eagleton, *Against the Grain*
AO   = Deleuze and Guattari, *Anti-Oedipus*
AP   = *Aesthetics and Politics*
B   = Morris, "Banality in Cultural Studies"
BCS   = Fiske, "British Cultural Studies and Television"
C   = Marx, *Capital*
CCA   = Haug, *Critique of Commodity Aesthetics*
CE   = Smith, *Clint Eastwood*
CP   = McGuigan, *Cultural Populism*
CPES = Baudrillard, *For a Critique of the Political Economy of the Sign*
DE   = Adorno and Horkheimer, *Dialectic of Enlightenment*
DM   = *Deconstructing Madonna*
ED   = Savage, *England's Dreaming*
F   = Freud, "Fetishism"
FC   = Adorno, "Fetish Character in Music"
G   = Marx, *Grundrisse*
GP   = Lewis, *Gender Politics*
HS   = Foucault, *History of Sexuality*
LC   = Bhabha, *Location of Culture*
LM   = Jameson, *Late Marxism*
M   = *Madonnarama*
MC   = *Madonna Connection*
MCM   = Tester, *Media, Culture, and Morality*
MCMC = Miller, *Material Culture and Mass Consumption*
MFI   = Kellner, "Madonna, Fashion, Image"
MH   = Jameson, "Marxism and Historicism"
MM   = Adorno, *Minima Moralia*
MP   = Baudrillard, *Mirror of Production*

MPM = hooks, "Madonna: Plantation Mistress or Soul Sister?"
ND   = Adorno, *Negative Dialectics*
NP   = Deleuze, *Nietzsche and Philosophy*
OW   = Spivak, *In Other Worlds*
P   = Jameson, *Postmodernism*
PDM = Habermas, *Philosophical Discourse of Modernity*
PM   = Adorno, "On Popular Music"
PP   = hooks, "Power to the Pussy"
PS   = Hegel, *Phenomenology of Spirit*
QN   = Berlant and Freeman, "Queer Nationality"
R   = Plotnitsky, *Reconfigurations*
RC   = Kaplan, *Rocking around the Clock*
RMW = Kemple, *Reading Marx Writing*
RRF = Mercer, "Reading Racial Fetishism"
SH   = Plotnitsky, *In the Shadow of Hegel*
SL   = Hegel, *Science of Logic*
SLT = Appadurai, *The Social Life of Things*
SM   = Derrida, *Specters of Marx*
TC   = Fiske, *Television Culture*
WA   = Benjamin, "Work of Art in the Age of Mechanical
       Reproduction"

Excursion

> The final trait of effective history is its affirmation of knowledge as perspective.
>
> —Michel Foucault, "Nietzsche, Genealogy, History"

> To solve the puzzle is to travel, he'd said, or something like that. The box, it seemed, was not just the map of the road, but the road itself.
>
> —Clive Barker, "Hellbound Heart"

Triptik

Genealogy—as Foucault remarks in "Nietzsche, Genealogy, History"— aims to excavate the history of metaphysical concepts (say, negation) and to accent its perspective, those passions and preferences such as affirmation that motivate it. In this sense, genealogy is not so much a matter of origin (*Ursprung*) as descent (*Herkunft*).[1] Hegel, Marx, Adorno—these discursive figures therefore represent the "isolation of different points" or scenes in the history of the logic of negation, scenic points that are also always the historiographic effect of certain figures of discourse such as substitution, displacement, and reversal—systematic reversal, as in Marx after Baudrillard.

This book assumes, then, the form of a genealogy, though it might more accurately be described—if it were not so routinely reviled as yet another instance of mass culture—as an excursion. Which is another way of saying that the working hypothesis of this text, something like a traveler's rule of thumb, has been that the *excursus* or peregrination is as important as the destination (and digression, or what Melville calls

1

"sinning," as much to the point as progression). Still, given that this particular excursion is an extended and at times difficult one (the initial section on Hegel, for example, represents something of a steep incline), the following synopsis is offered as a map of sorts or, if you will, a triptik.

* * *

The introduction, "From Adorno to the Clash," exploits the notion of dance music in order to flesh out Adorno's critique of mass culture in addition to more recent, Adorno-inspired readings of popular music (i.e., the Clash as sirens of the culture industry). In its essayistic movement, "From Adorno to the Clash" also recapitulates in a slightly different key a number of major motifs developed in the body of the text: general economics, (commodity) fetishism, the work of critical reaffirmation, and what Meaghan Morris calls "voxpop" theory.[2]

In a reversal of sorts of the first movement of the book (which rotates from Hegel to Adorno), the introduction tacks—in midcourse, as it were—from Adorno to Hegel and, in a minor echo of the movement of the introduction itself, from Adorno to Barthes, where Barthes figures not only as an alter ego of Adorno (not for nothing is the first, alphabetical entry of *The Pleasure of the Text* "affirmation")[3] but as one of the unanxious precursors of the "readerly" pleasures of voxpop theory (the "anti-hero" as the "reader of the text at the moment he takes his pleasure").[4] It will perhaps come as no surprise if I add that, true to the postmortem-like structure of the preface, "From Adorno to the Clash" is at least occasionally distinguished by that owlish aftersight which comes, as Hegel knew, with retrospection.

As for the "body" proper of the book, Part One takes up the thread of the concept of negation as it appears in Hegel's preface to the *Phenomenology* and then—in what I take to be an early, paradigmatic moment in this discursive history—Hegel's discussion of "something" in *The Science of Logic*, a moment that Adorno will later turn to in an attempt to redeem what, since Plato, the dialectic perennially eradicates: the particular.

If Marxism marks a break with Hegel (and is, as such, post-Hegelian), Adorno's negative dialectics represents Marxism in, to revise Fredric Jameson, a quintessentially late, Hegelian guise. The focus in this first section is thus primarily on *Negative Dialectics* where I read Adorno's complex, ambivalent relation to Hegelianism in terms of his characteristically hyper-Hegelian accent on negation. At the same time, in order to mark the limits of Adornian critique (and as a counter to his aporetic, tortured understanding of the dialectic), I also enlist Habermas's critique of Adorno in *The Philosophical Discourse of Modernity*. Question: What position does Adorno arrive at in *Negative Dialectics* and *Aesthetic Theory*, and if it is as "uncomfortable" a place as Habermas says it is, how can one hold it? Moreover, if one can only occupy this negative place when it is "at least minimally plausible that there is *no way out*," is there a way out (*euporia*) and, if so, is it the way back or the way forward?[5] In other words, is the way forward the way back—to the project of modernity (to, say, Hegel)—or is the way forward, *pace* Habermas, the way of postmodernity?

After Habermas, whose work represents one of the most compelling attempts to delimit the usefulness of a strictly negative dialectics (arguing as he does that negativity without any trace of affirmation leads, literally, nowhere), I turn to both *the* precursor of postmodernity and Habermas's primary philosophical antagonist, Nietzsche.

"Affirming Affirmation," the third installment of Part One, opens with Nietzsche's critique of Hegel in *Ecce Homo*, then offers a reading of what is arguably the definitive poststructuralist interpretation of Nietzsche and the concept of affirmation: Deleuze's *Nietzsche and Philosophy*. Though nothing would appear to be further from the prosaic, negative labor of Hegelianism, late or otherwise, than the Nietzschean play of "becoming active," a question nevertheless insinuates itself: Could it be that this declared difference is a phantom one, a mere hallucination of the dialectic? Put another way, does Deleuze's philosophy of denegation, diametrically opposed as it appears to be to Adorno's negative dialectics, represent the other of the *prima dialectica*, or do Adorno's and Deleuze's projects in fact mirror each other in their philosophical exorbitance?

If the answer to this last question is, as I suspect, an affirmative one, it may well be time to think the concept of affirmation outside the logic of negation (at least as it has traditionally been thought from Hegel to Adorno) and beyond as well Deleuzian affirmation (which successfully escapes the negativity of late Hegelianism only at the price of evacuating any and every trace of critique). Rather more to the point, given the cultural-economic changes wrought by global, post-Fordist capitalism, a critical-dialectical notion of affirmation must actively come to terms not only with the classical Hegelian concept of negation but the dominant concept-metaphor of the discourse of Marxism, what Guy Debord calls "our old enemy": the commodity.[6]

Since a renewed sense of affirmation must also be distinguished from, in particular, the sometimes reflexive discourse of negation associated with the Frankfurt School, Part Two begins with an examination

of the most influential attempt—at least within the Frankfurt School—
to think the problem of affirmation, Herbert Marcuse's "Affirmative
Character of Culture."

While Marcuse performs the by-now familiar negative critique of
commodity culture, his work nonetheless remains pertinent because it
broaches—in a distinctly *pre*-postmodernist vein—the problem of the
body. That is to say, Marcuse's attention to the materiality of the body
reintroduces, if only implicitly and obliquely, one of the master concepts
of the discourse of classical Marxism, the *commodity-body* (where the
commodity refers to exchange- and the body to use-value). A number
of conceptual possibilities as well as critical opportunities devolve from
this proposition. For instance, if the commodity is a body and the body
a commodity (and the history of bodies cannot therefore be disassoci-
ated from the history of fetishism and capitalism), what can a critical-
affirmative concept of "commodity fetishism" do for us?

Now, since it may not be obvious why it is crucial to rethink the
orthodox account of commodity fetishism as it intersects with the discourse of the body, in the fourth segment of Part Two, "Hard-Core
Commodity Aesthetics," I take up an especially revealing text—W. F.
Haug's Adornian analysis of the cover of The Rolling Stones' *Sticky
Fingers* (designed by none other than Andy Warhol, the irrepressible
impresario of pop art)—in order to demonstrate the limits of the Frankfurt School critique of mass culture, where mass culture is itself figured
by that most fetishistic of body-parts, the phallus. The question that
guides my reading of Haug is: Can the *Sticky Fingers* cover be reduced
to its commodity-fetishistic status and, if so, what does this negative
determination elide?

Having illustrated some of the problems with the Frankfurt School
position on consumer culture, in the fifth segment of Part Two I turn
to Marx—or, more precisely, to Marx after Baudrillard—in order to
formulate a general economy of the *commodity-body-sign* (where sign-
value is the supplement or super-signifier of use-exchange-value). The
point here is not so much to deconstruct the ostensibly restricted political economy of use-value, as in Baudrillard, as to figure a way to
produce an alternative conception of consumption as "cultural sign
labor." This is not, it is important to emphasize, yet another version of
cultural populism. Indeed, precisely because of the excesses associated
with reception and audience studies, I return towards the end of Part
Two, in "Consumption *Redux*," to Marx's programmatic remarks on
productive consumption in the *Grundrisse* and *Capital* in order to situate my affirmative reading of "commodity fetishism" within a determinate, critical context.

In the very last segment of Part Two, I return as well to the issue of production, reworking sign-value in terms of the still resourceful concept of contradiction as well as, equally or more importantly, the "real" logic of capitalism: the production of *surplus*-value. This segment on the so-called *rapports de production* serves a dual purpose: to punctuate the uncritical drift towards affirmation in contemporary cultural theory and, at the same time, to proffer a more flexible model of the economic than is offered in either classical Marxism or recent cultural studies. Moreover, since a general (political) economy of "commodity fetishism" must, as I see it, be dialectically attentive not only to production and consumption but, in addition to this conventional binary opposition, distribution and circulation, the conclusion to this segment considers the political implications of the determinate realization of sign-value, in particular what Marx calls the "total circuit of capital."

If Part Two effects a turn from the philosophical scene of negation vs. affirmation to the political-economic terrain of commodity fetishism and the related issues of consumption and commodification, Part Three turns to the work of art—or what I call the *art-commodity*—in an age of electronic reproduction.

This is, I take it, the postmodern problematic, where the issues of consumption and commodification cannot be disengaged from what Jameson calls the media-market or, from a rather more medium-delimited perspective, televisuality.

With this televisual imperative in mind, I direct my attention to an exemplary, if controversial topic, MTV and, more specifically yet, Madonna. As I am rather less interested in MTV or Madonna *per se*, though, than in the various theoretical debates that these events have provoked, it would probably be more accurate to say that the object of my analysis in Part Three is not so much MTV or even Madonna as so-called "Madonna Studies," the history of which mini-discipline I read as a symptomatic figure of the current, banal/fatal state of critical and cultural theory.

For many cultural critics on both the left *and* right, of course, Madonna Studies is the first and last word of barbarism, political barbarism for the left, cultural for the right. In other words, Madonna Studies is not so much suspect as criminal. A number of troubling questions nonetheless remain: Has a crime in fact been committed and, if so, what kind? Is Madonna an accomplice to this crime against (high) culture, or simply a sign of the times? Is every act of consumption an act of complicity, so much so that we are always already unwitting agents of what Baudrillard calls, after both Hegel and Marx, the "cunning of capital"?[7] What, ultimately, *is* the meaning of that corpus that is Madonna?

While the first segment of Part Three, "*Corpus Delicti*: The Rise of Madonna Studies," conducts an overview of the initial academic appropriation of Madonna represented by the work of, among others, John Fiske and E. Ann Kaplan, the second segment—"Madonna Overdrive"—reviews *The Madonna Connection* in order to examine the role of the (star) commodity-body-sign in the context of what I have come to think of as the second moment of Madonna Studies. The third and final segment of Part Three, "The Fatality of Madonna Studies"—which recollects Baudrillard as well as Meaghan Morris's 1988 essay, "The Banality in Cultural Studies"—maps the complicated relation not only between fatality and banality in the third moment of Madonna Studies but, more generally, between Madonna Studies and cultural studies (where cultural studies itself enjoys a complicated relation to critical theory).

On a rhetorical note, I might add that the recourse in the final segment of Part Three to the word *fatality* as opposed to, say, *fall* (as in "The Rise and Fall of Madonna Studies") is intended not simply as a polemical insistence on what Adorno calls the "preponderance of the object" (the object, like the repressed, is what returns, and "Madonna" is arguably just such a fatal object), it is also intended as an ironic reminder that any narrative or periodization of either Madonna or Madonna Studies (not to mention critical theory or cultural studies) is just that, a narrative or story, one way to think historical change. One net effect of this stress on historicity is that "The Fatality of Madonna Studies" refocuses the picture of Madonna presented in the preceding two segments even as it foregrounds the trajectory of the book itself: from Hegel to Madonna.

Of course, from the perspective of classical critical theory, the itinerary of this book from philosophy to mass-popular culture can only mean one thing: the eclipse of negation and dialectics, art and good taste—in sum, the autumn of engaged critique and the consequent, not-so-slow death of cultural politics in any meaningful sense. The evidence would appear to lie all around us like so many pulp-fiction bodies, the resurrection of affirmative culture and conspicuous consumption, bathos and banality and the ruses of Capital itself, albeit with a fatal, postsituationist twist: after Madonna, the Queen of MTV, the new "empire of the spectacle."

While this particular argument obviously speaks to a certain "obscene" strain of contemporary culture, popular-cultural phenomena are rarely, it seems to me, as simple as they appear or, for that matter, as received wisdom would have us believe. Bluntly, even if Madonna Studies were only a simulacrum of a simulacrum, Material Girl dressed up in the trendiest, state-of-the-art discourse, even this negative proposition as well as the affirmative object to which it refers would still need to be read and re-read, submitted anew to the work of the dialectic in all its detail and force, determinations and counterdeterminations.

Such, at least, is the premise of this book.

Introduction

> People want to have fun.
>
> —Theodor Adorno, "Popular Music"

> From the first it has been the theatre's business
> to entertain people, as it also has of all the
> other arts. It is this business which always
> gives it its particular dignity; it needs no other
> passport than fun. . . .
>
> —Bertolt Brecht, *A Short Organum
> for the Theatre*

From Adorno to the Clash

I want to begin this introduction by saying what this book, Madonna aside, will not be about: it will not be about "popular music." Though I admire people who can write intelligently and persuasively about the subject (no mean achievement, this), I have not endeavored to write specifically about Madonna's music for any number of reasons, not the least of which is that I decided many years ago to leave at least a couple areas of my everyday life uncolonized by academic analysis. This is, I realize, a pretty indefensible position for a cultural critic, but there it is: when I listen to pop music, I just wanna have fun—not unlike, I suspect, a lot of folks.

There is of course one real, disciplinary snag with this position, especially if, as Andrew Blake has observed, cultural studies has a "problem" with music.[1] Now, I do not think I have a problem with music (unless the above critical renunciation can be said to constitute a problem), but I will plead guilty to the specific charge of attending more to the "specular" as opposed to "sonic" aspects of the so-called Madonna

9

Phenomenon. Still, Blake's critique of cultural studies—that its problematic relation to music is a direct result of various theoretical crutches ("the historical, literary, political and psychoanalytic")[2]—seems a little wrong-headed to me, since Madonna Studies can be said to be a response, however musicologically underdeveloped, to the whole problem of popular culture understood as a secret, repressed figure of Culture itself.

Adorno's shadow looms large here. On one hand, for all his left-mandarin elitism, Adorno knew, like Brecht, that "people want to have fun"; on the other hand, "light" or popular music for Adorno was always only the dialectical truth of state monopoly capitalism.[3] In other words popular or, more generally, "entertainment music" (*Unterhaltungsmusik*) was the "unproductive" correlate of the monopolistic mode of production, which mode engenders, in turn, "fears and anxiety about unemployment, loss of income, war" (PM 310). Hence the absolute symmetry or, for Adorno, "harmony" between the consumption and production of popular music (PM 310). As he remarks in "Popular Music": "The people clamor for what they are going to get anyhow" (PM 310).

Now, the "problem" with Adorno's analysis, it seems to me, is not so much its complete, functionalist reduction of the sphere of consumption to the mode of production (though this critique is accurate enough)[4] as that, rather more particularly, just such an economistic reduction cannot hope to describe, let alone explain, the textual specificity of any given pop song—say, to offer a pointedly gendered example, Cyndi Lauper's "Girls Just Want to Have Fun" (1983).[5] If one of the problems of Adorno's argument against popular music is that it analytically reproduces, seemingly despite itself, that economic logic of abstraction or "standardization" of which it is ostensibly a critique, Blake's "musicological" critique of Madonna Studies elides the economic even as it rhetorically reinscribes it. So, in "Madonna the Musician" (1993), Blake insists that "music has been, and remains, the sonic base on which the visual superstructure is built."[6] In sum, while Adorno can only see in the pulse of popular music the "dull compulsion of economics" (Marx), Blake—his invocation of the classical Marxist trope of the base and superstructure notwithstanding—cannot "hear" the economic in the sonic.

The elision of the economic here is especially problematic inasmuch as no one, I imagine, would want to dispute that Madonna's music is intimately tied to the music industry and, more generally, transnational capitalism. (Time Warner, which is the parent company of Madonna's Maverick and which merged in 1995 with the Turner Broadcasting System, is one of the largest corporations in the media-entertainment world.) Without dismissing Blake's argument, one might argue that the real problem for popular-cultural critics is not so much the music (whether "high" or "low" as in Adorno)[7] nor, for that matter, "the" economic as finding or inventing an analytical and phenomenological language that does justice to that composite of art and commerce which is popular music.

Of course, this has arguably been *the* problem since, say, the middle 1930s when Adorno and Benjamin first began their "lover's quarrel" about the status of the "work of art in the age of technical reproduction."[8] In fact, Adorno's now notorious response to Benjamin, entitled "On the Fetish Character in Music and the Regression of Listening" (1938)—which essay was published, like Benjamin's now celebrated essay on reproducibility, in the *Zeitschrift für Sozialforschung*—appears in retrospect as a pretext of sorts for Adorno's slightly later essay on popular music as well as his *Philosophy of Modern Music* (1948), the latter of which includes a chapter on "light music."[9] But before I take up the "Fetish Character" essay, let me be clear about what is at stake in the preceding remarks on popular music.

Although there are any number of different media one could adduce in order to focus the various issues that animate this book (e.g., film, TV, MTV), popular music is especially apposite because it constitutes an especially charged instance of popular culture. Thus, with respect to the three main foci of this book (the philosophical problem of negation versus affirmation, the question of a general economy of commodity fetishism, and the cultural-political phenomenon of Madonna Studies), popular music is particularly appropriate because it's difficult—at least for most people—to be dispassionate about popular music;[10] because popular music—whatever one thinks or feels about it—has, as Adorno argues, a determinate relation to the capitalist mode of production and, a fortiori, commodity fetishism; and, most obviously perhaps, because both Madonna Studies and Madonna proper cannot be divorced from the whole question of popular music.

Moreover, popular music—as my opening epigraphs I hope indicate—invariably raises the issue of pleasure or, better yet, "fun," which raises in turn the complicated and recently much worried-over issue of the relation between production and consumption. The latter, not simply economic, issue is absolutely central to the theoretical concerns of this book since the opposition between consumption and production can be said to inform, even if only tacitly, the current antagonism between critical theory and cultural studies, where the cultural populism of Anglophone cultural studies is sometimes seen as the "optimistic" answer or retort to the Germanic pessimism of the Frankfurt School.

"Into the Groove": Dance, Distraction, Reproduction

In "The Work of Art in the Age of Mechanical Reproduction" (1936), Benjamin made the case that the "dominant" state of reception in modern culture was "distraction" (*Zerstreuung*), which he felt was not only pervasive in "all fields of art" but was "symptomatic of profound changes in apperception."[11] Although Benjamin was not entirely sanguine about the progressive potential of the new media (for example, in a letter to Adorno he argued that the emergence of "sound" would undermine the "revolutionary primacy of the silent film"),[12] he did believe not only that the technical reproducibiity of art would liberate it from "cult value" and auratic ritual but that the "decay" or "destruction of aura" would eventuate in a new, non-elitist function for art, one based on "politics" (WA 224)—on, that is to say, mass, democratic access. In the latter "political" scenario, the charactistic mode of reception would not be contemplation (as in Kant)[13] or even concentration (as in Adorno) but participation (as in Brecht); with this shift in the mode of reception, the public would not only displace the author, becoming an "expert" critic in its own collective right, but at any given moment the reader would be ready, as in the later Barthes, to "turn into a writer" (WA 232).

One can see here—writ small, as it were—the eventual turn to reception in media and cultural studies. As for critical theory, it perhaps goes without saying that Adorno (who owed rather more to Kant than to Brecht, to substantially understate the matter) did not find Benjamin's argument—in particular his theory of distraction—convincing.[14] Where distraction for Benjamin found its "true means of exercise in film," the same claim could also be made, according to Adorno, for popular music: "the apperception of the cinema in a condition of distraction is just as valid for light music."[15] There is a definite twist to Adorno's reformulation, however, since what for Benjamin was a positive or at least potentially positive phenomenon was, for Adorno, almost wholly pejorative.

Indeed, Adorno extends his rather severe critique of Benjamin by linking distraction to jazz,[16] where the latter is understood—albeit somewhat eccentrically, at least today—as popular (dance) music: "the usual commercial jazz can only carry out its function because it is not attended to except . . . as an accompaniment to dancing" (FC 288).[17] What Adorno says about light music—"it is fine for dancing but dreadful for listening" (FC 288)—is, needless to say, precisely the sort of thing that has been said about Madonna's music. Moreover, what was true for jitterbug jazz is even truer, one imagines, for Madonna's music: unlike avant-garde or "serious" music,[18] which encourages concentration, popular (dance) music almost demands to be consumed in a state of distraction,[19] the effects of which distracted listening, for Adorno, can only be "regressive."

In the "musical" context I have been developing here, it is difficult I think to underestimate the impact of the Adorno-Benjamin debate about concentration and distraction—or, more generally, elite and popular culture—on the discourse of critical media and cultural studies. The title of Andrew Goodwin's 1992 book on MTV, *Dancing in the Distraction Factory: Music Television and Popular Culture*—which echoes W. F. Haug's notion of the "distraction industry" (which itself echoes Adorno and Horkheimer)[20]—neatly sums up a number of issues played out in the above debate: MTV, dancing, popular culture, the distraction factory.

This set of terms (and it feels very much like a set) brings us back full circle to the beginning of this introduction and Adorno's position on popular music. Admittedly, the terms are not identical: where Adorno's audience was the "radio generation" (FC 312), Goodwin's is that abhorrent thing, the MTV generation; where Adorno's topic is the culture industry, Goodwin's is the post-Warhol distraction factory. This said, the terrain in both cases is mass or popular culture or, more precisely perhaps, what I prefer to think of as *mass-popular culture*. Finally, there is the issue of dancing, an especially critical one in this context not simply because of its currency in Goodwin's and Adorno's work[21] but because Madonna's music—in particular, her early music—is, first and foremost, "dance music."

If Madonna's career is inconceivable outside of that musical-industrial phenomenon known as the "dance single"—consider, for instance, "Holiday" (1983) or, to cite another one of my personal favorites, "Into the Groove" (1985)—*dance music* is central, it is clear, to the Madonna phenomenon. I mention this here because in the now extensive literature on Madonna, only Cindy Patton in her essay "Embodying Subaltern Memory" (1992)—as I demonstrate in more detail in Part Three of this book—has begun to articulate the cultural and proto-political effects of dance culture.[22]

Unlike Adorno, whose argument in the "Fetish Character" essay bears an obvious, if complex, debt to the Platonic notion of imitation ("People do not dance or listen 'from sensuality,' and sensuality is certainly not satisfied by listening, but the gestures of the sensual are imitated" [FC 292]), Patton proposes that the "subaltern" interest of Madonna-style voguing (as opposed to, say, *Saturday Night Fever*-style disco) lies precisely in its mimetic character. As she observes of the New York club scene in the late 1980s and early 1990s: "Young gay men and women were coming out through their imitation of . . . Madonna" (MC

86). That is to say, via an elaborate process of mimicry (which involved, among other things, imitating Madonna who in turn was imitating gay black and Latino drag queens who in turn were imitating . . .), gays and lesbians were effectively learning to "remember their bodies" (MC 86).

The Body in Adorno, Adorno's Body

This is, as it were, the rub, especially if one remembers that commodity fetishism (as in Marx's classical account) or reification (as in Lukács) has traditionally been thought of as a form of forgetting.[23] Similarly, for Adorno, perpetual distraction, or what he calls *deconcentration*, is *the* precondition for that fetishistic forgetting prompted by mass music—as, for instance, in sweet as opposed to hot jazz. More to the point, if Adorno recognizes what he and Horkheimer in the *Dialectic of Enlightenment* (1944) call the "importance of the body,"[24] this body is understood less as a figure of that *promesse de bonheur* or possibility of true happiness associated with serious art than with the mere pleasure (*Vergnügen*) associated with mass amusement or entertainment.[25] To say this, however, is not to claim that Adorno's understanding of the corporeal was ascetic in the conventional sense, since Adorno's asceticism was, like almost everything else in his work (and, one sometimes imagines, his life), thoroughly subjected to the prism of dialectical thinking.[26]

Indeed, Adorno's brief for asceticism as an anticapitalist practice must itself be situated in a determinate historical context. As he put it in *Minima Moralia* (1951), "ascetic ideals constitute today a more solid bulwark against the madness of the profit-economy than did the hedonistic life sixty years ago against liberal repression."[27] Hence the tactical use-value of what, in another fragment, he termed—with true dialectical relish—*barbaric asceticism* (MM 50). In this political-historical context, it is important to recall that Adorno's ascetic-barbaric prescription for "intellectual production" was issued in the immediate wake of the Second World War (Adorno's model was, ironically enough, Stravinsky's *Histoire du soldat*); moreover, this prescription was predicated on a psychosexual reading of modern culture: where the work of art is "ascetic and unashamed," the culture industry is "pornographic and prudish" (DE 140). More generally, if the work of art is characterized, as Adorno understood it to be, by sublimation, the culture industry or its synonym, the pleasure industry, is characterized by repression: what the culture industry really delivers, then, is not pleasure, as it promises, but pain or, more properly, that mix of pain-pleasure that is masochism. Accordingly, when the body is mobilized in late capitalism,[28] whether in the sphere of labor or of leisure, it always already appears for Adorno under the sign of sadomasochism.

I will return to this sadomasochistic dynamic—which receives exemplary expression in Adorno's "Fetish Character" essay—in a moment, but it is crucial to recall how sexuality and, rather more specifically, the body are constellated in Adorno. To remember this particular body is, I want to argue, to endeavor to reclaim that materiality—as in the preferred figure of this book, the commodity-*body*-sign—which has been lost or repressed in the classical conception of commodity fetishism. It is also to contest the figuration of the body in Adorno (and, more generally, in Marxism), but—and this is the crucial difference—on Adorno's own late-Marxist terms.

If the body is associated here, as it is in classical Marxism, with the concept of use-value, the answer to the riddle of commodity fetishism for Adorno is not regression (to, say, the immediacy of use-value) but supercession of the commodity-form or what, in another letter to Benjamin, he calls the "liquidation of phantasmagoria" (AP 127). However, part of the epistemological perversity of "commodity fetishism" for me, as it was for Benjamin, is that its bewitching, phantasmagoric character resists absolute dialectical supercession or liquidation.[29] The answer to the problem of commodity fetishism is therefore not liquidation or supercession, but—as Adorno himself puts it—"*more* dialectics" (AP 124).

This "more" involves, among other things but most especially, the concept of *sign-value*, without which—as my portmanteau term *commodity-body-sign* suggests—neither the postmodern body nor commodity can adequately be understood. Thus, with respect to the issue of the body, one of the working hypotheses of this book is that the body in late capitalism is always already *mediated* by the commodity or, more precisely, the commodity-sign economy.[30] Moreover, despite the naturalist equation between the body and use-value in classical Marxism, the body—at least as I understand it here—is precisely that which exceeds any strict, restricted economy of utility. Though a certain Hegelian impulse is, as I indicated above, at work in Adorno's formulation of use-value, a general-economic determination of the body is not inconsistent with another strain of his work, which shares an elective affinity with Benjamin's interest in the "liberation of things from the curse of being useful."[31] In other words, if, on one hand, Adorno himself could be positively "barbaric" on the subject of modern music (having claimed that, among other things, there was no decent popular music after the nineteenth century, Mozart's *Magic Flute* being the last great instance of the reconciliation between the higher and lower arts),[32] on the other hand, he was absolutely adamant about the conceptual limits of use-value, arguing that the mere concept does not constitute a sufficient critique of the commodity, "but only leads back to a stage prior to the division of labor" (AP 114).

As this last passage makes clear, Adorno's theory of commodity fetishism eschews, then, any simple, unmediated notion of use-value;[33] indeed, one might argue that this same complex notion of use-value is what enabled him to comprehend the historical progression of the commodity-form up to and including late Fordism. Consider, for instance, the following passage from "The Culture Industry" that, in its stress on reception and status, prestige and consumption, prefigures both Bourdieu and Baudrillard: "What might be called use-value in the *reception* of cultural commodities is replaced by exchange-value. . . . The use-value of art, its mode of being, is treated as a fetish; and the fetish, the work's social rating (reinterpreted as its artistic status), becomes its use-value" (DE 158). This strikingly contemporary account of commodity fetishism also appears—in an even more suggestive, sophisticated form—in the earlier "Fetish Character" essay: "If the commodity in general combines exchange-value and use-value, then *pure use-value*. . . . must be replaced by *pure exchange-value*, which precisely in its capacity as exchange-value deceptively takes over the function of use-value" (FC 279, emphasis mine). The interest of this passage—at least from a general-economic perspective—is that Adorno is working here at the very limits of a restricted economy of commodity fetishism, a classical economy he inherits from both Marx and Lukács.

More specifically, if one way to render the limits of this restricted economics is, as I suggested earlier, to read "pure exchange-value" as *sign-value*, another related way is to *re*-conceive the body as use-value, which can be said to both proceed and succeed—if not, strictly speaking, supercede (*aufheben*)—the commodity-form. Here the body—understood, as in the "Fetish Character" essay, as exchange-value or pure use-value—is that part or image, *la part maudite*, for which there is no whole or original nor, for that matter, *telos* (unless death or, more precisely, that ultimate perversion which is the death drive, can be said to possess a *telos*).

The Body in Dance

For all his dialectical ingenuity, even genius, Adorno could not quite affirm this fantasmatic body, which is, as it were, "beyond the pleasure principle."[34] Adorno knew better than most that in order to do "justice to *his* object and to *himself*" (emphasis mine), the "dialectical critic must both participate in culture and not participate."[35] However, despite this credo (which is not without a gendered dimension—hence the above italics),[36] Adorno was unable to understand the sort of "fun" (*Spaß*) that I for one associate with the *body in dance*. Indeed, it might not be too much to say (to risk a hyperbole) that Adorno's body— except in that reverse fetishization which is disgust or in that ascetic renunciation which is utopianism—was dead to the music, *dance* music.

Again, it is not so much that Adorno completely ignored the body and its pleasures—after all, even in the "Fetish Character" essay what enjoyment there is in light art is located in "immediate bodily presence" (FC 274)—as that given the "love-hate relationship with the body" that Horkheimer and he detected, like Foucault, in the discourse of the Enlightenment, he was alternately fascinated and appalled by the body moved by music, the body *in* dance. Thus, in an extraordinary passage in the "Fetish Character" essay, he submits that the dance music of jazz jitterbugs is "stylized like the ecstasies savages go into in beating the war drums," its convulsive character "reminiscent of St. Vitus' dance or the reflexes of mutilated animals" (FC 294). In fact, unlike Patton, for whom the mimesis of dance music can have a subversive, even sex-liberatory effect (I'm thinking here of her reading of Madonna's *Vogue*), mimicry for Adorno is the sign *par excellence* of what he calls the "atomistic espressivo of debased music," and debased music in turn— *dance* music—a pathetic imitation of real desire: "Dance and music copy stages of sexual excitement only to make *fun* of them" (FC 292, emphasis mine). Here, it is as though Adorno were invoking Brecht— as he in fact does throughout the "Fetish Character" essay[37]—only to invert him, since for Adorno neither dance nor music nor, say, "sport" (FC 287) is finally any "fun" at all, obeying as it does the regresssive, sadomasochistic rhythms of the monopolistic mode of production.

This, then, is the punishing and ultimately self-flagellating dynamic of the culture industry, a dynamic that rhetorically dominates the analysis of mass culture in "The Fetish Character" essay: the apparent fun of jitterbugging obscures the real sociosexual dynamic being played out (where the ecstatic masochism of the dancers is merely the flip or *B* side of the disciplinary sadism of the "system"). Having said this, I would be remiss, though, if I did not mention that Adorno's critique of popular music is not without a certain irony, and a rather fine one at that. For instance, it is not for nothing that the "Fetish Character" essay begins with an observation about the "decline of musical taste," this complaint being, according to Adorno, as old as human history itself (FC 270). Adorno's irony is also apparent in his recollection of Plato's irony in *The Republic*—as in the sheer mischievousness of the flute-player Marsyas being summarily "flayed by the sober-sided Apollo" (FC 272)—as well as in his severe, epigrammatic judgment on the Platonic utopia: "Plato's ethical-musical program bears the *character* of an Attic purge in Spartan style" (FC 272). As the last passage highlights, Adorno is by no means solely on the side of the Platonic gods or Kantian angels; indeed, given his allusion to "Pan's bewitching flute" and the "dance of the Maenads" (FC 278), Adorno is no doubt thinking of the late great Titian painting where our eyes are drawn not to Apollo or even Pan but to Marsyas, whose golden opalescent body is hung upside down like some ungodly carcass.[38]

And yet, if Adorno did not believe that the solution to the declining musical consciousness of the masses—or, more generally, to the problem of commodity fetishism—lay in the past, I also think it's safe to say that he could not bear to contemplate the stamp of the commodity-form in the popular music of his time (and, in this, could be said to have possessed something of the hypersensitivity that one associates with Nietzsche's ear). Indeed, even modern music, whether jazz or classical, Stravinsky or Schoenberg, "good bad music" or "bad good music," was an unfailing index, according to Adorno, of the decline of Western civilization (to anticipate my turn to punk at the conclusion of this introduction).[39] As for popular dance music, which for Adorno was bad "without exception,"[40] it was only redeemable—if redeemable at all—via critical negation or social change, *revolutionary* social change.

After Hegel: From Adorno to Barthes

With the last ultra-utopian negation in mind, I might observe that although the genealogy of this book begins with Hegel—with, that is to say, the dialectic and the philosophical concept of negation—the *Geist* or "spirit" that haunts the discourse of contemporary cultural studies, including and especially Madonna Studies, is not so much Hegel as Adorno, not least because Adorno, like Marx, radicalizes Hegel. Take, for instance, the following passage from the "Fetish Character" essay, which remains as acute today as when Adorno first composed it:

> The positive aspect for which the new music has been praised—vitality and technical progress, collective breadth and relation to an undefined practice, into whose concepts there has entered the supplicant self-denunciation of the intellectuals who can thereby finally end their social alienation

from the masses in order to coordinate themselves politically with contemporary mass consciousness—this positive is negative, the irruption into music of a catastrophic phase of society. The positive lies locked up solely in its negativity. (FC 297)

In the *Phenomenology of Spirit* (1807), Hegel wrote that the "true" is the "bacchanalian whirl in which no member is not intoxicated."[41]
    Unlike Hegel, whose dialectic points inexorably forward to that moment when what Adorno calls "bacchantic agitation" gives way suddenly, as in a cinematic dissolve, to a picture of the Spirit, still and sober as Apollo himself, Adorno sees things in a different, negative-dialectical light. For Adorno, the only positive—that is to say, good—thing about the new mass music is its catastrophic aspect. Alas, if it is true that negation is the key to revolutionary transformation ("The positive lies locked up solely in its negativity"), postmodern intellectuals would appear to have completely abandoned their critical posts: rather than negate the fetish character of contemporary music, they blithely *affirm* it, an especially hypocritical form of self-denunciation, according to Adorno, as it also allows them to end their historical "social alienation from the masses" (FC 297).
    While there is more than a grain of truth to Adorno's indictment here of the new, postmodern "class" of intellectuals, against this particular Adorno, the Adorno of the "Fetish Character" essay, one might juxtapose the Barthes of *Mythologies* (1957), the last essay of which, "Myth Today," concludes with its own negative-dialectical proposition: "tomorrow's positivity is entirely hidden by today's negativity."[42] That is, if Barthes could write—very much in the critical spirit of Adorno—that the measure of the mythologist's alienation was his constant oscillation between the "object and its demystification,"[43] Barthes is closer to us, or so it seems to me (and this is in part an historical claim), because the difference between "ideology and poetry" or, more properly, commodity and work of art was not nearly so absolute for him as it was for Adorno (for whom poetry, among other things, was well-nigh impossible after Auschwitz).[44]
    The difference between the Barthes of *Mythologies* and the later Adorno—say, the roughly contemporaneous Adorno of *Minima Moralia* (1951)—is reflected in the very different tone of the two books, a difference that, however slight it may appear at times (given their mutual denunciation of mass bourgeois culture), nevertheless seems like all the difference in the world. Unlike Adorno, Barthes, writing at the advent of the consumer society in postwar France, captures both the poetry

and ideology of capitalism (not, I might add, unlike the Marx of the *Manifesto*). Though Barthes can be just as judgmental as Adorno about the technology of affluence (jets, cars, and domestic gadgets),[45] he can also wax positively poetic about mass-produced objects such as the new Citroën ("I think that cars today are almost the exact equivalent of the great Gothic cathederals").[46] More exactly, if on one hand Barthes presents a "world transformed by the mendacious, interested magic of 1950s consumerism," a world of "consumer-dopes" not unlike the pod-people depicted in 1950s sci-fi classics like *Invasion of the Body Snatchers* (1956), on the other hand, Barthes's rhetoric in *Mythologies* (1957)—engaged, playful, mercurial—reflects a very real fascination with the manifold fetish-objects of the "culture industry."[47]

Compared to this relatively gay reading of consumer society (in both the Nietzschean and queer senses),[48] Adorno's attitude towards the new, emerging mass culture in *Minima Moralia* is not only wholly negative but decidedly melancholy: "The change in the relations of production themselves depends largely on what takes place in the 'sphere of consumption,' the mere reflection of production and caricature of true life" (MM 15). Indeed, in a letter that foreshadows the Barthes of *Mythologies* (whose allusions to Brando and Hepburn, *The Lost Continent* and *Julius Caesar*, echo in turn the *Cahiers du cinéma*), a perplexed Benjamin queried Adorno about his "completely negative" reading of music in the "Fetish Character" essay:[49] "Do you see any positive elements in the 'decline of sacral reconciliation?' " (AP 141).

Benjamin is clearly thinking here of that lyrical destruction of the sacred—recounted in "The Work of Art in the Age of Mechanical Reproduction"—which is the poetry of the cinema. In response, Adorno might well have pointed to the conclusion to the same "Fetish Character" essay where he praises the popular music of the Marx Brothers' films as farce (FC 297). Yet even this negative-dialectical reading of popular music as farce merely underlines, it seems to me, the "tragedy" of Adorno's cultural politics. For the fact that music as a whole has, according to Adorno, become comic in the modern, commodity-fetishistic phase confirms not so much the general listener's as Adorno's own profound social—and, as I suggested earlier, *historical*—alienation.

General Economics

Although commodity fetishism is of course one privileged figure of alienation (indeed, it is *the* master figure of alienation in Marx), this book has been motivated, at least in part, by the desire to understand it as a function not of modernity (as in Adorno) but of postmodernity or, from a more political-economic perspective, post-Fordism. In other words, after *inter alia* the fall of communism (a topic I will take up in more detail below), it is I think imperative at this point in time to begin to think "commodity fetishism" without reducing it to a unilateral determination (as in Adorno's work, which can be said to be marked by negation in the last instance) or, equally importantly, without eliminating the concept entirely (as in some recent versions of media and cultural studies). Simply put, one of the aims of this book—in addition to conceiving the body in relation to the postmodern sign and post-Fordist commodity—has been to fashion a sense of "commodity fetishism" that is at once negative and affirmative or, in a word, dialectical.

Lest there be some confusion on this score, a word about dialectics is perhaps in order here.[50] Athough the genealogy that comprises the first part of this book begins with Hegel, my use of the word *dialectic* and its synonyms in what follows is intended not so much in the strict, Hegelian sense—except occasionally and then usually in the classic, restricted sense (very roughly speaking, *position, negation, negation of the negation*)—as in the more general, Adornian or deconstructive sense (i.e., the "negative in the positive" or the "positive in the negative"). My sense of the dialectical is, then, a radically delimited one, since dialectics for me is governed neither by the logic of sublation nor, more generally, by the sort of teleological understanding of history associated with the "notion" of *Aufhebung*, whether Hegelian (i.e., the phenomenological progress of Spirit) or Marxian (i.e., communism as the historical sublation of capitalism).

The role that classical, Hegelian dialectics plays in contemporary critical theory—a reduced role that is exemplified in Adorno's work (as I demonstrate in the second section of Part One)—is, needless to say, a function of a number of political, historical, and theoretical forces. With respect to theory, for instance, one of the most powerful critiques of dialectics as well as Marxian political economy has been developed in the micro-discourse of general economics, the critique of which is reflected in the subtitle of this book—*Towards a General Economy of "Commodity Fetishism"*—where what Derrida calls the "regime of quotation marks" ("commodity fetishism") signals both a reconsideration *and* reconfiguration of the classical-Marxist reading of commodity fetishism.

Having broached the subject of general economics, however, I hasten to add that a general (political) economy of "commodity fetishism" also involves an apparent or real contradiction (or both at once, as I want to argue), since general economics can also be said to constitute the theoretical other of any political economy, including and especially a classically restricted one such as commodity fetishism. As Arkady Plotnitsky explains in *In the Shadow of Hegel* (1993): "At stake [*en jeu*] in the question of general economy is the possibility of theory—*general economy*—that relates to the irreducible, unaccountable loss in representation and meaning in any interpretive or theoretical process."[51] Yet if the genealogy of general economy presented in *In the Shadow of Hegel* begins, as in this book, with Hegel and Marx, what is really at issue or stake for Plotnitsky is not so much the possibility of a general political economy (which is also necessarily a restricted economy, since value—or at least one of its forms, surplus-value—is restricted) as a "general economy of all meaning, including the interpretive or theoretical, rather than only *political-economic* considerations" (SH 10, emphasis mine).

General economy refers, then, not only to that which cannot be reduced to political economy; it is precisely that which cannot be accounted for, or recompensed, in *any* economy. Given this logic of indeterminacy, there can be no such thing, strictly speaking, as a Marxian general economy, since Marxism, like Hegelianism, is a political economy.[52] Indeed, according to Plotnitsky, precisely because of Marxism's methodological insistence on dialectics, it is difficult to imagine it constitutively transforming itself in order to "compensate" for its historical-theoretical defeat at the hands of other competing, general-economic theories such as deconstruction (R 256).[53]

Plotnitsky, it should be obvious, is rather more pessimistic about the theoretical potential of Marxism than I am, though he does observe in *Reconfigurations* (1993), if only in passing, that some form of political economy might be "indispensable for a kind of *general* political economy that one needs as *theory*" (R 190, emphasis mine). While Plotnitsky does not pursue this particular and, I think, crucial suggestion about general economy, it's very much the sense in which I understand the term— general economy as, in other words, general (political) economy—except that I would want to argue something like the dialectical obverse of the above position: that a restricted political economy like Marxism or, rather more to the point, *post*-Marxism is indispensable for any general economy that one needs as practice, *political* practice.[54]

In this particular context, it's also worth noting that the force of the last "political" claim does not derive simply from the irreducibility of restricted economics, about which Plotnitsky himself is perfectly clear: "any general economy depends on restricted economies for its functioning" (R 15). Rather, the claim for the critical irreducibility of Marxism is that unlike, say, deconstruction, it has produced the most sustained critique of political-*economic* force (where, again, surplus-value is understood in the restricted sense as the asymmetricality of capitalist exploitation). Put another way: if, as Plotnitsky observes, a condensed way to understand economics is as the "play of forces" (*das Spiel der Kräfte* [R 14]), what is "at stake" (*en jeu*) in economics for me—as it was for Marx (as opposed to, say, Nietzsche)—is not so much the play (*jeu*) of forces as the force or violence, the violent economic force, of this *Spiel*.

The Work of Affirmation

One of the retrospective ironies of Plotnitsky's work, in particular *In the Shadow of Hegel*, is that while it tends to privilege Derrida's work and deconstruction in general at the expense of the discourse of Marxism, in the meantime Derrida himself has returned in *Specters of Marx* (1994) not only to the specter of Marx but to that specter which is communism. Europe of course is a very different place than when Marx first penned the opening lines of the *Manifesto* in 1847 (one thinks immediately of the European Economic Community), while the apocalyptic fall of communism in Eastern Europe and the subsequent, ostensibly triumphant rise of capitalism there and elsewhere (most notably, China) have made past crises of Marxism pale in comparison.[55] The title of the companion volume to the Derrida, *Whither Marxism?* (1994), is instructive in this regard, since the antique term *whither* begs to be read as a not-so-buried pun, where what has withered away since 1848 is not the capitalist state, as Marx predicted, but Marxism itself.

Clearly, what we are talking about here is a death—a symbolic death.[56] Hence the stress in Derrida's book on the "work of mourning," as if the corpus of communism, Marxism, had finally been buried along with the body of Marx himself.[57] The consequences of this "second death" would appear to be as obvious as the print on a Coca-Cola can: if Marxism is dead, then capitalism must be alive, or—to attempt to do typographic justice to its current, Frankensteinian status—ALIVE! Drawing cannily on, among other things, the Freud of "Mourning and Melancholia" (1917), Derrida registers the spectral mood of the present, "mournful" conjuncture:

> There is today in the world a dominant discourse . . . on the subject of Marx's work and thought. . . . This dominating discourse often has the manic, jubilatory, and incantatory form that Freud assigned to the so-called triumphant phase of mourning work. The incantation repeats and ritualizes itself, it holds forth and holds on to formulas, like any animistic

magic. To the rhythm of a cadenced march, it proclaims: Marx
is dead, communism is dead, very dead, and along with it its
hopes, its discourse, its theories, and its practices. It says: long
live capitalism, long live the market . . . ![58]

Now no one, I think, would deny that capitalism has entered a new,
dominant-hegemonic phase both in theory and practice (though the
reality, as the residents of the former East Germany would no doubt
testify, clearly lags well behind the rhetoric). The only question is: How
dead, exactly, is Marxism?

The great interest of Derrida's *intervention*—a much-abused
Althusserianism that, in the present context, seems somehow right (since
much of the force of *Specters of Marx* derives from its polemical-
conjunctural character)—is its obstinate evocation of the continuing
vitality of Marxism. In fact, if the "work of mourning" that currently
confronts the (post-) Marxist Left is a negative, albeit necessary, moment in its continuing quest to remain historically viable, this moment
of negation is also—true to the logic of deconstruction—the precondition for another, equally necessary moment, what I call the *work of
affirmation*. Do not misunderstand me (as Nietzsche was fond of saying): there can be no question of a simple affirmation of, among other
things, Derrida's reading of Marxism. Even an affirmative deconstruction
as bracing as Derrida's in *Specters of Marx* cannot do justice to the
decisive, determinate character of Marxism, which turns not only on
the question of political economy but, more specifically yet, the unequal
social relations that result from the forcible extraction of surplus-value.

Given this difference, *constitutive* difference, Derrida is nevertheless especially eloquent at this particular moment in the history of
Marxism on what he calls its "spirit": "There is no inheritance without
a call to responsibility. An inheritance is always the reaffirmation of a
debt, but a critical . . . *reaffirmation*" (SM 92, emphasis mine). Here
Derrida proposes what I call *critical* re-affirmation.[59] As opposed to a
simple affirmation of Marxism or the sort of double affirmation that
Deleuze develops in *Nietzsche and Philosophy* (which I discuss in the
last section of Part One), the work of critical re-affirmation understands
the still vibrant specter of Marxism to be the "*spirit* of Marxist cri-
tique" (SM 68, latter emphasis mine). This, the critical spirit or spirited
critique of Marxism is what *lives on* (unlike, say, the dead letter of
communism).

Finally, though the editors of *Whither Marxism?* contend that it is
time to "begin to address questions about the connection between the
death of communism and the fate of Marxism,"[60] it seems to me that

one would also do well to refrain from positing a too-simple, causal relation between these two terms or formations. For if it is true that communism, one historical form of Marxism, has recently been reduced, like Lenin's corpse, to an eternally embalmed state, now bereft even of its residual symbolic aura, this is by no means necessarily the "fate of Marxism." Though there may well be a certain fatality to Marxism (where, for example, Marxism is understood as that bad, exorcized object that will come back to haunt capitalism, Marxism as both conscience *and* unconscious of capitalism), Marxism is not I think fatalistic in the pejorative, Hegelian sense since at its historical-materialist best, it has always already been open to the question not only of historicity but futurity. To recollect Derrida once again (as well as to invoke, rather more subversively, the Sex Pistols): "no future, no future without Marx" (SM 93).[61]

If the fate of Marxism is not in fact the same as the fate of communism, the critical question therefore becomes: Which spirit or, more properly, spirit*s* of Marxism should we *re*-affirm?

Psycho-Marxism

This question is, needless to say, an enormous one, and as befits a collective, historical project such as Marxism, I do not presume to offer *the* answer. However, another of the working hypotheses of this book is that if Marxism is to continue to survive, to live on, as a critical discourse, it must actively continue to engage and articulate itself with other theoretical discourses. One such discourse is psychoanalysis, which enjoys, not unlike deconstruction, a unique, supplementary relation to Marxism. Indeed, according to Plotnitsky, general economy is intimately related to a "certain irreducible-structural unconscious" (R 21), so much so that there can be no question of a general economics—or, in this case, a general (political) economy—without a thoroughly radicalized "concept of the Unconscious" (SH xii). Moreover, precisely because of this relation of complementarity, the concept of "commodity fetishism" offers an especially fertile discursive constellation in which to explore the relation between Marxism and psychoanalysis, where the conceptual switch-point between the two discourses is, of course, fetishism.

Now, the concept of fetishism has attracted a lot of critical attention of late (to the point, in fact, where one might well talk about a certain fetishization of fetishism),[62] but one way, it seems to me, to get at the current discursive surplus on fetishism might be to ask: What, exactly, is the *force* of the concept of fetishism? For William Pietz, who has authored a series of influential articles on the topic, the force of the concept lies less in the fetish-object itself than in the rich history of its descriptions. More importantly, while Pietz's work effects an exhaustive excavation of the discursive history that accounts for much of the interdisciplinary interest of the concept, he also solicits the various social formations that have constituted its material conditions of possibility. Hence, in "The Problem of the Fetish, I" (1985), he observes that the term *fetishism*—unlike, say, that of the *suman*—is not only a colonialist concept-metaphor but simultaneously "speaks" and suppresses its specific, cultural conditions of possibility (i.e., the Portuguese moment of West African history).[63]

The colonialist conditions of possibility of fetishism as a discourse (where fetishism is a Western, not to say Eurocentric, discourse *par excellence*) also underscore a larger, theoretical point: that if there is in fact, *pace* Pietz, a general theory or economy of fetishism, such a general-economic theory must scrupulously attend to the constellation—at once historical and social, material and institutional—that has accreted around the concept of fetishism like so many magnetic filings. This constellation is, needless to say, an extremely varied, multidisciplinary one, ranging as it does from philosophy to art history, feminist film theory to gay/lesbian studies.[64] At the same time, invaluable as these various disciplines and micro-discourses have been for my thinking about fetishism, it should become clear in the course of this book that I am ultimately less interested in the concept of fetishism per se—as it is developed in, say, anthropology or psychoanalysis—than in the restricted discourse of commodity fetishism as well as, equally importantly, the valence or determination of this concept-metaphor in any given discourse.

Take, for instance, the very different appraisals of fetishism in the work of Homi Bhabha and Kobena Mercer. In "The Other Question" (1983), Bhabha presents an extremely provocative interpretation of fetishism, rendering it in terms of a chiasmatic structure of stereotypical discrimination where the metaphor of *dis*avowal is to the metonymy of avowal as the narcissism of imaginary identification is to its "alienated" other, aggressivity.[65] One consequence of this admittedly complicated formulation is that it allows Bhabha to avoid simplistic—that is to say, simply negative—readings of the stereotype (as, for example, "the setting up of a false image which becomes the scapegoat of discriminatory practices" [LC 81]). Indeed, as Bhabha ably demonstrates, the racist, stereotypical discourse of colonialism is rather "more ambivalent" than heretofore acknowledged, so much so that colonial discrimination can be said to be a product of both projection and introjection, "metaphoric and metonymic strategies" (LC 81).

Though Bhabha's work is clearly cognizant, as the above synopsis illustrates, of what he elsewhere calls the split, "enunciatory space" of fetishism,[66] in a later essay, "Signs Taken for Wonders" (1985), he nonetheless opposes the fetish to the hybrid, arguing that the difference between the two formations depends on when, exactly, the intervention of difference occurs: whereas the hybrid happens, as it were, after the perception of difference, fetishism occurs *prior* to this differential moment (LC 115). Bhabha's analysis here not only conceptually subordinates fetishism to hybridity, it attributes to hybridity a political effectivity that fetishism, for all its multivalence, cannot be said to possess. More to the point perhaps, while there may well be an undecidable relation between the two terms in Bhabha's work,[67] his reading of fetishism in "Signs Taken for Wonders" itself conforms to and confirms the general, stereotyptical discourse of fetishism: to wit, however ambiguous or undecidable one initially finds the "idea" of fetishism, one must eventually subordinate and suppress it (in this particular case, to the analytically superior category of hybridity). Indeed, in this "repressed" sense, it might not be too much to say that the fetish, like the *pharmakon*, is a dangerous concept.

A different—and, frankly, less snarled (though equally intricate)— assessment of fetishism can be seen in Mercer's double essay, "Reading Racial Fetishism: The Photographs of Robert Mapplethorpe."[68] Where the first part, "Imaging the Black Man's Sex" (1986), references Bhabha's "Other Question" in order to broach a determinate, negative judgment on, among other things, Mapplethorpe's black male nudes ("Mapplethorpe silently inscribes the ambivalent disavowal found in the most commonplace of utterances, 'I'm not a racist, but . . .' " [RRF 318]), the second part, "The Mirror Looks Back: Racial Fetishism Reconsidered" (1989), entails a "partial revision" and *re*-evaluation of Mapplethorpe's work: "the biographical dimension of Mapplethorpe's relations with the black models enables a revision of racial fetishism that challenges the view that fetishism necessarily indicates a conservative politics" (RRF 322).

Mercer's diptych on Mapplethorpe is, it seems to me, an extraordinary work of cultural theory, not least because it performatively stages its topic—fetishism. But given this book's critical-affirmative position on "commodity fetishism," what I find even more striking about Mercer's essay is his petition for the renewed "relevance of 'fetishism' in cultural criticism" (RRF 307). In other words, unlike Bhabha's "Signs Taken for Wonders," which sets up an external opposition between fetishism and hybridity (where, for instance, fetishism "lacks" the proto-political efficacy of hybridity), Mercer's essay displaces even as it reverses his

earlier, strictly negative determination of Mapplethorpe's racial fetishism and, in doing so, not only critically reinscribes the discourse of
fetishism but, immanent gesture that it is, effectively problematizes the
general, historical-theoretical repudiation of fetishism as such.

Though Mercer's defense of fetishism is obviously close to the
political and theoretical concerns of this book, I do not want to suggest
that it is a matter somehow of choosing between a "good" as opposed
to "bad" fetishism. In fact, given my commitment to the concept of
"commodity fetishism" as well as the practice of *critique*, it is important I think to note that the second, "positive" part of Mercer's essay
is symptomatic in its own right, reproducing another, equally stereotypical trajectory. Specifically, if in the first part of "Reading Racial Fetishism" Mercer explicitly addresses the commodity aspect of commodity
fetishism ("sexual fetishism dovetails with commodity fetishism to inflate
the valorization of print texture in art photography as much as in
fashion photography" [RRF 316]), in the second, *pro*-fetishism part,
this particular political-economic address completely drops out, as if the
turn in his essay from a negative to an affirmative conception of fetishism necessitated a turn away from the *commodity*-fetish.[69]

Rather more specifically, I want to suggest that Mercer's deconstructive position on spectatorship—that the meaning of Mapplethorpe's
work "depends on the identity that different audiences and spectators
bring to bear on the readings they produce" (RRF 325)—reflects a more
general (and, I think, problematic) paradigm-shift in Anglophone cultural studies from production to consumption or, more precisely, from
class to identity politics.[70] This shift to consumption-as-reception has in
turn been tied to the issue of populism, *cultural* populism, where "the
people" have become the symbolic place-holder for that loneliest of
moments: the economic in the last instance.

Vox Pop Theory

With respect to British cultural studies at least, the theoretical modula-
tion from an insistence on "encoding" to "decoding" has a distinct
history, which (for the sake of brevity) can be summed up in the following three catchphrases: "authoritarian populism," "economic populism,"
and "cultural populism." The first, authoritarian populism, refers to
Stuart Hall's extraordinarily prescient reading of Thatcherism as an
"inspired" and, ultimately, dominant-hegemonic discursive mix of populism and authoritarianism;[71] the second, economic populism, refers—in
the words of Frank Mort—to the "vaunted economic successes" of the

Thatcher government from 1985 to 1988;[72] and the third, cultural populism, refers—according to Jim McGuigan—to the intellectual assumption that the *"symbolic experiences and practices of ordinary people are more important analytically and politically than Culture with a capital C."*[73]

If, to attend to the last of these formations, the history of cultural populism can be said to have begun in 1979, it can also be said to have reached its apex in 1989 with the publication of Hall and Martin Jacques's *New Times: The Changing Face of Politics in the 1990s.* In an earlier essay, "The Culture Gap" (1984), Hall had laid down the consumptivist line that would eventually culminate, in 1989, in the New Times Project first announced in the pages of *Marxism Today:* "Consumer capitalism works by working markets; but it cannot entirely determine what alternative uses people make of the diversity of choices and the real advances in mass production which it also always brings."[74]

In the late 1980s, John Fiske's work on mass-popular culture pursued Hall's thesis to its logical and, for some, absurd conclusion. In fact, Fiske's reading of Madonna—which followed on the heels of a number of earlier, left-feminist responses to her work[75]—almost completely closed the culture gap between the financial and cultural and, in the process, became a locus classicus of sorts for the case against cultural populism. But the real reductio ad absurdum of cultural populism was no doubt the chapter titled "Shopping for Pleasure" in Fiske's *Reading the Popular* (1989). There, citing Pressdee and de Certeau, Fiske claimed that proletarian shopping—or, more properly, window shopping with no intention to buy—could be said to constitute an "oppositional politics" (since the sensuous consumption of images and mall space does not result in the creation of profit, as is the case with commodities).[76]

As I observe in the first segment of Part Three, Fiske's work, for all its hyperbole, is hardly unique when it comes to extolling the oppositional pleasures of consumption and "people's capitalism." It is important to remember, though, that even as Fiske's work exemplifies the limits of a one-dimensional affirmation of reception, other work in cultural studies has managed to steer a middle ground between the Scylla of consumptivism and the Charybdis of productivism. Indeed, as Michael Bérubé wittily explains in "Pop Goes the Academy" (1993), work in cultural studies generally falls into three camps:

> Camp one, reacting to a previous generation of dour mass-culture theorists and Frankfurt School killjoys, holds that the masscult audience is in some way *empowered* by consump-

tion and actively creatively "produces" the text/artifact/prac-
tice under scrutiny. Camp two, skeptical of the utility of
emphasizing consumer empowerment, replies that camp one
is fooling itself: in the United States, theorizing "agency" and
"pleasure" in consumerism tends to align you with cable
companies (more channels! more power!) and the Reagan-
era FDA, which argued that consumers were too smart, too
product-literate to need accurate product labels.[77]

If camp one is associated with cultural industrialism and camp two with
cultural populism, camp three is composed of work that "rejects the
extreme formulations of camps one and two."[78]

Bérubé references Laura Kipnis's essay on *Hustler* and Janice
Radway's work on the Book-of-the-Month Club, but another, better
example of this third camp for me—which is to say, within the local
context of this introduction (i.e., popular music)—is Tricia Rose's *Black
Noise* (1994), which persuasively argues the case for rap against, among
other critics of mass music, Adorno.[79] The problem, as Rose sees it, is
how to account for the appeal of black popular-cultural practices such
as rap that not only privilege repetition but are also unequivocally
positioned within the system of capitalist commodity production. Though
Rose recognizes that black culture does not supercede commodification
and therefore can hardly be said to exist outside, or completely in
opposition to, mass-cultural industries (BN 72), she nonetheless contends that to understand repetition simply as a function of industrial
production, as for example Adorno's work does, is to underestimate the
way in which it simultaneously represents collective resistance to the
system. Rose's conclusion, which sets her squarely within camp three
(and which marks her distance from classical Marxism), is a call for
"readings of commodification that can accommodate multiple histories
and approaches" (BN 72).

The interest of Rose's position—as opposed to, say, Fiske's—is
that it represents a genre- and medium-specific return to the issue of
production. More generally, Rose's work suggests that a return to production must involve not only an historically informed recognition of
where both critical theory and cultural studies (as well as Marxism)
have been, it must also be responsive to the conjunctural demands of
the present, post-communist moment. Two examples of recent work in
what one might call *critical cultural studies* that satisfy this double
demand with real theoretical flair are Paul Smith's *Clint Eastwood: A
Cultural Production* (1994) and Jostein Gripsrud's *Dynasty Years:
Hollywood Television and Critical Media Studies* (1995).

In the introduction to his monograph on Eastwood, Smith invokes the spirit of Adorno, insisting that the recent demonization of the Frankfurt School involves a gross misreading of its position on mass audiences and popular-cultural texts since, according to Smith, the "function of the culture industry is always dialectically bound up with audience reaction and that, even if there is no predictable transcendent moment in that dialectic, a film or any other kind of cultural text directs a certain set of possibilities towards its readers."[80] In addition to Smith's emphasis here on what he calls the "intendment" of popular-cultural texts, he also offers an especially discerning reading of the location of Eastwood's independent production company, Malpaso, within the larger, corporate Hollywood community (where the patronal, family business of Malpaso, assuming the heroic role that the small embattled homestead plays in spaghetti westerns, functions as a perfect alibi for the corporate interests of Hollywood [CE 67]). The point for me is that, while Smith is careful to elaborate the site-specific conditions of reception of Eastwood's films as well as their "cotextual histories," he is also concerned—true to his spirited invocation of Adorno—"not to forget that movies and movie stars are particular kinds of commodity produced for profit under the particular conditions of a specifiable stage in the history of U.S. capitalism" (CE xii).

As with *Clint Eastwood*, *The Dynasty Years* was written, according to its author, to counter the ritual denunciation and widespread dismissal of the Frankfurt School in Anglo-American media and cultural studies as well as in mainsteam mass communication research.[81] Gripsrud's study of *Dynasty*, however, is not simply a defense of Adorno & Co., but a vigorous critique of the "popular celebration of the sovereign audience" that has developed in media and cultural studies over the last fifteen years or so (from, roughly speaking, 1979 to 1994). Thus, while *The Dynasty Years* can certainly be said to constitute a form of reception research, the critical accent in the book is less on reception *per se* than on the relative importance of the "role of production in the process of media communication."[82]

If both *Clint Eastwood* and *The Dynasty Years* effect a return of sorts to the Frankfurt School position on mass-popular culture, neither text represents, it is important to add, a simple, uncritical reappropriation of Adorno.[83] Rather, the overt recourse to Adorno and the Frankfurt School in *Clint Eastwood* and *The Dynasty Years* constitutes a response to a felt theoretical demand for what Gripsrud calls "production studies," a demand that is especially palpable in the context of such popular-industrial modes as "generic" American cinema and television (e.g., western and prime-time soap opera respectively). Moreover, whether one is reading the complicated relation of Sergio Leone's subaltern spaghetti westerns to the American film industry in the 1960s or the controversial "cultural debate of the ages" that *Dynasty* provoked in Norway in the 1980s, the question of production today is inevitably bound up, as both Smith and Gripsrud contend, with the postmodern global economy (CE 16).

If both Smith's and Gripsrud's work can be said to supply a nuanced defense of Frankfurt School critical theory in order to produce a more balanced critique of Hollywood film and television (more balanced, that is, than what has passed as critique in recent, reception-dominated media and cultural studies), not every return to Adorno has been as felicitous. A case very much in point is Keith Tester's *Media, Culture, and Morality* (1995), which takes a very dim—make that, *grim*—view of cultural studies: "Cultural studies is a discipline that is morally cretinous because it is the bastard child of the media it claims to expose."[84] The issue of bastard children aside (which trope has, it seems to me, an unfortunate Victorian ring to it), the notion of cretinism that provides the moral ballast for Tester's criticism of cultural studies derives—according to Tester himself—from the *Dialectic of Enlightenment*: "In the light of the work of Adorno (and of course Horkheimer) it is not too unreasonable to claim that the media make us cultural cretins, utterly unable to make any sensible discriminations of value" (MCM 57).

Now, assuming (if only for the sake of argument) that everybody is a cretin because of the mass media, what, one wonders, are the general implications of this mass-cultural pathology? I quote the following passage in its entirety not simply because it constitutes the pretext for the above claim about the alleged cretinism of cultural studies, but because it underscores the moral and political stakes of Tester's *prise de position*:

> Contemporary culture is not just one in which it is impossible to provide a reasoned argument for why something is culturally bad. It is also a culture in which it is impossible to say for sure why something like ethnic cleansing in the former Yugoslavia is bad. Indeed, these two different responses of the dull acceptance of what happens might be attributable to the same factors. Moreover I wish to contend that the debates and subject matters which are conventionally associated with the discipline called cultural studies . . . are amongst the prime culprits for this state of affairs coming to pass in universities and the media's own reflections on

their own impact. Today's students and lecturers now spend all their time and energy talking abut Mills & Boon romances or Levi jeans commercials—and meanwhile rape goes on in Bosnia. (MCM 3)

The problem with Tester's critique here—aside, of course, from the fact that he attributes entirely too much influence to cultural studies (one can only wish it had this sort of cultural-political impact!)—is that it's rather difficult to trust the moral-categorical pronouncements of someone who exhibits such a crude understanding of the phenomena under review. (Tester never seems to have learned one of the core premises of Adorno's work: that a political determination of culture is possible only if, and when, "it is mediated through the *total social process.*")[85]

Tester claims, for instance, that "cultural studies is a discipline built around a narrative theme (the theme of popular culture) which is incapable of sustaining any kind of *critique* of the institutional arrangements and practices of everyday life" (MCM 9); instead, cultural studies merely reveals and revels in the "fetishization of everyday life" (MCM 76). Though Tester's argument against commodity fetishism is not without a certain satiric point,[86] all too often he's content to make ontological assertions about cultural studies (as if Smith's and Gripsrud's work, for all its interest and investment in popular culture, were not unambiguously indebted to Adornian critique). Not surprisingly, given Tester's curious claim about the popular-culture "plot" of cultural studies, he's also content to make extraordinarily sweeping generalizations about the various mass media.

The latter tendency is perhaps most evident in the chapter titled "The Culture Industry" in *Media, Culture, and Morality* where Tester applies Adorno's analysis of American jazz in the 1930s and 1940s to the British punk band the Clash in the 1970s and early 1980s. Tester concedes at the very outset that his reading of the history of punk represents an "application" of Adorno's point of view to something "about which he could know and therefore write absolutely nothing" (MCM 45).[87] However, despite this *caveat*—which would stop most cultural critics dead in their tracks—Tester proceeds, undeterred, with his Adorno-inspired critique of the Clash as a paradigmatic instance of the rise and fall of punk.[88] Forget about the fact that jazz and punk are two very different genres of popular music. Forget about the fact that we are talking here about two very different national-historical moments. What according to Adorno goes for jazz, goes, *mutatis mutandis*, for punk—at least according to the gospel of Tester.

More specifically, Tester's negative commodity-fetishist analysis
turns on a line from the Clash's "White Man in Hammersmith Palais"
(1978)—"You think it's funny, turning rebellion into money"—which,
according to Tester, reflects not only the downward spiral of punk but
the virtual "destruction of everything punk could and should have been"
(MCM 45). Tester never says what exactly punk could and should have
been (the Clash as musical Bolsheviks?), but he nevertheless maintains
that, despite the critical tenor of "White Man in Hammersmith Palais,"
the Clash's career embodies the "movement from rebellion to money"
(MCM 45). In other words, *after* 1978, the Clash fell prey, ironically
enough, to their own corporate-economic critique.[89] Invoking the scarlet
letter of Adorno and Horkheimer, Tester concludes: "what happened to
the Clash is, in fact, symptomatic of all rebellion and innovation in a
world where art is dominated by the culture industry" (MCM 43).

Tester's recourse to the word *all* here is, it seems to me, more
symptomatic than the object of his critique, since even as it reduces the
Clash's music to the absolute zero-degree of cultural-industrial reproduction, it also subjects them to a critical burden that no one musical
group should be compelled to assume. Morever, if the above scenario
about art in an era of cultural-industrial reproduction is in fact the case,
analysis of popular music should arguably *begin*—not end—with this
hypothesis. In short, Tester's "tale" about the Clash (which tends to be
dominated, as does the *Dialectic of Enlightenment*, by a Spenglerian
notion of *Verfallsgeschichte*) is a familiar, not to say hackneyed one, full
of rhetorical sound and fury but signifying virtually nothing in the way
of real insight about the Clash or punk, popular music or the music
industry as a whole. Indeed, I don't think it's too much to say that
Tester's rise-and-fall story of the Clash's career—from, as it were, clash
to cash—betrays an "out-and-out romanticization" of popular music,[90]
as if punk were not always already situated within what Marx calls the
"cash nexus."

The Clash's persona, of course, occasionally invites the sort of art-
romantic reading that Tester indulges in (as almost all rock music tends
to do, including and especially punk), but if his critique does justice to
this aspect of the Clash, what one might call the romance of revolution,
it utterly misses out on the ferocious and self-reflexive irony of their
music, an irony—not unlike Adorno's—that is ferocious precisely because it is so self-reflexive.

Remember, if you will, the mini-narrative of the song in question:
the speaker is attending an all-night reggae concert at the Hammersmith
Palais and discovers that he is the only "white man" present (a loaded
racial situation prefigured in the earlier Clash single, "White Riot"

[1977]).[91] The result is predictable enough, as Jon Savage comments in *England's Dreaming* (1991): "Here is the perennial problem of the kneejerk white approach to black culture, which holds that what is in fact pop and highly mediated, is 'authentic,' the voice of struggle" (ED 488). Savage himself passes on a number of crucial details of "White Man in Hammersmith Palais" (for example, right before Joe Strummer repeats the line "It's funny, turning rebellion into money," the irony is underscored by a very audible laugh), but unlike Tester, he *listens* to the music, and the music speaks volumes.

In fact, since I promised at the very beginning of this introduction not to talk about music, allow me to cite Savage again on the musical counterpoint of "White Man in Hammersmith Palais": "The song moves from confusion to despair as Strummer realizes that unitary rhetoric pales before the reality of state power. But like all great pop records, the music subverts the song's lyrical message: at the time Strummer realizes the limits of his well-intentioned rhetoric, the group's music is their most full, sympathetic fusion of Punk and Reggae to date, with its dub-like space, the slightly phrased hi-hat and the plaintive, melodica-style harmonica" (ED 488). Here, Savage communicates the tense, explosive contradictions of "White Man in Hammersmith Palais"—not only the contradiction between the white male desire for roots rock rebel[92] and the rather messier facts of black cultural production such as British reggae[93] but the contradiction between the message of the lyric and the subversive music, the well-intentioned rhetoric and the reality of the moment: England fast asleep and dreaming even as it's on the brink of awakening into that long and, for some, nightmarish counterrevolution that would be Thatcherism.

For Tester, of course, it is all downhill for the Clash after 1978: "to see how quickly rebellion is turned into money, listen to the Clash album of 1977 and then to *Sandinista!* of 1980" (the latter of which, according to Tester, is "impotent nostalgia," all conformity and standardization [MCM 43]).[94] Though this comparative critique is no doubt intended as a stinging critique, à la Adorno, of the logic of commodity fetishism at work even in punk, that most revolutionary of postwar, popular-musical genres, Tester's take on the Clash is itself fetishistic through and through, deaf as it is not only to the real, material contradictions of commodity culture but to history itself, which rarely conforms—even in retrospect—to our grand narratives. If in fact there is a "story of the Clash," it can only be found, or so it seems to me, in the historical pulse of their music, where the philosophical differences between negation and affirmation, art and commodity fetish, or—in the cultural-political terms of "White Man in Hammersmith Palais"—money and rebellion, are submitted to the estranging rhythms of rock and reggae, backbeat and dub.

Indeed, as Savage chronicles, the stormy contradictions that both drove and eventually undermined punk were manifest as early as 1978, when with violence in the streets and on the stage, the Sex Pistols having split up and, in the process, having "ripped the heart out of any remaining 'movement' " (ED 488), the possibilities for punk that had seemed so tangible the year before—a fusion of political *and* aesthetic radicalism—vanished overnight. Fully fledged rock stars, attended by their "customary entourage of lads, liggers and Rock'n'Roll poseurs," the Clash—on trial more than ever for "trying to bring down pigeons with air rifles" (ED 488)—nonetheless managed to capture the lightning-like volatility of the moment in their music. "No pop performer has sounded more completely alone," according to Savage, than the speaker of "White Man in Hammersmith Palais" who, at the very end of the song, as a lone guitar solos in the background, scans a hostile dance-hall for that very *commodity* that was in such short supply in 1978 (ED 488): "Oh please mister, just leave me alone: I'm only looking for fun. Looking, looking, looking. Looking for fun. . . ."

Part I

For those who do not know the Hegelian
language, we shall give the consecrating
formula—affirmation, negation, and negation
of the negation.

—Karl Marx, *The Poverty of Philosophy*

From Negation to Affirmation

Working in and for the Negative: On Hegel's Dialectic

In order to understand the role that the concept of affirmation has
played in contemporary critical theory and cultural studies, as in
Marcuse's phrase the "affirmative character of culture," it is important
to understand something of the history of the concept of negation. That
history begins with Hegel.

In the preface to the *Phenomenology of Spirit* (1807), Hegel
insists—recollecting Spinoza (*omnis determinatio negatio est*)—that understanding is philosophically insipid, a matter of mere edification, if
one does not take into account pain, patience, and seriousness: "the
work of the negative."[1] More specifically, spirit—for Hegel, the philosophical power *par excellence*—"is not . . . the positive that looks away
from the negative. . . . The spirit is this power only by looking the negative in the face and abiding with it" (PS 50).

Yet if spirit realizes its truth "only by finding itself in absolute dismemberment" (PS 50), analytic understanding—even the sort of negative analysis that characterizes Kant's *Zerrissenheit* in the three *Critiques*—is not enough. One must take another step up the ladder of knowledge, and that step is the second negative, the negation of the negation or, in terms of the trajectory of Hegel's own work, the *Logic* itself.[2]

In the *Science of Logic* (1812–16), the sequel to the *Phenomenology* and part of the announced but never completed *System of Science*, Hegel defines the difference between reason (*Vernunft*) and understanding (*Verstand*): where understanding fixes what it determines, reason is both negative *and* positive, positive "because it generates the universal and comprehends the particular therein," negative—and, consequently, *dialectical*—"because it resolves the determinations of the understanding into nothing."[3] Indeed, reason is ultimately spirit (*Geist*), since it supercedes both "positive reason" (as exemplified in Kant) as well as "merely intuitive understanding" (as in those philosophies of intuition or *Anschauung* associated with the German Romantics). This reason-as-spirit is, in turn, negativity as such.

In the introduction to the Greater *Logic* (which concerns itself not so much with consciousness, as in the *Phenomenology*, as with the "forms of consciousness"), Hegel presents his concept of negation and thereby distinguishes his understanding of the dialectic from that of Plato and, in particular, Kant:

> All that is necessary to achieve scientific progress—and it is essential to strive to gain this quite *simple* insight—is the recognition . . . that what is self-contradictory does not resolve itself into a nullity, into abstract nothingness, but essentially only into the negation of its *particular* content, in other words, that such a negation is not all and every negation but the negation of a specific subject matter which resolves itself, and consequently is a specific negation [*bestimmte Negation*] . . . . Because the result, the negation, is a *specific* negation it has a *content*. It is a fresh Concept [*Begriff*] but higher and richer than its predecessor; for it is richer by the negation or opposite of the latter, therefore contains it, but also something more, and is the unity of itself and its opposite. (SL 54)

Unlike Plato who, according to Hegel, regarded the dialectic only in its abstract negative aspect (as, that is to say, an external activity), and unlike Kant who grasped that the dialectic in its positive aspect is "nothing else but the *inner* negativity of the determinations [of reason] as their self-moving soul" (SL 56, emphasis mine) yet was nonetheless unable to advance beyond Plato's limited understanding of dialecticity as, say, a mode of refutation,[4] Hegel conceives the dialectic as the speculative comprehension (*Begreifen*) of opposites in their unity: the positive in the negative or, to echo Marx's *Poverty of Philosophy* (1847), the affirmation in the negation. Hence, in the section on "Something" in the *Logic*, Hegel argues that "negation is determinate being, not the supposedly abstract nothing but . . . as it is in itself, as affirmatively present, belonging to the sphere of determinate being" (SL 115).

Though it is obviously impossible to do justice to the scope, let alone complexity, of even a small part of the *Logic*, I have chosen the above passage not only because it looks forward to a crucial moment in Adorno's *Negative Dialectics* (to which we will turn in a moment) but, more importantly, because "something" represents, according to Hegel, "the *first negation of negation*" (SL 115). In other words, the self-movement of something re-presents, as it were, the genesis of that "scientific" logic which is the dialectic itself.

Yet, as Hegel explains in the section on "Determinate Being," negation in general "is as little an ultimate for [speculative] philosophy as reality is for its truth" (SL 113). In this sense, the negativity that drives the dialectic is as little about affirmation (being) as it is about negation (nothing); rather, the dialectic aims precisely to reconcile this contradiction and is therefore ultimately more about what Hegel calls the second negation, or the negation of the negation.

Now, inasmuch as the concept of contradiction is decisive for the Hegelian dialectic and radically differentiates it from formal logic (what for formal logic is unthinkable is, for Hegel, precisely what the dialectic *thinks*), I want to conclude these preliminary remarks on Hegel—which constitute this book's genealogical point of departure—by citing a passage from the last chapter of the *Logic* titled, appropriately enough, "The Absolute Idea":

> Now the negativity just considered [second negation] constitutes the *turning point* of the movement of the Concept. It is the *simple point of the negative relation* to self, the innermost source of all activity, of all animate and spiritual self-movement, the dialectical soul that everything true possesses and through which alone it is true; for on this subjectivity alone rests the sublating [*Aufheben*] of the opposition between Concept and reality, and the unity that is truth. The *second* negative, the negative of the negative, . . . is this sublating of the contradiction, but just as little as the contradiction is it an *act of external*

reflection, but rather the *innermost, most objective moment* of
life and spirit, through which a *subject,* a *person,* a *free being,*
exists. (SL 835–36)

To use Hegel's language in anticipation of Adorno's, the negation of the
negation—the *turning point* of the movement of the concept (*die
Bewegung des Begriffes*)—is the unity or dialectical identity of the identical and the non-identical or, in the language of this book, the affirmative
and the first negative. As Hegel himself puts it, the Concept is "*alike* the
universal that is in itself [*an sich*], *and* the negative that is for itself [*für
sich*], *and* also the third, that which is both in and for itself [*an und für
sich*], the *universal* that runs through all the moments" (SL 837–38).
Here, in the conclusion to the *Logic,* Hegel fulfills Spinoza's sublime
demand: that thinking "consider everything under the form of eter-
nity"—that is to say, "as it is in the absolute."[5]
    At the very same time (to reverse critical gears), if the Absolute
Idea designates the apotheosis of the Hegelian dialectic,[6] Hegel's theoretical absolutism could also be said to constitute a form of positivism
or "bad" universalism. More to the point of this book, if postmodernism is itself—as Fredric Jameson suggests—a belated instance
of positivism,[7] what good is an absolute affirmation that for all its
negativity rehearses the ancient subsumption of the particular under
the party of the universal?

Late Hegelianism: On Adorno's Negative Dialectics

> Through the absolute rule of negation the
> movement of thought as of history becomes,
> in accordance with the pattern of immanent
> antithesis, unambiguously, exclusively,
> implacably positive.
>
> —Theodor Adorno, *Minima Moralia*

> We remain contemporaries of the Young
> Hegelians. . . .
>
> —Jürgen Habermas, *The Philosophical
> Discourse of Modernity*

If Slavoj Žižek's work offers the most recent and compelling defense of
the Hegelian dialectic,[8] Adorno's work—for all *its* obvious indebtedness

to Hegel—represents, it seems to me, an even more searching reading of his dialectic, so much so that it may well be time to read Hegel not only *with* Lacan (as Žižek suggests) but *after* Adorno.[9]

After Hegel, then, Adorno. In the preface to *Negative Dialectics* (1966), Adorno revises Plato and Hegel as well as the whole of that philosophical tradition that has sought dialectically to "achieve something positive by means of negation," via—in particular—"the thought figure of a 'negation of negation.' "[10] In a paradoxical formulation that is characteristically Adornian, Adorno comments that the aim of *Negative Dialectics* is to free dialectics from affirmation without "reducing its determinacy" (ND xix).

I will return to the question of determinacy in a moment, but first it is imperative to stress the destructive, even deconstructive, character of Adorno's *negative*-dialectical project. From the latter, Derridian perspective, negative dialectics as the anti-system or *Unphilosophie* it is, is a wholesale assault on the philosophical valorization of affirmation or, more precisely, positivity: the "place" of that which is (*positivus*). Indeed, such is the negativity of the dialectic in Adorno that he can claim, against Hegel, that "dialectical logic is more positivistic than the positivism that outlaws it" (ND 141).

While the excessive formality of Hegel's logic—as evidenced, for example, in *The Science of Logic*—suggests a certain, stubborn faith in the positivities of "dialectical logic," this is not to say that Hegel, or at least the young Hegel, did not understand the value of negativity. As Adorno maintains with respect to his own preferred, negative-dialectical mode of analysis, the positive announced in the preface to the *Phenomenology* is to "such analysis, as it was to [Hegel], the negative" (ND 38). In other words, the "positive for the young Hegel does not think," since it is precisely thinking that causes negation, "negative motion" (ND 38). And yet, the positive does not simply disappear in the Hegelian dialectic, and this is true whether one considers its end or its origin. For if there is Being at the end of the dialectic, it is also always there at the beginning. Appropriately enough, the first triad of the *Logic* begins not with something but Being, where something signifies, for Adorno, the "cogitatively indispensable substrate of any concept, including that of Being" (ND 135).

Given Adorno's critique of Hegel's originary and teleological identitarianism, the question is: What is the relation between negative dialectics and that something which escapes the Concept (*Begriff*)? More specifically, if negative dialectics does not—despite its anti-systematic thrust—seek to posit another ontology, not even an anti-ontology, what *is* its aim?

The answers to these particular questions can, I think, be found in "Critique of Positive Negation," that section of *Negative Dialectics* where Adorno decisively articulates his break with Hegel and what one might call Hegel's *positive* dialectics. Significantly, this section is also the location of one of Adorno's fiercest attacks on the fetish of affirmation, what he calls the "fetish of the irrevocability of things in being" (ND 52):

> The nonidentical is not to be obtained directly, as something positive on its part, nor is it obtainable by a negation of the negative. This negation is not an affirmation itself, as it is to Hegel. The positive, which to his mind is due to result from the negation, has more than its name in common with the positivity he fought in his youth. To equate the negation of the negation with positivity is the quintessence of identification. . . . (ND 158)

"Something positive"—that something which can be obtained immediately—is not the same, finally, as that non-identity which Hegel found unbearable and of which the word *something* is, according to Adorno, a reminder.

Moreover, since this non-identical something cannot be obtained as a result of the law of double negation either, one can therefore say, as Adorno does, that the "anti-dialectical principle"—that formal-mathematical logic which takes "minus times minus for a plus" (ND 158)—resides where one least expects it: at the very heart of the Hegelian dialectic. Indeed, it is against just such a sublative, logical-dialectical operation that Adorno *re*-affirms the force of the negative: (in)definite or (in)determinate negation.[11] This adamant, even revolutionary, refusal to sanction things as they are—whether the indifference of an original positivity (Being) or the "happy" state of affairs realized by positive negation (from a finalist, world-historical perspective, the Absolute Idea)—this refusal constitutes, according to Adorno, "the decisive break with Hegel" (ND 160).

Still, having done this, having, that is, arrested the dialectic in order not to erase that something which resists its consequence-driven conceptuality, where does one go? What, if anything, remains?

Something, of course, remains. As Adorno aptly puts it: "What is, is more than it is" (ND 161). But however one names this "more" (Adorno, like Derrida, has many names for it—difference, non-identity, the preponderance of the object), the constellation is one "place" where it can be located.[12] To be sure, in Adorno's later work—in, to be specific, the posthumously published *Aesthetic Theory* (1970)—Adorno will argue that the work of art is the locus of determinate negation; in *Negative Dialectics*, though, the question of aesthetics is bracketed and the accent is not so much on the (art-) object as the subject. "To use the strength of the subject to break through the fallacy of constitutive subjectivity"—this, according to Adorno, is his task (ND xx).

And yet, whether the non-positivistic "place" of something is dialectically determined as the art-object or the "objective" subject (and given Adorno's own unique genius for reading: "It is when things in being are read as a text of their becoming that idealistic and materialistic dialects touch" [ND 52]), the negative "position" that both his aesthetic theory *and* critical philosophy perform would appear to be a precarious, not to say impossible, one to sustain. More importantly perhaps, even if one can sustain this high-wire act (as Adorno seemingly could, even as the German student movement of the 1960s climaxed around him), the question of politics—or, at least, the question of a less radically delimited politics—remains.[13]

To invoke Peggy Lee: Is that all there is?[14]

Now, to pose such a question is not to suggest that negative dialectics is merely a species of deconstruction, since—to counter a common enough comparison—there is a world of difference between Adorno and Derrida.[15] While it is true that Derrida has insisted as early as the skirmish with Houdebeine and Scarpetta in *Positions* (1967) on the necessity of an affirmative, positively displacing deconstruction, his "position" on this issue has remained, as it were, flexible: "Why not leave *open* . . . this question of the position, of the *positions* (taking a position: position (/negation)? position-*affirmation?*"[16] In other words, if Derridian deconstruction is not without a certain affirmation, this "position" nonetheless appears to be devoid of precisely the sort of determinacy that distinguishes Adornian dialectics—which is to say, it's ultimately not much of a position.

Unlike Derrida, Adorno—even at his bleakest, as in *Minima Moralia*—harbors a position or "place," even if it is, as Lukács said, "the Grand Hotel Abyss." In fact, with Benjamin in mind and Lukács aside, it might not be too much to say that for Adorno the only viable position in a world dominated by the violent, equivalential logic of the commodity is precisely Utopia, "no place." Hence the finale of *Minima Moralia*: "The only philosophy which can be responsibly practiced in face of despair is the attempt to contemplate things as they would present themselves from the standpoint of redemption."[17]

For all its messianic aura, however, this redemptive standpoint is not the dialectical opposite of what Jameson calls "cynical empiricism"

(LM 131), since it is not so much a utopian possibility as what one might call a *utopian impossibility* or *negativity*. In this sense, Adorno's negative dialectics is itself utopian because, unlike Hegel's or Lukács's, it will not—by definition—"come to rest in itself, as if it were total" (ND 406). At the same time (to attend to that "satiric positivism" which is for Jameson the negative other of utopian possibility), there is, as it were, no determinate affirmation for Adorno. Another, rather more specific way to put this would be to say that Adorno's negative-dialectical philosophy of positionality is itself a function, at least in part, of quite concrete cultural-political conditions of possibility.

Accordingly, in order to do justice to, say, Adorno's work before the war and his expatriation to America, it is necessary to take the following historical realities into account: the "Stalinization of the KPD in the mid 1920s," the "increasingly sclerotic and conservative behavior of the SPD and many of the trade unions" in the same period, and the "utter debacle and destruction of the Left in the wake of the Nazi seizure of power."[18] The historical irony here, of course, is that *after* the fall of the Third Reich, Adorno was—if possible—even less sanguine about the future of the Federal Republic. As a so-called "mandarin of the left" whose cultural politics were a product of the Viennese avant-garde and, in particular, the Schoenberg society, Adorno was thoroughly dismayed by the way in which postwar Germany, under the impact of administered, American-exported capitalism, was rapidly colonizing what was left of those feudal, precapitalist enclaves of Europe that had once been the source of the haute bourgeoisie as well as a certain aristocratic classicism.[19]

Yet if Germany in the 1950s was a simulacrum of America in its state-monopoly phase, America between the wars was, for Adorno, a bad Grade-B movie.[20] Which brings me to the following working hypothesis: in terms of a postmodern theory of affirmation at least, any estimation of Adorno's corpus must take into account not only the above historical contexts (Weimar Germany, émigré America, Adenauer Germany) but, as I've remarked in the introduction, his position on mass culture. It's also worth remarking, I think, that if the "culture industry" is generally a synonym for mass culture (and mass culture should therefore be distinguished from both folk and popular culture[21]), the origins of the *Kulturindustrie* were inscribed for Adorno in the prehistory of modernism—in, that is to say, *pre*-modernism or, to be more specific yet, in the Germany of the Second Reich, the paradigmatic figure of which imperial period was Wagner himself, the "author" of the *Gesamtkunstwerk*.

In fact, in his book on Wagner, Adorno comments that given the "operatic" origins of the culture industry, Wagnerian opera represents the origin of the "art work of the future" or: the "birth of film out of the spirit of music."[22] Hence the following audiovisual passage from "The Culture Industry," a passage that in retrospect looks more and more like a *locus modernus*—for Adorno:

> Television aims at a synthesis of radio and film, and is held up only because the interested parties have not yet reached agreement, but its consequences will be quite enormous and promise to intensify the impoverishment of aesthetic material so drastically, that by tomorrow the thinly veiled identity of all industrial culture products can come triumphantly into the open, derisively fulfilling the Wagnerian dream of the *Gesamtkunstwerk*—the fusion of all arts in one work. The alliance of word, image, and music is all the more perfect than in *Tristan* because the sensuous elements which all approvingly reflect the surface of social reality are in principle embodied in the same technical process, the unity of which becomes its distinctive element. This process integrates all the elements of production, from the novel (shaped with an eye to the film) to the last sound effect. It is a triumph of invested capital, whose title as absolute master is etched deep into the hearts of the dispossessed in the employment line; it is the meaningful content of every film, whatever plot the production team may have selected.[23]

Given the above dyspeptic vision of television, one can only wonder what Adorno would have made of MTV. As for Madonna, I don't think we have to wonder: he's still turning over in his grave.

And yet, administered and manipulative as the culture industry may be (as in Saturday morning children's programming, to take an especially obvious and egregious example),[24] Adorno and Horkheimer's depiction of the culture industry as enlightened mass deception has become increasingly less persuasive as postmodernism has itself become the cultural dominant of everyday life in North America. Even the late Adorno of the "Culture Industry Reconsidered"—which, irony of ironies, was first delivered on the Hessian Broadcasting System in 1963 as part of the International Radio University Program—even *this* Adorno now seems as historical as the technologism of the chronologically earlier triumvirate of Brecht, Benjamin, and Kracauer.[25] The catchwords of the late Adorno may well be status quo and conformity rather than barbarism and fascism, but the message remains the same: "the masses are not the measure but the ideology of the culture industry."[26]

However, if it is true that cultural-industrial objects are, as Adorno insists, "commodities through and through" and the masses merely an "object of calculation," how do these same products—ostensibly served, like McDonald's hamburgers, to the millions from above—accomplish their work as ideology? As Gramsci among others has taught us, ideology works precisely because it speaks to us, to our needs and fantasies; moreover, these desires, however much they are a function of mass media manipulation, are also always in some sense "objective." The last suggests that, *contra* Adorno, the culture industry in fact fulfills certain public functions, satisfying cultural needs (not all of which, it is important to note, are false or retroactive) and, more importantly yet, that the mode of reproduction—the process whereby social contradictions are reproduced as ideology—is also frequently a "field of contest and struggle."[27]

Though the last proposition has become something of a commonplace in current critical theory, it is no less true, it seems to me, for all that. That is to say, it is still important to recognize that any reading that neglects the specific conditions of reception of a given text, mass or otherwise, risks the kind of "mandarin" abstraction and knee-jerk negativity that marks Adorno's work at its worst (e.g., "Every visit to the cinema leaves me, against all my vigilance, stupider and worse" [MM 25]). The extraordinary German reception of the American miniseries "Holocaust" (1979) is a case in point,[28] since as Andreas Huyssen has shown, its effects can in no way be reduced, *pace* Adorno, to the mercenary intentions of the production team that selected it. Indeed, as I will argue in detail and at length in the second part of this book, production and consumption are never—to echo Adorno himself—identical. From a reception perspective, then, the classic cultural-industrial thesis with its stress on domination and manipulation, regression and infantilization, betrays an almost absolute negativity with respect to "mass" vis-à-vis "elite" culture, the dialectic of which cultures must be continually refigured if one is to avoid compulsively repeating their repressed history.

This said, there is also little doubt that Anglophone cultural studies and its neo-Gramscian optimism would benefit from a strong dose of Adornian pessimism. (This is Jameson's lesson, as we shall see in a moment, though Gramsci's slogan was itself eminently dialectical.) The real issue, though, is less pessimism or optimism *per se* than the relative use-value of negativity. That is to say, if on one hand the accent on negation in Adorno's work promises to retain a determinate critical utility in a new world order dominated more and more by the logic of capital, on the other hand Adorno's philosophical discourse of modernity is itself subject not only to the site-specific pressures of any given historical moment (for instance, so-called postmodern capitalism) but those cultural and institutional preconditions out of which that work emerged in the first place. The critical question concerning Adorno, then, is not so much *Is that all there is?* as *What, exactly, can his work do for us today?*

It is within just such an effective-historical context that Habermas's critique of Adorno acquires, it seems to me, its full force. It is not simply that Habermas was Adorno's assistant and thus knew his work from, as it were, the inside, nor that Habermas is the heir apparent of the Frankfurt School (a dubious honor, for some). Rather, it is that Habermas's historically specific subject-position places him in a unique, though by no means absolute, position to both respect *and* contest the question of Adorno. The critical fruits of this positionality are evident in the following passage from *The Philosophical Discourse of Modernity* (1985) where Habermas describes that hyper-reflexive, post-Hegelian position that Adorno's work repeats, compulsively, like some sort of spiritual exercise:

> [H]e makes the performative contradiction within which [the self-referential critique of reason] has moved since Nietzsche, and which he acknowledges to be unavoidable, into the organizational form of indirect communication. Identity thinking turned against itself becomes pressed into continual self-denial and allows the wound it inflicts on itself and its objects to be seen. This exercise quite rightly bears the name negative dialectics because Adorno practices determinate negation unremittingly, even though it has lost any foothold in the categorical network of Hegelian logic. . . . (PDM 185–86)

In lieu of the positivistic fetish of affirmation, Adorno offers, as we have seen, the fetish of demystification. At the same time, the only thing that remains from this unremitting operation of determinate negation, at least according to Habermas, is a residual, aesthetically certified faith in reason, *deranged* reason, one that has been "expelled from the domains of philosophy and become, literally, utopian" (PDM 186). In just this sense, the utopian destination of *Negative Dialectics* is, precisely, nowhere.[29]

This is not, of course, to suggest that Adorno's work is devoid of dialectical usefulness. In fact, for the Jameson of *Late Marxism* (1990), Adorno's introspective, antipositivist dialectic, frustrating and infuriating as it is, is just what we need today, a "joyous counter-poison and

a corrosive solvent to apply to the surface of 'what is' " (LM 249)—
where "what is" is postmodernism itself. Then again, unlike Habermas,
Jameson believes that the discourse of capital-logic so pervasive in Adorno
points to an impending Hegel revival: not the "idealist-conservative
Hegel who *preceded* the writings of Marx's first great work, the unpub-
lished commentary on *The Philosophy of Right*" but an "unfamiliar
materialist-mathematical Hegel, one who comes *after* the *Grundrisse*"
(LM 241).

But who is this unfamiliar Hegel if not the Hegel of the *Logic*?
And who is the Adorno of *Late Marxism* if not the Hegel who comes
after the Marx of the *Grundrisse*?[30]

We seem to have come viciously full circle here, since Jameson's
Adorno—who appears to be a late (young) Hegelian—looks an awful
lot like Žižek's Lacanian Hegel. And yet, it is precisely at this point—
where the specter of absolute negativity begins to rear its Medusa-head
(whether Žižek's Lacan, Jameson's Adorno or, for that matter, Derrida's
Marx)—that it is useful, or so it seems to me, to invoke the Habermasian
verdict on negative dialectics: "Today the *situation of consciousness* still
remains one brought about by the Young Hegelians when they dis-
tanced themselves from Hegel and philosophy in general" (PDM 53). In
other words, one does not have to endorse Habermas's notion of communicative rationality and everything it entails to appreciate his attempt
to *re*think and thereby to *dis*place that Hegelianism that haunts Jameson's
Adorno. Put another way, inasmuch as Habermas's critique of that
"present-open-to-the-future" which goes by the name of postmodernism
is predicated on—as the above passage indicates—a critical reading of
young Hegelianism, that same critique is, paradoxically enough,
Adornian. Indeed, Habermas's project to re-claim the claims of reason
is a persistent endeavor to answer that question which Adorno's work
poses so singularly and insistently: Can dialectical reason play any role
save that of negation?

In an interview titled "The Dialectics of Rationalization" (1981),
Habermas queries: "Is it not possible—*pace* Adorno—to explicate a
concept of communicative reason that can stand against Adorno's nega-
tivism, so that it contains what Adorno believed could only be made
visible indirectly, by implication, through continual and consistent negation?"[31] Having posed this question, though, Habermas almost immediately concedes (in an afterthought that speaks volumes) that Adorno
would no doubt have disagreed with him, since even the above formulation would have been—in the last analysis—"too affirmative." One
might therefore say (and here I go well beyond both the letter *and* spirit
of Habermas's work) that the philosophical discourse of modernity in

Adorno, precisely because of its intimate analytical relation to modernism, does not adequately explain either the cultural discourse of
postmodernism or, for that matter, the historical project of postmodernity
(the latter of which must itself be distinguished from that postmodernization associated with what—in my more polemical moments—
I prefer to think of as *late* late capitalism).

In sum, if the cultural-economic discourse of postmodernism ex-
poses the philosophical and political limits of a strictly negative, late
Hegelian project such as Adorno's, perhaps it is time to reconsider that
post-Hegelian project which Habermas refuses and which appears under the dark, mercurial sign of Nietzsche:[32] the *play* of affirmation.

Affirming Affirmation: On Nietzsche and Deleuze and Guattari

> My formula for greatness in a human being
> is *amor fati*: that one wants nothing to be
> different, not forward, not backward, not
> in all eternity. Not merely bear what is
> necessary, still less conceal it—all idealism
> is mendaciousness in the face of what is
> necessary—but love it.
>
> —Nietzsche, *Ecce Homo*

> Affirmation as object of affirmation— this is
> being. In itself and as primary affirmation, it
> is becoming. But it is being insofar as it is the
> object of another affirmation which raises
> [*élevè*] becoming to being or which extracts
> the being of becoming. This is why affirmation
> in all its power is double: affirmation is
> affirmed.
>
> —Deleuze, *Nietzsche and Philosophy*

If, as I suggested in the preceding segment, Adorno's work represents a
break with Hegel's philosophy of history, it should not be surprising—
given what one reader has called Adorno's "melancholized Hegelianism"[33]—that Nietzsche constitutes one of his principal antecedents. In
fact, one has only to recollect Adorno's determination of *Minima Moralia*
as melancholy science (*die traurige Wissenschaft*) with its ironic inversion of Nietzsche's *Gay Science* (*Die Fröhliche Wissenschaft*) to register
his influence on Adorno.

To assert this particular filiation between Adorno and Nietzsche is
not, however, to sublime the *difference* between Hegel-Nietzsche, which
is absolute. In his retrospective reevaluation of *The Birth of Tragedy*
(1872) in *Ecce Homo*, that canniest of proleptic texts, Nietzsche writes:

> Taken up with some degree of neutrality, *The Birth of Trag-*
> *edy* looks quite untimely: one would never dream that it was
> begun amid the thunder of the battle of Worth. . . . it smells
> offensively Hegelian. . . . An "idea" [*Idee*]—the antithesis of
> the Dionysian and the Apollonian—translated into the realm
> of metaphysics; history itself as the development of this "idea";
> in tragedy this antithesis is sublimated [*aufgehoben*] into a
> unity; and in this perspective things that had never before
> faced each other are suddenly juxtaposed, used to illuminate
> each other, and comprehended [*begriffen*]. . . .[34]

"It smells offensively Hegelian"—the mephitic note is characteristically
Nietzschean, as is the extended metalinguistic conceit and the sarcastic
allusion to the "birth" of the *Phenomenology* (which Hegel had completed almost fifty years before, in 1806, in Jena, while the French took
the city). One can also glimpse here, in Nietzsche's critique of Hegel,
that disruptive, iconoclastic will-to-deterritorialization which will later
inform the discourse of poststructuralism as well as the conventional
wisdom about its genesis or genealogical origin: Nietzsche not so much
as the antithesis (*Gegensatz*) as the non-dialectical Other of Hegel.

The latter convention is, of course, a rather recent invention and
is due in no small part to the work of Gilles Deleuze, in particular his
Nietzsche and Philosophy (1962). Citing Foucault, Cornel West sums
up the consequences of the Deleuze-effect for the Nietzsche-text:

> Deleuze was the first to think through the notion of differ-
> ence independent of Hegelian ideas of opposition, and that
> was the start of the radical anti-Hegelianism which has char-
> acterized French intellectual life in the last decades. This
> position [which] . . . we now associate with postmodernism
> and poststructuralism [goes] back to Deleuze's resurrection
> of Nietzsche against Hegel. Foucault, already assuming this
> Deleuzian critique, was the first important French intellec-
> tual who could *circumvent*, rather than confront, Hegel, which
> is why he says we live in a "Deleuzian age." To live in a
> Deleuzian age is to live in an anti-Hegelian age so that one
> does not have to come to terms with Lukács, Adorno or any
> other Hegelian marxists.[35]

In this post-Hegelian context, one might cite as well the preface to *Anti-Oedipus* (1972) where Foucault, reciting those principles that make the Deleuze and Guattari text a post-Salesian "guide to everyday life," issues the following non-fascist demand: "Withdraw allegiance from the old categories of the Negative (law, limit, castration, lack, lacuna), which Western thought has so long held sacred as a form of power and an access to reality."[36]

Now, if the discourse of negation cannot be laid simply at the door of Hegel (as Foucault's parenthetical makes clear), Hegel and not, say, Freud or Lacan is the manifest antagonist of *Nietzsche and Philosophy*. Thus, in "Against the Dialectic," Deleuze argues not only that Nietzsche's philosophy remains abstract and incomprehensible if we miss its habitual, Hegelian targets but that "anti-Hegelianism runs through Nietzsche's work as its cutting edge" (*comme le fil de l'agressivité*).[37] Indeed, the specificity of Nietzschean empiricism can best be seen, according to Deleuze, in its uncompromising understanding of the "role of the negative."

For Hegel, of course, the negative occupies the paramount position: it is that which drives the dialectic. The decisive term of this dialectic is in turn *aufheben*, which—as Hegel notes in *The Science of Logic*—has the twofold meaning of "to preserve, to maintain" and "to cause to cease, to put an end to."[38] With this double sense in mind, one might therefore say—as Hegel does—that there is nothing without negation. Yet as Deleuze demonstrates in his practical reading of Spinoza's *Ethics*, one might also say, after Spinoza, that negation itself is nothing.[39] Such an "empiricist" perspective represents a radical critique not only of Hegelian dialectics but of any philosophy of negation, effectively undoing it at its origins—which is to say, *at the roots*.

Not unlike Spinoza (Nietzsche, like Hölderlin and Kleist, is, for Deleuze, a Spinozist), Nietzsche flatly denies the *absolute* value of negation and its conceptual-lexical correlates. To positive negation or the "positivity of the negative," Nietzsche "posits" affirmation: "the negativity of the positive" (NP 180). As Deleuze puts it: "Nietzsche's 'yes' is opposed to the dialectical 'no'; affirmation to dialectical negation; difference to dialectical contradiction; joy, enjoyment [*jouissance*], to dialectical labor; lightness, dance, to dialectical responsibilities" (NP 9).

While the antithetical tenor of this passage, not to mention Deleuze's description of Nietzsche's philosophy as an anti-Hegelianism, suggests that Nietzsche produces a mere reversal of Hegel, Nietzsche's "semiology" constitutes, according to Deleuze, a thoroughgoing critical *displacement* of Hegelian dialectics (since the negative is not simply denied but delimited). For instance, in "Active and Reactive" (where becoming-active and becoming-reactive signify the affirmative and the nihilistic respectively), Deleuze maintains that Nietzsche's interest in the active, affirmative power of negation is not, strictly speaking, re-active: "Negation, by making itself the negation of reactive forces themselves, is not only active but is . . . *transmuted*. It expresses affirmation and becoming-active as the power of affirmation" (NP 70). In other words, Nietzsche does not simply oppose affirmation to negation (or difference to dialectical contradiction); he interrogates that hierarchy or "binary machine" in which the negative has traditionally been established as the good, the high, the noble, etc.[40] Consequently, affirmation is not a vulgar, passive aspect of negation; rather, the negative becomes, via the process of transmutation, an affirmative power.

Now, if affirmation is not simple—if, in other words, it is neither a "function of being" (NP 183) nor a reactive inversion of negation— it must perforce be double. For the negation of the negation, then, what Deleuze calls the "syllogism of the slave" (NP 121), Nietzsche substitutes the affirmation of affirmation—which is to say, the affirmation both of becoming *and* the being of becoming. The net effect of this synthesis, according to Deleuze, is that *affirmation itself is affirmed*, a double affirmation that comprises the "power of affirming as a whole" (NP 186). Given this double affirmation, it is clear not only that there can be no possible compromise, as Deleuze says, between Hegel and Nietzsche, but also that Nietzsche's philosophy, like Adorno's, constitutes an "anti-system" that aims to "explore all the mystifications that find a final refuge in the dialectic" (NP 195).

Deleuze's conclusion: though the history of philosophy has been characterized by negation and reaction, by—in a Nietzschean word— nihilism, this long story (*longue histoire*) itself has a "conclusion" (*achèvement*): that point, dependent on the Eternal Return, when negation suddenly turns back on the forces of reaction and, changing quality, *becomes* active, "now only the mode of being of affirmation as such" (*plus que la manière d'être de l'affirmation comme telle* [NP 179]). This, then, is the Nietzschean moment in all its paradoxical splendor, a moment beyond negation when difference is pure affirmation and Dionysus dances lightly but joyfully on the grave of a Spirit whose resurrection in the form of the Absolute is only a bad dream, "an ass's idea" (NP 181).

* * *

Now, before I broach a brief critique of Deleuze's delirious neo-Nietzscheanism (which we see here in all its rhetorical force), I would be remiss if I did not mention where his philosophy of affirmation leads.

I am referring of course to that extraordinary assemblage, *Anti-Oedipus* (1972), where Deleuze and Guattari construct that "long road" stretching from Spinoza to Nietzsche and beyond. By way of illustration, here are Deleuze and Guattari on the Nietzschean schizo-subject:

> The subject spreads itself out along the entire circumference of the circle, the center of which has been abandoned by the ego. At the center is the desiring-machine, the celibate machine of the Eternal Return. A residual subject of the machine, Nietzsche-as-subject garners a euphoric reward (Voluptas) from everything this machine turns out. . . . It is not a matter of identifying with various historical personages, but rather identifying the names of history with zones of intensity on the the body without organs; and each time Nietzsche-as-subject exclaims: "They're *me*! So it's *me*!" No one has ever been as deeply involved in history as the schizo, or dealt with it in this way. He consumes all of universal history in one fell swoop. (AO 21)

This is not, I should note, an innocent citation, as it is part of a much longer passage that Fredric Jameson cites in "Marxism and Historicism" (1979). More to the point, this passage highlights that voluptuous textual intensity of which *Anti-Oedipus* is, as Jameson says, the "most powerful contemporary *celebration*" (emphasis mine).[41]

The telltale word here is *celebration*, the sense of which is ambiguous, if not pejorative, since celebration—for a negative-dialectical critic like Jameson—is an especially uncritical mode of affirmation. Still, as any reader attentive to the subtext of *Postmodernism, or, The Cultural Logic of Late Capitalism* (1991) can attest, Jameson's critique of Deleuze and Guattari is also already predicated on the phenomenological truth of *Anti-Oedipus*, which articulates, according to Jameson, a whole new, properly postmodernist gamut of effects ("dizziness, loathing, nausea, and Freudian decathexis" [MH 161]). True to his recuperative version of dialectical critique, Jameson observes in his concluding remarks on *Anti-Oedipus* that the malaise that distinguishes postmodernism signals an authentic contact with the object of Deleuze and Guattari's existential historicism, "which has now become but another moment of our own past and which we live, in the no less vital mode of the negative" (MH 161–62).

Jameson's move here—reading the affirmative, celebratory thematics of *Anti-Oedipus* as a negative instance of a more general, authentic mode of historicity—is quintessentially Jamesonian. Yet salutary as just such a gesture is (in a Deleuzian age, Hegelianism of any sort has, to be sure, a certain, polemical-tactical effect), this move also *re*-institutes precisely the sort of universalist theory (i.e., Marxism as the "semantic horizon" or "master code" of all semiosis) which Deleuze and Guattari's work explodes into so many schizzes and escape-lines, flow-breaks and rhizomes.

In fact, from a schizo-molecular perspective such as that of Deleuze and Guattari, Jameson's militantly molar, not to say "paranoid," Marxism would appear to be merely another, albeit renovated, philosophy of negation. But if Deleuze and Guattari sometimes appear to be Nietzschean vitalists in late-capitalist guise, the following passage from *Anti-Oedipus* suggests that to read their work simply from a negative-dialectical standpoint, as Jameson does, is not only to mistake its claims of generality but to misread its political implications as well:

> So what is the solution? Where is the revolutionary path?. . . To withdraw from the world market, as Samir Amin advises Third World countries to do, in a curious revival of the fascist "economic solution"? Or might it be to go in the opposite direction? To go still further, that is, in the movement of the market, of decoding and deterritorialization? For perhaps the flows are not yet deterritorialized enough, not decoded enough, from the viewpoint of a theory and practice of a highly schizophrenic character. . . . The truth is that we haven't seen anything yet. (AO 239–40)

Not to arrest the process of decoding and deterritorialization but to accelerate it, this is Deleuze and Guattari's maximalist slogan, a maxim so outrageous on the face of things as to be beyond belief: Are we really supposed to take this *programme* seriously?

The answer is, I propose, yes *and* no. If, on one hand, the positive or affirmative position signals an effort on the part of Deleuze and Guattari to conceive a space beyond the restricted, Oedipal economies of "law, limit, castration, lack, [and] lacuna,"[42] on the other hand, the antithetical position effectively points up, not unlike negative dialectics itself, the critical *indifference* of a strictly affirmative project.[43] To recollect Jameson, what is the (political) use-value of a model, like Lyotard's in *Économie libidinale* (1974),[44] "made up of nothing but positivities"?

Now, to accuse Deleuze and Guattari of the sin of the Same may seem contradictory, especially given their programmatic insistence on difference, but their work is ultimately not as free of metaphysical postulates as it advertises (or as I have, for tactical reasons, suggested).

For instance, the ontologization of desire at work in *Anti-Oedipus* (Desire as the Eternal Return of the Same) can itself be read as so much residual Hegelianism, one that is always already operative, albeit in a different "ontological" form, in *Nietzsche and Philosophy*.[45] Moreover, if Deleuze's project represents both a critique of Hegelian reification and a valorization of normative, non-negative affect, this philosophy of affirmation and its "vision of precultural libidinal chaos" also engenders its own kind of reification: becoming-active as the invariant, ahistorical structure of the Law of Desire.[46]

From another, more site-specific perspective, Deleuze and Guattari's program of desiring-production—including and especially such concepts as the Body without Organs and the "plane of consistence" in, respectively, *Anti-Oedipus* and *A Thousand Plateaus* (1980)[47]—itself presupposes a nomadic, topo-geological conception of Desire that is a "function," in turn, of a certain stage in the *history* of exploitation. Amin's anticapitalist recommendation—that the Third World should withdraw from the world market—may not represent a viable or even sensible solution to the problem of colonialism (in fact, it would no doubt be counterproductive in every sense of the word); however, to argue that the answer is to accelerate the decoding logic of capital—as Deleuze and Guattari do—is to rather willfully ignore what Gayatri Spivak calls the "epistemic violence of imperialism."[48]

We haven't seen anything yet. So Deleuze and Guattari declare, taking us castrated, privatized subjects of postmodernity to task for not taking up the "task of schizoanalysis." Yet even as one concedes the force of their schizophrenic critique (psychoanalysis is inconceivable, as they show, without some notion of surplus-value), the truth is that we have seen quite enough already, especially *if* one bears the above epistemic violence in mind. In fact, given the last barbaric scenario—so-called peripheral Fordism or, rather more pointedly, what Alain Lipietz calls "bloody Taylorism"[49]—it seems to me that Deleuze and Guattari's philosophy of Desire-as-denegation demands not so much a programmatic counter negation as a counterdiscourse that explicitly takes into account the political-economic preconditions of desire, what one might call the *culture of capitalism* (where the global or transnational culture industries are inconceivable without that extraction of surplus-value associated with neo-colonialism).

For it is only when one attends to specific historical and economic-institutional conditions of possibility that the problem of affirmation for contemporary cultural theory begins to assume its determinate but not prohibitive disposition: how to avoid the lure of a molar, monolithic totality, so-called total affirmation, as well as an equally "totalitarian," because politically inflexible, molecularity; or, in the philosophical ideolect of this book, how to think affirmation without reinscribing an infinite dialectics of negativity (as in Hegel and Adorno respectively) or, what is ultimately the other side of the same coin, a delirious, neo-Nietzschean will-to-affirmation (as in Deleuze and Guattari).[50]

Transit

> Critical problematization continues to do battle against ghosts. It fears them as it does itself. The specter itself, the red specter, has been in effect disencarnated. As if that were possible. But is that not also possibility, precisely [*justement*], virtuality itself? And to understand hisory, . . . must one not reckon with this virtualization? To the point that it is then impossible to discern between the specter and the specter of the specter . . . ? Not the night in which all cows are black, but grey on grey because red on red.
>
> —Derrida, *Specters of Marx*

From Negation/Affirmation to Critical Affirmation

Whether the logic of negation is understood in its originary Hegelian form or in that late, non-synthetic version that goes by the name of negative dialectics, the history of this logic from Hegel to Adorno illustrates the limits of any dialectic that privileges either the false, because teleologically recuperated, positivities of sublation or the super-reflexive gyrostatics of negativity "for itself." The play of affirmation associated with the work of Nietzsche would appear to represent a displacement of, if not an escape from, these negative-driven dialectics, but even Deleuze's concept of double affirmation indicates that this militantly anti-Hegelian practice is subject to the same limits as its Adornian, late Hegelian other.

Though the above discourses sometimes suggest that the answer to the aporia of negation/affirmation lies with logic, the classical Marxist position has always been that the solution to any social problem—and the issue of affirmation is ultimately a social rather than philosophical problem—does not lie simply with what Gayatri Spivak calls "mere

philosophical justice."[1] In other words, the problem of affirmation cannot be divorced from, among other things, its historical conditions of
possibility. Thus, in a now familiar move that explicitly acknowledges
its discursive debt and in the process affirms the possibility of a materialist dialectic, Fredric Jameson reiterates Marx's "definitive" recon-
struction of Hegel's distinction between "individual morality" (*Moralität*)
and the "very different realm of collective social values and practices"
(*Sittlichkeit*):

> In a well-known passage Marx powerfully urges us to do the
> impossible, namely, to think [the historical development of
> capitalism and the development of a specific bourgeois cul-
> ture] positively *and* negatively all at once; to achieve, in
> other words, a type of thinking that would be capable of
> grasping the demonstrably baleful features of capitalism along
> with its extraordinary and liberating dynamism simultaneously
> within a single thought, and without attenuating any of the
> force of either judgment.[2]

According to Jameson, the Marx and Engels of the *Manifesto* (1848)
"teach the hard lesson of some more genuinely dialectical way to think
historical development as change"—more genuinely dialectical, that is,
than either Hegel's or Nietzsche's, Adorno's or Deleuze's way.

The object of this austere dialectical imperative, however, is not
industrial capitalism (as in Marx) but late capitalism, which represents
the so-called third, multinational mutation of capitalism (as in Jameson).
And yet, if—as Andreas Huyssen observes in "Mapping the Postmodern"
(1984)—the culture of postmodernity "must be grasped in its gains as
well as in its losses, in its promises as well as in its deprivations," one
of the primary effects of postmodernism is that the "relationship between progress and destruction of cultural forces, between tradition and
modernity, can no longer be understood today the same way Marx
understood it at the dawn of modernist culture."[3] Indeed, for Huyssen,
the relation between culture and capitalism has radically changed, so
much so that Jameson's rather orthodox, economistic logic of late capitalism must itself be reconceived in order to account for this changed
relation.

Accordingly, Huyssen in the conclusion to his essay advances his
critique of both a strictly negative *and* classical-dialectical postmodernism
of resistance: "Resistance cannot be defined simply in terms of negativity or non-identity *à la* Adorno, nor will the litanies of a totalizing,
collective project suffice. At the same time, the very notion of resistance

may itself be problematic in its simple opposition to affirmation. After all, there are affirmative forms of resistance and resisting forms of affirmation."[4] Although Huyssen adds that the last may be more of a semantic problem than a problem of practice, his concluding chiasmus— "affirmative forms of resistance and resisting forms of affirmation"— perfectly captures the logical complexity of postmodernism even as it marks the limits of just such an abstract formulation. The latter bears repeating because even Huyssen's mapping of the postmodern—still one of the most nuanced and dialectical readings of postmodernism to date— reflects, it seems to me, a residual modernist politics: a "good" alternative postmodernism *versus* a "bad" affirmative postmodernism. Seemingly despite itself, then—despite, that is, the subtlety of its conclusion— "Mapping the Postmodern" ends up rehearsing the Frankfurt School critique of affirmation.

Indeed, inasmuch as this critique remains influential, if only as a ghost to be ritually and uncritically exorcised in the recent cultural-populist phase of cultural studies, I want to briefly take up the essay from which, together with Adorno's work, so much of the cultural critique of affirmation derives: Herbert Marcuse's "Affirmative Character of Culture" (1937). I might add that this turn represents not only a return to the question or logic of negation (from which, it is clear, there is no escape), but a turn to a topic that I will argue is central to the problem of affirmation: the commodity-body (*der Körper der Ware*).[5]

Part II

Every attempt to sketch out the counterimage of affirmative culture comes up against the ineradicable cliché about the fools' paradise.

—Herbert Marcuse, "The Affirmative Character of Culture"

Hysteria was interpreted . . . as the movement of sex insofar as it was the "one" and the "other," whole and part, principle and lack.

—Michel Foucault, *The History of Sexuality*

The Commodity-Body-Sign

Turn: From "Affirmative Culture" to the Hysteria of Castration

Affirmative culture—what is it? What, to be exact, does such a culture *affirm*?

According to Marcuse, affirmative culture is that "culture of the bourgeois epoch which led in the course of its own development to the segregation from civilization of the mental and spiritual world as an independent realm of *value*" (emphasis mine).[6] More specifically, affirmative culture certifies the value of culture as such (*Kultur*)—of, in other words, spiritual values such as the Good, the Beautiful, and the True—against those material values that define civilization (*Zivilisation*). In an epigram: *Geist* is good, body bad. Or, as Marcuse himself puts it: "in affirmative culture, the 'soulless' regions do not belong to culture [but] like every other commodity . . . are openly abandoned to the economic law of value" (ACC 117).

Yet if affirmative culture is the culture of a particular epoch, it is clearly not that mélange of cultures we associate today with the word

61

culture, as in postmodern culture.[7] In this sense, affirmative culture is not only class culture but, by definition, bourgeois culture. Hence, as in the second, interrogative section of the *Manifesto* where Marx and Engels call for the abolition of the various bourgeois forms of society (education, private property, etc.), Marcuse asserts that the point is not to demolish culture as such but to abolish its affirmative, bourgeois character, which must appear utopian—at least from the standpoint of the interest of the status quo—since culture in Western thought has always meant affirmative culture (ACC 129).

But for all its negativity, Marcuse's negative reading of affirmative culture is by no means monolithic since the body for him can provide an anticipatory memory of non-affirmative culture. That is to say, when the body becomes an instrument of pleasure rather than an instrument of labor (when, in other words, the production of pleasure is not in the direct service of profit and reproduction), it counters that systematic commodification of bodies (i.e., wage-labor) from which the affirmative-cultural ideal derives its force.

Still, if the body can adopt a positive or liberatory role, it also always bears the burden of—as Marcuse's own negative-driven dialectic implies—the surplus-repressive aspects of commodification. Accordingly, in what I take to be an exemplary text in this regard (since the accent, despite the above negativity, is on the positive position), Marcuse's *Essay on Liberation* (1969) proposes that the counterrevolution is rooted in second nature, in—to be precise—that social instinctual structure which materializes with the advent of consumer capitalism and its aggressive libidinal politics.[8] If a new culture is therefore to emerge, it is necessary to transform not only the old, exploitative modes of production, but to create new, non-dominative modes of consumption and thereby new instinctual needs and satisfactions as well—in a word, a *new subject*.

Now, Marcuse's vision may well be utopian (in the pejorative sense), but for all its limitations, not the least of which is the habitual Frankfurt School valorization of the aesthetic,[9] it still speaks to us, it seems to me, because spectacular consumption has in fact become—at least for some of us in the first world—second nature and, more importantly perhaps, because liberatory strategies of the sort essayed in Marcuse's later work remain an increasingly valuable resource for the "new" New Left.

As for the other, rather less utopian reading of the body, there is of course Foucault who, writing from a very different moment in history—in the wake, that is, of Paris 1968—describes a political technology of the body where docility, not joy, is the end of the "ends of man": "The historical moment of the disciplines was the moment when an art of the human body was born, which was directed not only at the growth of its skills, nor at the intensification of its subjection, but at the formulation of a relation that in the mechanism itself makes it more obedient as it becomes more useful."[10] From these projects of docility-utility, these *disciplines* (the art of distributions, the composition of forces, etc.), the man of modern humanism is born: man as an unholy effect of the disciplinary body.

While *Discipline and Punish* (1975) details just how repressive Marcuse's repressive society is, it is clear—if only in retrospect—that Foucault's discursive-productive philosophy in all its Nietzschean affirmativity is rather closer to Deleuze than it is to Marcuse. At the same time, if Foucault's early work owes an obvious debt to Deleuze,[11] the later Foucault of *The History of Sexuality* (1976) is nevertheless determined to demystify any philosophy of liberation, whether Deleuzian or Marcusian, that is predicated upon an economy of scarcity. So, Foucault remarks that if the first phase in the deployment of sexuality revolved around the classical-capitalist problem of labor capacity (the imperative to constitute a labor force and insure its reproduction), the second phase was absorbed with an entirely different problem, what Foucault calls "hyper-repressive desublimation" or the "theme of a sexuality repressed for economic reasons."[12] As one might suppose given the general, polemical repudiation of Marxism which animates his project from the start,[13] Foucault invokes one of Marcuse's signature themes ("repressive desublimation") only to categorically refute it. Thus, though the proper name in the conclusion to "The Deployment of Sexuality" is Wilhelm Reich, it may as well be Marcuse: "The fact that so many things were able to change in the sexual behavior of Western societies without any of the promises or political conditions predicted by Reich being realized is sufficient proof that this whole sexual 'revolution,' this whole 'antirepressive' struggle, represented nothing more, but nothing less—and its importance is undeniable—than a tactical shift and reversal in the great deployment of sexuality" (HS 131). So much, Foucault seems to say, for sexual liberation—or, at least, any liberatory movement whose politics are based on a negative interpretation of power-desire (e.g., repression).

This position raises, in turn, the following great question: "By what spiral did we come to *affirm* that sex is *negated*?" (HS 9, emphasis mine). This question, it is clear, is the genealogical point of departure for *The History of Sexuality*. And to his credit, Foucault in attempting to answer it not only delimits the usefulness of various research sentences—power represses sex, law constitutes desire, etc.—but productively reinscribes the discursivity of sex-desire, the latter of which is not so much *a* discourse on sex as a series of discourses of sexuality.

More specifically, if the promise of liberation is, for Foucault, a false promise (since power is not simply external to desire), the affirmative position that accompanies the other, constitutive reading of power in the juridical history of the West—"you are always already trapped" (HS 83)—is, *pace* Lacan, equally spurious. As Foucault argues in, among other things, the conclusion to *The History of Sexuality*, the flashpoint for the counterattack against that regime of power-knowledge which currently sustains the discourse on human sexuality is not sex-desire but bodies and pleasures. Therefore, if it is indeed true that our liberation is not in the balance ("Tomorrow sex will be good again"), what is? In addition, if the Age of Repression and that era of high capitalism with which it was historically implicated are now over, what would a "history of bodies" tell us or, more to the point, *do* for us?

First, Foucault again: in *The History of Sexuality* he distinguishes four relatively autonomous strategic unities which have produced specific mechanisms of power-knowledge about sex, the first of which is the *hysterization of women's bodies* (HS 104). This latter process defines sexuality for women not only as that which is common to both men and women as well as that which produces woman's body, "ordering it wholly in terms of the functions of reproduction" (HS 153), but—and this is the particular hysterical deployment I want to focus on here—as that which "belongs, *par excellence*, to men, and hence is lacking in women" (HS 153). If the first of these micro-discourses refers to the general sexualization of women and the second to their necessary role in the sociosexual reproduction of society, the last alludes, not so surprisingly, to the "whole" thematics of castration.

Freud, Marx, Baudrillard, or That "Surplus" Which Is Sign-Value

> Freud turned the theory of degeneracy inside out, like a glove. . . .
>
> —Foucault, "Confession of the Flesh"

> It is an enchanted, perverted, topsy-turvy world, in which Monsieur le Capital and Madame le Terre do their ghost-walking as social characters and at the same time directly as mere things.
>
> —Marx, *Capital*, Vol. 3

> The term "fetishism" almost has a life of its
> own.
>
> —Jean Baudrillard, *For a Critique of the
> Political Economy of the Sign*

Though the thrust of Foucault's historiographic project is to dispute the sexual-political economy of scarcity in general (the Law-as-lack) and the mytheme of castration in particular, the fact that sexuality is—as Foucault himself attests—originally, historically bourgeois also confirms, it seems to me, the considerable historical impact of the discourse of castration. I am less interested in this discourse, however, than in the way it operates in certain "perversions," in, to be precise, fetishism— *the* model perversion, for Foucault (HS 154).

For example, it is well-nigh impossible to overestimate the *value* of this particular "aberration" for psychoanalysis. But don't take my word on it, take Freud's: "No other variation of the sexual instinct that borders on the pathological can lay so much claim to our interest as this one, such is the peculiarity of the phenomena to which it gives rise."[14] Accordingly, insofar as fetishism is itself an instance of sexual overvaluation, Freud's valorization of it in the *Three Essays on Sexuality* (1905) is worth remarking not simply because it evokes the whole machinery of repression but because it ostensibly "proves" one of the master tropes of the discipline of psychoanalysis: the existence of the castration complex (*die Existenz des Kastrationskomplexes*).[15] The castration complex can, in turn, be reduced—without I think doing too much violation to Freud's text—to the following negative thesis: "a woman has no penis" (*das Weib [besitzt] keinen Penis* [F 199]).

With this strategic reduction in mind, one might say that if fetishism is the negation of castration, this negation also always affirms the existence of that which fetishism serves to deny. As Freud himself puts it: "Aversion [*Entfremdung*] from the real female genitals [*wirkliche weibliche Genitale*], . . . remains as an indelible stigma of the repression [*Verdrängung*] that has taken place" (F 200). In other words, fetishism is not simply a negation of the negation (of, that is to say, castration) but an affirmation of sexual difference as such (so-called primary castration).[16] Put another, more orthodox way, the fetish is at once a substitute for the woman's (mother's) phallus (*der Ersatz für den Phallus des Weibes [der Mutter]*) as well as a displaced index of that *complex* of organs which distinguishes the woman's body, where the former complex is not, *pace* Freud, simply the clitoris, the real little penis (*der reale kleine Penis*) but the "clitoris *and* vagina, the lips *and* the vulva."[17]

Now, to broach such a reading of Freud is, I might add, neither to attempt to recuperate classical psychoanalysis and its phallogocentric economy nor, for that matter, to consolidate Foucault's critique of this particular discipline of desire in _The History of Sexuality_ (1978). Hence (to expatiate on the latter), if it is true—as _The History of Sexuality_ argues—that the discourse of Freudianism is itself repressive (since it represents yet another moment in the deployment of sexuality), Foucault's own polemical, productive-affirmative reading of sexuality seriously misreads the very real force of repression, which classical psychoanalysis has historically been at pains to test and contest.[18]

Unlike Foucault, Jean Baudrillard, or at least the Baudrillard of _For a Critique of the Political Economy of the Sign_ (1972), is rather less dismissive of psychoanalysis and is consequently more sensitive to its theoretical resources. In, for instance, "Fetishism and Ideology" he submits that among the social sciences, only psychoanalysis has escaped that vicious circle of magical thinking which inevitably seems to trap whoever tries to re-function the concept-metaphor of fetishism. In fact, for Baudrillard, the psychoanalytic definition of fetishism as a "perverse _structure_" makes possible a general economy of perversion that can help explain the "generalized 'fetishization' of real life" associated with the emergence of late capitalism.[19]

I will take up Baudrillard's general theory of perversion in more detail below, but I want first to review Marx's understanding of _commodity fetishism_, since this economic concept is not only one of the master-concepts of Marxism but also one of the objects of Baudrillard's critique of the political economy of the sign.

The centerpiece of the Marxian analytic is, of course, the section on the secret of the fetishism of commodities (_der Fetischcharakter der Ware_) in the first volume of _Capital_. There, Marx contends that the mystical, enigmatic character of commodities originates not in their use- but their exchange-value (_Gebrauchswert/Tauschwert_). Moreover, precisely because the commodity represents a _perversion_ of that article of utility from which it derives its interest or use-value,[20] it is a very queer thing (_sehr vertracktes Ding_ [C 61]).[21] Thus, in an extraordinary passage, Marx writes that if commodities could speak, they would say: "Our use-value may be a thing that interests men. It is no part of us as objects" (C 83). And in his almost equally extraordinary reading of Baudelaire, Benjamin adds that when the "commodity whispers to a poor wretch who passes a shop-window containing beautiful and expensive things," these fetish-objects are not interested in the "poor" subject of consumption: "They do not empathize with him."[22]

For Marx as for Benjamin, then, commodity
to constitute a negation of exploitation—a negat
the (abstract) human labor-power incorporated i
this negation not only effects the "erasure of a ge
of a history,"[23] but is itself an instance of alier
goods and services he consumes, becomes a thing:
being as with the commodity" (C 23). At the same time (to attempt to
problematize what I take to be a residual naturalism in Marx), commodity fetishism also always testifies to the *"detour of exchange."*[24]
This general or elementary logic of substitution suggests, in turn, that
commodities can function as fetishes only because use-value itself is a
thing that interests men. In other words, that "original" article of utility
which subjectively incarnates use-value is always already an *object* of
exchange. In fact, from this last, critical perspective, one can say—as
Baudrillard does—that the commodity-fetishist metaphor and its restricted economy naturalizes rather than historicizes utility, since use-
value itself is only the *"satellite* and *alibi* of exchange value" (CPES
139).

Furthermore, from another, general-economic perspective (given,
that is, a sumptuary as opposed to subsistence or exchange economy),
the commodity-body assumes a different character or, more to the point,
form. To wit: if the "logic of the commodity and political economy is
at the very heart of the sign" (i.e., the sign-form traverses both the
object- and commodity-form) and if the "structure of the sign is at the
very heart of the commodity form" (i.e., a general sign-code differentially structures the exchange of both the commodity and article of
utility [CPES 146]),[25] then sign-value (*valeur signe*) can also be said to
re-affirm the body of the commodity. In just this sense, sign-value is,
strictly speaking, a super-signifier of use-exchange-value, where—and
this is crucial for a political-materialist sense of fetishism—the signifier
is itself not without a certain materiality, however "synthetic."

I will return to the problem of sign-value a little later in this
segment (a problem that any general theory of fetishism which proposes
to retain a critical purchase on capital must, it seems to me, assume),
but I would only observe here that the concept of sign-value does not
wholly negate the concept of use-value. Though Baudrillard's work tends
to valorize sign-exchange-value (*valeur d'échange signe*) at the expense
of use-value in order to argue for the "beyond" of sign-value (symbolic
exchange is, for Baudrillard, *au-delà de la valeur*), Spivak, among others, has persuasively argued the case for the theoretical utility of use-
value. As she observes in "Scattered Speculations on the Question of
Value" (1985), use-value is simultaneously "outside and inside the system

alue determinations" and, consequently, "puts the entire chain of alue into question" (OW 123). The result of this tactical deconstruction of use-value and consequent textualization of value in general is what Spivak calls, after both Marx and Derrida, the "economic text 'under erasure' " (OW 168). Hence, where Baudrillard speaks of sign-value, Spivak speaks of ~~use-value~~ (where the concept is put under erasure [*sous rature*]) or "use-value" (where it is submitted to what Derrida calls the "regime of quotations").

The interest of Baudrillard's semiurgic critique of political economy— and, in particular, his concept of sign-value—is that not unlike Spivak's deconstructive re-conceptualization of use-value, it articulates a new, distinctive "moment" in the history of the commodity-body. This moment is, of course, postmodernity or, to accent its "aesthetic" aspect, post-modernism, which period constitutes, according to Jameson, the "cultural logic of late capitalism." At the same time, sign-value—which for Baudrillard is linked to the simulacrum—is, by definition, beyond both use-value and any economic theory such as Jameson's which deploys the economic (here "late capitalism") as a "concept of the last resort" (OW 168). Indeed, if, as Spivak claims, the "logical progression to accumulation can only be operated by its own rupture, releasing the commodity from the circuit of capital production into consumption as a *simulacrum* of use-value" (OW 167, emphasis mine), then sign-value is, *stricto sensu*, the simulacrum of use-value, or: a commodity-body-*image*.[26]

Contemporary culture affords many examples of this spectacular body-image (see, for example, Madonna), but the most historically fraught example of this material simulacrum—at least in the context of commodity fetishism—may well be the phallus, inasmuch as the phallus is that (body) part which, however fantasmatic, sutures the "whole" scene of castration: no phallus, as it were, no castration. Put another way: if fetishism is, as Metz says, the "perversion par excellence,"[27] then the phallus is the ultimate *objet petit a.*

While there are any number of critical conclusions to be drawn from this proposition, not the least of which is that psychoanalysis is itself a massively fetishistic discourse,[28] I want to focus in what follows less on the strict, restricted psychoanalytic understanding of fetishism than the way in which the classical-Marxist concept of commodity fetishism has been mobilized to explain, or *explain away*, what I call the postmodern phallus, where the phallus functions not only as "part" of the general economy of the commodity-body-sign—an economy that bears, as we have seen, a perverse relation to the restricted economy of classical Marxism—but as "part" of another, non-restricted economy, the economy of the work of art or *art-commodity.*

Commodity-as-Art, Art-as-Commodity: Warhol's Coca-Cola Bottles, Shoes and Soup Cans

> You can be watching TV and see Coca-Cola, and you know that the President drinks Coke, Liz Taylor drinks Coke, and just think, you can drink Coke, too. A Coke is a Coke is a Coke and no amount of money can get you a better Coke . . . .
>
> —Andy Warhol

In "Capitalism, Modernism, Postmodernism" (1984), Terry Eagleton contends that the aesthetics of postmodernism represent a "dark parody" of the anti-representationalism of the early twentieth-century avant-garde. According to this parodic logic, postmodernism lays bare not so much the commodification of the artefact as the aestheticization of the commodity: "To say that social reality is pervasively commodified is to say that it is always already 'aesthetic'—textual, packaged, fetishized, libidinized; and for art to reflect reality is then for it to do no more than mirror itself, in a cryptic self-referentiality which is indeed one of the inmost structures of the commodity fetish."[29] The net effect of this "perverse," insidious process of postmodernization is that the commodity has become an artefact, and the artefact, in turn, a commodity.

The problem with this argument (Eagleton's implicit, uncritical reliance on reflection theory aside), is that it rather willfully presents what W. J. T. Mitchell calls a " 'vulgar' notion of art as commodity," a notion that rather conveniently suppresses Marx's claim that a "commodity is something like a work of art."[30] That is to say, if the commodity-fetish cannot be thought without its dialectical other, the artefact or work of art, only a genuinely "dialectical image"—as Benjamin's work suggests—can capture the art-commodity in all its "polyvalence": "as object in the world, as re-presentation, as analytic tool, as rhetorical device, as figure," and, most importantly perhaps, "as a Janus-faced emblem of our predicament, a mirror of history, and a window beyond it."[31] While such a multiplex notion of the art-commodity may not be consonant with the canons of classical Marxism (and, as such, a case of incorrigible reversion), it better articulates, or so it seems to me, the dynamic complexity of the postmodernist object of knowledge.

The following illustration indicates, I think, what is at stake in just such a re-articulation. In "Capitalism, Modernism, Postmodernism,"

Eagleton resurrects Marx's critique of commodity fetishism as well as the legacy of modernism and, in particular, the historical avant-garde in order to pronounce a determinate, negative judgment on postmodernism: "in dreaming that art might dissolve into social life, [William Morris] turns out . . . to have been a true prophet of late capitalism: by anticipating such a desire, bringing it about with premature haste, late capitalism deftly inverts its own logic and proclaims that if the artefact is a commodity, the commodity can always be an artefact" (AG 133). As the above allusion to the English utopian-socialist Morris hints, Eagleton's abstract-universal critique of postmodernism would appear to be fueled by a reactionary nostalgia, as if art in the era of late capitalism were more a matter of handicraft than mechanical, even robotic, reproduction. Still, in a critical world where the Soviet avant-garde remains the talisman of the revolutionary art of the twentieth century as well as the touchstone of an authentically political art, the camp and kitsch that allegedly characterize postmodernism constitute a very poor pastiche indeed. In a period: "Mayakovsky's poetry readings in the factory yard become Warhol's shoes and soup cans" (AG 133).

It is a sordid little story, this fall into postmodernism.

If Eagleton's general brief against postmodern theory (Deleuze et al.) is not without polemical interest, the same, alas, cannot be said of his case against contemporary art, since to compare the "farce of a Warhol" to the "tragedy of a Mayakovsky" (AG 133) is merely to reproduce the pieties of orthodox polemic in lieu of a more genuinely dialectical reading. Jameson's concluding remarks on Warhol in *Postmodernism* also reflect a similar aesthetic bad faith: "Warhol's Coca-Cola bottles and Campbell soup cans—so obviously representative of commodity or consumer fetishism—do not seem to function as critical or political *statements*" (P 58, emphasis mine). On the plus side, however, the specificity of Jameson's readings of individual works of art, not to mention his obvious and extensive familiarity with postmodernism, productively "deconstructs" the austerity of his political program.

Indeed, for Jameson (who is especially good on visual culture), to *read* Warhol—"the central figure in contemporary visual art" (P 8)—is to confront one of the central and most intractable issues of postmodernism: "Warhol's work . . . turns centrally around commodification, and the great billboard images of the Coca-Cola bottle or the Campbell's soup can, which explicitly foreground the commodity fetishism of a transition to late capital, *ought* to be powerful and critical political statements. If they are not, then one would surely want to know why, and one would want to begin to wonder a little more seriously about the possibilities of political or critical art in the postmodern period of late capital" (P 9).

Figure 2.1 *The art-commodity, or "work of art in the age of mechanical reproduction"*: Andy Warhol, *100 Cans* (1962), oil on canvas, 72 x 52 in., Albright-Knox Art Gallery.

Whether any art ought to constitute a statement, political or otherwise, remains, it seems to me, a very real question. With respect to a critical-affirmative theory of postmodernism, though, one thing is clear: if it is to remain both persuasive and critical, it will need to be *more*, not *less* dialectical. It will need, in other words, to believe less in the rhetoric of consumerism and alienation, reification and "false consciousness," and wonder a little more seriously about pleasure and desire, consumption and commodification—about, that is to say, "commodity fetishism."

Hard-Core Commodity Aesthetics: Warhol's *Sticky Fingers* and the Popular-Cultural Phallus

> Everybody tries to imitate Andy Warhol but they don't get the point. The point is that it's what's up front that counts.
>
> —Lester Bangs, *Psychotic Reactions and Carburetor Dung*

Although Baudrillard's notion of a general economy of perversion or fetishism represents an overt critique of the restricted economy of classical Marxism as well as the almost equally restricted economy derived from Mandel that underpins Jameson's understanding of postmodernism as the cultural logic of late capitalism, one of the peculiar "qualities" of the concept of sign-value is that it represents both a negation *and* affirmation of the commodity-body—of, that is to say, use-value (body) and exchange-value (commodity).

This, the super-sublative status of sign-value can perhaps best be seen in the post-Frankfurt School account of commodity fetishism that appears in W. F. Haug's *Critique of Commodity Aesthetics* (1971). For Haug, commodity fetishism—or, more properly, commodity aesthetics— sublimates the contradiction between the commodity's use-form (the commodity-*body*) and its exchange-form, that "aesthetic promise" or "*appearance* of use-value" which defines the commodity as such. The result is an aestheticization of the commodity whereby the "skin" of the commodity—true to the increasing abstraction and rationalization characteristic of monopoly capitalism—becomes more and more detached from its "body": "What appears here, reflected in the modification of the commodity's skin and body, is the fetish character of the commodity in its monopolistic peculiarity."[32]

Haug's general position, it is clear, represents an Adornian, negative-dialectical twist on Marx's *Capital*; at the same time, it also raises a number of questions, such as: What would it mean to read the commodity-body given a critical-affirmative sense of consumption and commodification? What, exactly, is the significance of the commodity-body in the increasingly implosive, hyperreal space of postmodernity? Finally, if—according to the "perverse" economy of postmodernity—the commodity is always already an artefact or work of art, what is the fate of the body?

One of the working hypotheses of this book is that the body in late capitalism is not only inevitably caught up in the restricted circulation of exchange-value, but that exchange-value as well as the originary use-value from which it presumably derives its utility cannot be disentangled from the discriminatory economy of sign-value, of prestige and taste—of, in a word, *distinction*.[33] Moreover, if "society is never a disembodied spectacle,"[34] then a general theory or economy of the body—what Foucault calls an anatomo-politics—will necessarily be imbricated with the government of the body or the body politic. In sum, if the work of affirmation will necessarily be concerned with the simultaneous commodification and aestheticization of the body, it will also need to concern itself with the question of how social institutions rethink the body (which is of course the Foucauldian project) as well as, most importantly perhaps, the question of how "we can rethink institutions with our bodies."[35] As the latter, plural emphasis intimates, the point of departure for a theory of affirmation remains the "fact" of bodies and pleasures, institutions and modes of (re-) production, or—rather more to the point (to recollect my discussion of fetishism)—specific commodities and sexualities, specific pleasures and (parts of) bodies.

Since it is historically the most privileged of body-parts, albeit one that has recently been subject to both intensive and extensive review,[36] one might well begin with that most imaginatively supercharged of part-objects, the phallus. So, in chapter 3 of *Commodity Aesthetics* (one of the subtitles of which is, appropriately enough, "The Penis Enters the Commodity Arena"! [CCA 78]), Haug takes up the discourse of the "male member" as it materializes in contemporary advertising. His concluding and, one imagines, conclusive example is the cover of the 1971 Rolling Stones album, *Sticky Fingers*, conceptualized and photographed by Andy Warhol.[37] The cover itself, which consists of a cropped shot of "skintight small-hipped jeans from the belt down to the upper thighs," reveals "every contour of the body," including and in particular the "penis" (CCA 86). True to the *trompe-l'oeil* spirit of the times (i.e.,

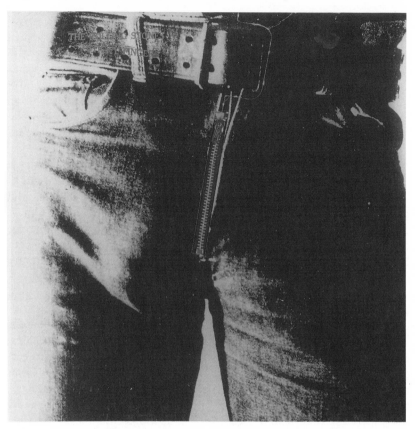

Figure 2.2 *The popular-cultural phallus:* cover of Rolling Stones' *Sticky Fingers* (1971), photograph by Andy Warhol.

pop art),[38] the cover also features a real zipper, a graphic trick that stylizes, according to Haug, "the promised content" (CCA 86).

Now, however one reads this cover, the combination of the *enfant terrible* of pop and the bad boys of rock is obviously a marriage made in commercial and even artistic heaven. But what, one wonders, is the message of this record cover? What does it promise, and does it in fact deliver on this promise? Here is the conclusion to Haug's commodity-aesthetic analysis:

> The buyer acquires the possibility of opening the package, and the zip and finds . . . nothing. It is a reversal of the tale of the Emperor's new clothes: the tale of the buyers' new bodies. They buy only packages which seem more than they

are. Warhol may present himself as an enlightened critic of
society, with his earlier signed replicas of soupcans, which
make a point by apparently accepting the dominant fraudu-
lence in society and pushing it to the limit, so that even the
most stupid can see what lies behind the advertisements.
(CCA 86–87)

Although this particular reading of Warhol appears, at first glance, to
be more nuanced than Eagleton's, Warhol unmasks commodity aesthetics, according to Haug, merely in order to allow its "mask to become
an even more sophisticated advertisement" (CCA 87). In fact, Haug—
reverting, like Eagleton, to a rigorously binary logic of repression and
liberation—contends that Warhol's cover-ad and its "penis joke" mo-
mentarily enlighten even the "most stupid" of consumers only to leave
him enchained in an inferno of cynicism and frustration from which
there is no escape.

Is there any better example of what, after Adorno, one might call
the affirmative dialectics of the art-commodity? For all its promise (here,
finally, is a commodity-body that wears its penis on its sleeve!), the joke,
as usual, is on the consumer: instead of a penis, the purchaser gets zip,
nothing, neither the small angry arousal of "enlightenment" (the false
magic of the commodity having been summarily exorcised like Macbeth's
ghosts) nor that true pleasure which, for Haug, is the real "reward"
of art.

Although Haug's commodity-fetishist analysis of Warhol retains a
residual, historical interest,[39] it is difficult to square the behavior of his
imputed buyer with what I take to be the rather more savvy consumption habits of the average consumer—or at least North American consumer—*circa* 1970. From another, less reception-oriented perspective,
Haug's analysis evinces a surprising literalism. One would think, reading his gloss on Warhol, that the promise of the *Sticky Fingers* cover is
a (real) penis rather than a record (since, according to Haug, "all one
gets one's hands on," finally, is "mere packaging" [CCA 87]). The
onanistic subtext of this passage aside (Haug's implied consumer-spectator
is, I've noted, characteristically masculine), such a reading consistently
conflates the penis with the phallus. In other words, if, as Lacan says,
the phallus "can play its role only when veiled,"[40] to insist on the penis,
as Haug does in his reading of Warhol, is to invoke a particularly crude
phallicism, as if it were somehow possible to skirt the differential "castration" of signification and access the penis-utility as such.

Haug, it is clear, is determined to demystify and thereby defuse
Warhol's penis joke ("The unmasked void appears to rebound on the
purchaser" [CCA 87]); however, the joke ultimately rebounds—true to

the redoubtable logic of fetishism—on Haug himself. Furthermore, given his masturbatory model of consumption (which I think unnecessarily demonizes consumption, to say nothing of masturbation),[41] is it any surprise that this perverse activity leaves the buyer in a state of unrequited acquiescence, ashamed and addicted, with no reward, no true pleasure—in a word, no satisfaction?

In the final analysis, Haug, for all his attention to *commodity-aesthetics*, is unable to adequately come to terms with the commodity-body-*sign*. Because he cannot, as it were, hear the *re* in "*re*cord," he is effectively blind to Warhol's penis joke and its visual semiosis, a conceit he literally fails to see (or, at least, fails to mention), since when one unzips the jacket of *Sticky Fingers*, one finds not only yet another cropped shot (a pair of men's briefs) but the following reproducible, flesh-colored "signature": *Andy Warhol* (and, below it, in smaller print) THIS PHOTOGRAPH MAY NOT BE—ETC.

Here, even as Warhol repeats the authorial stamp on the cover (*The Rolling Stones: Sticky Fingers*), the message parodically points up the serial, non-auratic status of this particular medium (i.e., mass-produced popular music). In fact, it might not be too much to say (at least with the earlier, Warhol-designed cover for the Velvet Underground's first LP in mind)[42] that to read the art-commodity simply as a object or article of utility is to make a serious category mistake—to mistake, in other words, a banana for a penis. For when you unzip the cover of *Sticky Fingers*, there is, inside, not nothing but something: (part of) a body or, more simply, a body-*image*.

This body-part or image is not, moreover, any "chance penis" (to recollect Freud). The package on the cover of *Sticky Fingers* may or may not be Mick Jagger's,[43] but given the Stones' highly sexual persona in 1971 (when they were moving from the violent mode of Altamont to what the album's designer, Craig Braun, has called a "more sexual mode"),[44] this particular crotch shot—like the Stones' logo which debuted at the same time ("a caricature of Jagger's lips and tongue")[45]— is a not-so-subtle signifier of Jagger and his exorbitant sexuality. The role of the phallus, then, is a starring one. And to raise this question, the question of *star*-images—which, as Richard Dyer notes, are always extensive, multimedia, intertextual[46]—is to engage the commodity-body-sign in all its interest and intensity, provocation and polyvalence.

The critical implications of such a counter-critique of Haug's reading of the *Sticky Fingers* cover are, I hope, clear: where the analytical focus is on the corporeal, readings like Haug's which posit an ideal or universal consumer-spectator not only *re*-fetishize the (star's) body but are methodologically incapable of accounting for the specific sorts of

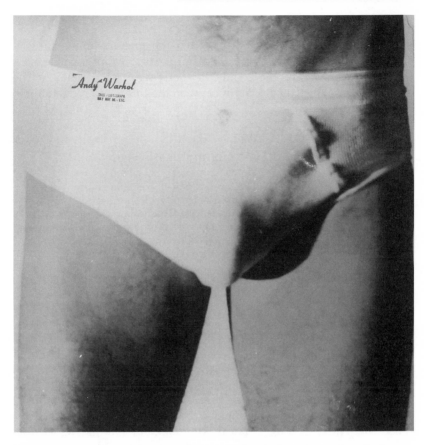

Figure 2.3 *A brief moment in the history of the phallus:* sleeve of *Sticky Fingers* (frontispiece).

"visual pleasure" spectacular bodies elicit. Consider, for instance, the question of female—not to say, gay[47]—spectatorship. What, after all, does it mean to do a reading of Warhol's penis joke, especially if one has actually listened to *Sticky Fingers* (say "Bitch"), and not broach the question of gender address—of, in other words, the (gay) female gaze?[48]

It perhaps goes without saying that it is extremely difficult to maintain a dialectical tension between the necessary demystification of the commodity-fetish and the equally necessary appreciation of its appeal, the power of its manifold pleasures. The example of Warhol's *Sticky Fingers* raises, however, the following critical questions: If the relation between negation and affirmation is in fact a tension (and not, therefore, a relation of balance but a constellation of forces, a *Kraftfeld*), how might one figure this "force-field" given the present conjuncture? In addition, if the art-commodity is itself a perverse figure of the general (political) economy of the commodity-body-sign, what can it tell us about the tense, mediated relation between the forces of production and consumption?

Marx after Baudrillard: The Commodity-Body-Sign

> The fetishization of the commodity is the fetishization of a product emptied of its concrete substance of labor and subjected to another type of labor, a labor of signification, that is, of coded abstraction (the production of differences and of sign values).
>
> —Baudrillard, *For a Critique of the Political Economy of the Sign*

Though the determinate reinscription of the classical theory of commodification in the *Critique of Commodity Aesthetics* reflects the kind of prescriptive negativity that dominates the work of the classical Frankfurt School,[49] Haug's explicit emphasis on what he calls the "general sexualization of commodities" (CCA 56)—together with Baudrillard's surmise about a general economy of perversion—allows one to begin to think the unthought of classical Marxism: an alternative, *critical-affirmative* conception of commodification. That is, rather than restrict commodification to reification (as, say, in Lukács), it makes more sense—or so it seems to me at this "late" date in the history of capitalism—to produce a concept of "commodity fetishism" that comprises both use- and exchange- as well as *sign*-value.

This said, it is perhaps not beside the point to reiterate that the point of this particular project—which is not without its polemical element—is to develop a genuinely more dialectical description of consumption and commodification in order to generate a more compelling *critique* of the limits of contemporary capitalism. More specifically yet, the task of a general-economic account of "commodity fetishism"[50] is to describe *and* explain the specific allure, produced today via packaging and advertising, marketing and publicity, that is the hieroglyph of the postmodern (art-) commodity.[51]

Therefore, to recapitulate the argument that I have developed so far with respect to commodity fetishism (see Figure 2.4): if in the language of classical psychoanalysis, fetishism represents a negation of castration as well as an affirmation of sexual difference as such (i.e., the complex of "real female genitals"), commodity fetishism—in the parlance of classical Marxism—constitutes a negation of exploitation as well as an affirmation of economic difference as such (i.e., value).[52] In addition to this logic, beyond what Baudrillard calls the restricted economy of ideological reproduction, the paleo-Marxist dramaturgy of projection and capture, alienation and appropriation, there is also what I want to call the *commodity-body-sign*, which appreciates commodification as cultural sign labor or the labor of signification (*travail de signification* [CPES 91, 93]).

Before I consider the impact of the concept of the commodity-body-sign on the question of consumption, though, a couple of caveats are in order. First, to take up Baudrillard's critique of Marxist political economy is not—I cannot emphasize enough—to endorse his hyperbolic critique of use-value and consequent sign fetishism: use-value, as I

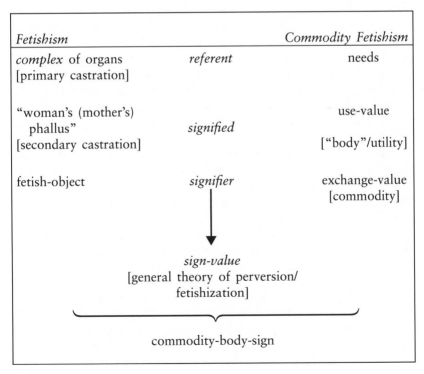

Fetishism		*Commodity Fetishism*
complex of organs [primary castration]	*referent*	needs
"woman's (mother's) phallus" [secondary castration]	*signified*	use-value ["body"/utility]
fetish-object	*signifier* ↓	exchange-value [commodity]

sign-value
[general theory of perversion/ fetishization]

commodity-body-sign

Figure 2.4

argued earlier, is not simply a mirage of exchange-value.[53] Moreover (to reverse tack), insofar as Baudrillard's theory of fetishization misprizes the by no means merely residual efficacy of use-value, the concept of sign-value must itself be scrupulously *re*-figured—that is to say, re-*worked*—if is to bear more than a purely rhetorical burden. (I will endeavor to do just this in the next segment.)

These caveats registered, it is important to remember that if the later Baudrillard's depiction of the mass media is even more monolithic and total-systemic than that of Adorno and Horkheimer (and therefore even less strategic because even more fatal), his work from the very beginning—from, to be precise, *Le système des objets* (1968) and *La société de consommation* (1970)—has always insisted, if only negatively, on the primacy of consumption. Such an emphasis assumes—at least as I read it here—that the subject of consumption[54] is inseparable from the classically privileged problem of production.

A critical re-conception of consumption also involves other, rather heterodox assumptions, the most important of which for me is a certain, discontinuous history of capital. For instance, one of the presuppositions of the critical-affirmative notion of commodification presented here is that late capitalism should be seen less as a continuation of classical or monopoly capitalism than as a "different 'order' of commodification," and that this last order is itself only one among several processes of de-differentiation at work in postmodernity as a whole (e.g., the de-auraticization of culture).[55] In other words, however one reads this general process of de-differentiation (whether positively or negatively, or both at once, as Jameson suggests), the emergence of post-Fordism suggests that from a demand as well as supply side, one would do well to think of the commodity (understood here in the received, pejorative sense associated with classical Marxism) as, *à la* Weber, an "ideal type." Simply put, with the advent of specialized and positional consumption, goods and services should be *read* as being more or less commodified rather than commodities as such. In this sense, the *work of affirmation* (to recollect and reverse Hegel) "demands" not only a critical-affirmative understanding of commodification but a general-economic "rhetoric of commodities," one that would better enable us to decode the *work of consumption*.[56]

The irony here (albeit one which exacts a certain dialectical imperative) is that in order to fashion a critical-affirmative sense of the commodity-body-sign at this particular moment in the history of critical theory and cultural studies, it is necessary—after Baudrillard et al.—to return to the beginning: to, in other words, the negative.

Consumption *Redux:* Cultural Populism, Consummativity, and the Consumptive "Beast of Burden"

> The saturated consumer is the spellbound avatar of the wage-laborer.
>
> —Baudrillard, "The Emergence of Consummativity," *For a Critique of the Political Economy of the Sign*

Jim McGuigan, responding to John Fiske's work on popular culture (in particular, Madonna), contends that "Fiske's television viewers, unlike Madonna, do not live in the material world."[57] By material, McGuigan is referring not so much to that ironic or parodic sense of the word invoked by, say, Madonna's "Material Girl" as the productive, anti-German idealist sense that distinguishes the discourse of classical Marxism. McGuigan is referring, that is to say, to *material* production, where production is, as he puts it, "distinct from productive consumption" (CP 74). Though McGuigan is surprisingly sympathetic to the critical promise of cultural populism (hence his counter-concept *critical populism* [CP 5]), he is nevertheless intent to interrogate the consumptivism associated with the recent, dominant strain of Anglophone cultural studies. Hence his effort to re-open the question of the "political *economy* of culture" (emphasis mine) which, according to McGuigan, the "new revisionists" of cultural studies have relegated to the garbage dump of history like so much Soviet-style heavy machinery.[58]

But given McGuigan's critique of cultural populism and attendant revalorization of the materiality of production, the question arises: What exactly is "the economic," with or without quotations?

Without quotations and at least with respect to the problem of consumption, the locus classicus remains Marx's "General Introduction" to the *Grundrisse*—in particular, the section on "The General Relation of Production to Distribution, Exchange, and Consumption." In this, the second section of the "General Introduction," Marx differentiates, like the classical political economists who are the object of his critique (e.g., Bastiat, Carey, Proudhon), between *consumptive production* and *productive consumption*, or production proper and consumption proper respectively.[59] Though not directly identical as in certain Hegelian political economists like Say and the *beaux penseurs socialistes*, there is a determinate relation or intermediary movement, according to Marx, between production and consumption: "Production furthers [*vermittelt*] consumption by creating material for the latter which would otherwise lack its object. But consumption in its turn furthers production, by providing for the products the individual for whom they are products" (G 24). *Ergo*: "Without production, no consumption; but, on the other hand, without consumption, no production" (G 24).

However, despite the symmetricality of this proposition, Marx's understanding of production/consumption falls squarely on the production side of the virgule—or so it would appear. In the *Grundrisse*, for instance, Marx submits that consumption "creates the *disposition* [*Anlage*] of the producer by setting him up as an aim and by stimulating wants," but production engenders consumption by (1) furnishing the latter with *material*, (2) determining the *manner* [*Weise*] of consumption, and (3) creating in consumers a *want* [*Bedürfnis*] for its products as objects of consumption (G 26). More simply, production produces the "object, the manner, and the desire [*Trieb*] for consumption" (G 26).

If the first of Marx's three-fold determination here of consumption is straightforward enough ("object"), the latter two—"manner" and "desire" respectively—are not nearly as simple with respect to the current micro-historical mode of production (i.e., late or transnational capitalism). That is to say, while the whole point of the "optimistic" cultural-populist movement in cultural studies has been to foreground the active, resistant, even transformative "manner" of consumption, the burden of Frankfurt School critical theory—at least as it has presently been codified—has been the different, rather "pessimistic" proposition that desire or, for Marcuse, "second nature" is itself a product of consumer capitalism. It will I hope have become clear by now that I do not share either of these theoretical positions, since neither cultural populism nor its apparent antithetical other, cultural industrialism, offers— at least on its own terms—a sufficiently complex account of consumption.

Still, if the cultural-populist stress on consumption is in part a response, however reactive and extreme, to the Frankfurt School emphasis on production, this last position derives, in turn, from the canonical, not to say orthodox, Marxist emphasis on the primacy of production. The critical passage here is the conclusion to the section on consumption in the *Grundrisse* where Marx lays down what has remained the classical position on productive consumption:[60]

> Consumption, as a natural necessity, as a want [*Bedürfnis*], constitutes an internal factor [*Moment*] of productive activity, but the latter is the starting point of realization and, therefore, its predominating factor [*übergreifendes Moment*],

the act in which the entire process recapitulates itself. The individual produces a certain article and turns it again into himself by consuming it; but he returns as a productive and self-reproducing individual. Consumption thus appears as a factor [*Moment*] of production. (G 27)

I do not think it is too much to say that if the subject of consumption does not, for Marx, fall completely "outside the scope of economics" (G 23), his reiteration of consumption as the finishing touch of production ("consumption gives the product the finishing touch by annihilating it" [G 24]) tends to reduce the play or agency of what he elsewhere calls the active subject (*das tätige Subjekt* [G 25]).

The Marx of the *Grundrisse* is not, of course, the only Marx. For instance, in the chapter on "Simple Reproduction" in *Capital*, he differentiates between productive consumption and individual consumption, noting that individual consumption is "totally distinct" from productive consumption (C 498). Moreover, while productive consumption has, according to Marx, a dual, properly dialectical articulation (the laborer's consumption of the means of production as well as the capitalist's consumption of this labor-power), individual consumption—or, in the language of *Capital*, the laborer's means of subsistence—refers to "what the laborer consumes for his own pleasure" *beyond* the surplus-value imperatives of the capitalist. From the last, non-economic perspective, one might therefore redefine individual consumption as "final consumption," in the strict sense that, situated as it is outside the realm of the circulation of value, it is "no longer defined by the internal logic of capital and its laws."[61]

More precisely, one might say à la Spivak that final, individual consumption—like use-value—is simultaneously inside *and* outside the circuit of capital, since the desire (*Trieb*) that drives individual consumption is itself subject, in however mediated a fashion, to the logic of capital.[62] This would appear to be the case in late, post-industrial as opposed to early, liberal capitalism where the object of the colonizing logic of capital is not so much the means of (mass) production as those of (mass) consumption. Indeed, Marx himself in *Capital* entertains the idea of a real—that is to say, substantial—increase in individual consumption of the sort now associated with the postwar, Keynesian Atlantic nation-state,[63] though he concludes in classical fashion that, in reality, individual consumption is ultimately unproductive even for the laborer ("since it reproduces nothing but the needy individual" [C 499]).

In sum, if Marx can certainly be said to have understood productive consumption, it must also I think be said that he did not appear to be especially interested in the *question* of final consumption, as the following passage from the first volume of *Capital* indicates:

> The individual consumption of the laborer, whether it proceed within the workshop or outside it, whether it be part of the process of production or not, forms . . . a factor in the production and reproduction of capital. . . . The fact that the laborer consumes his means of subsistence for his own purposes, and not to please the capitalist, has no bearing on the matter. The consumption of food by a beast of burden is nonetheless a necessary factor in the process of production, because the beast enjoys what it eats. (C 498)

One can readily appreciate Marx's point here—that the capitalist need not worry about the sphere of consumption since the laborer's basic instinct for self-preservation will insure that he survives for yet another working day—and still wonder at his determination of the proletarian as a beast of burden (*Lastvieh*) as well as his categorical disregard of the question of pleasure (*Vergnügen*), as if pleasure or enjoyment, not to mention *jouissance*, were only a factor or "moment" of the production process.

In order to complicate the above restricted picture of consumption, one must therefore turn, or return, to the Marx of the *Grundrisse*. While it seems to me that even in the *Grundrisse* Marx ultimately subordinates the sphere of consumption to that of production, his two-fold take on the topic nonetheless promises a more sophisticated account of consumption, one that does better descriptive justice to *homo cyberneticus* and the expanded reproduction of use-value that is the sign, however invidious, of the postmodern.

To wit, in the "General Introduction" Marx argues, first, that consumption itself *produces* production, since a product—as opposed to a mere natural object (*Naturegegenstand*)—only *becomes* itself, a product, in consumption (G 25). Thus, recollecting Aristotle, Marx writes that a "railroad on which no one rides, which is not consequently used up, is only a potential railroad (or is a railroad on which no one travels) and not a real one" (G 24). Put another way (to set the Marx of the *Grundrisse* against the Marx of *Capital*): a song—say, the Rolling Stones' "Beast of Burden"—only becomes a "real" song via the act of listening or reception.

Second, consumption, for Marx, also produces production by "providing the ideal, inward, impelling cause [*Triebenden*] which constitutes the prerequisite of production" (G 25). In other words, if production supplies the material object for consumption, consumption in turn furnishes the ideal object of production: its image (*Bild*), its want (*Bedürfnis*), its impulse (*Trieb*), and its purpose (*Zweck*). Most to the point perhaps (at least with respect to a less restricted, more general-economic reading of consumption), consumption provides the objects of production in a "form that is still subjective" (G 25). In a nutshell: "No needs, no production" (G 24).

I might add here that to reaccentuate this Marx, the Marx of the *Grundrisse*, is neither to re-privilege the sphere of consumption nor, even more regressively, the maximizing "rational choice" individual of micro-economics; rather, it is to maintain that without the "demand" of desire, not to mention need,[64] production itself would be without a purpose (G 24). In fine, the consumer is no beast of burden (though he may, at times, be a cultural dupe or dope) since there is all the difference in the world between animals and that *animal rationale* which is "man." As Marx himself says famously in the *Grundrisse*: "hunger that is satisfied with cooked meat eaten with fork and knife is a different kind of hunger from the one that devours [*verschlingt*] raw meat with the aid of hands, nail, and teeth" (G 28).

This difference—a culinary one, if you will[65]—is the difference between need and desire (or the raw and the cooked), and if the *Lastvieh* is therefore a creature of need, all teeth and cud, *Arbeiter(in)* is an altogether different creature, a "beast" who may well be, as Yeats says, "sick with desire/And fastened to a dying animal" but one who, even as he wolfs down (*verschlingt*) cooked meat with fork and knife to satisfy his hunger to stay alive, knows at the very same time that desire itself (*Trieb*) can never really be satisfied.[66]

Marx *avec* Duchamp: Socialized Consumption and De-Commodification

> At Marcel's request, [Alfred Stieglitz] agreed to photograph the *Fountain* for the frontispiece of [*The Blind Man*] . . . . He took great pains with the lighting, and did it with such skill that a shadow fell across the urinal suggesting a veil. The piece was renamed: *Madonna of the Bathroom*.
>
> —Beatrice Wood, *I Shock Myself*

While the preceding critique of Marx may suffer from a certain anachronistic character (since a Lacanian-inflected reading of consumption is obviously rather less applicable to the relatively scarce world with which

Marx was familiar than it is to our own, "affluent" one), recent work in Marxism and critical theory—work that is intimately familiar with postmodernism and poststructuralism—has steadfastly refused the above culturalist reading of Marx and chosen, instead, to pursue a different, "productivist" path. Jameson's work—as his political-economic formulation of postmodernism as the cultural logic of late capitalism perhaps suggests—is exemplary in this regard. Even as he recognizes, if only in passing, the epistemological problems that shadow the classical position on production, he nevertheless argues for the counter-hegemonic force of a certain productivism: "the affirmation of the 'primacy of production,' (whatever that might mean exactly), offers the most effective and powerful way of defamiliarizing ideologies of the market itself and consumption-oriented models of capitalism" (P 211). Indeed, for Jameson, the affirmation of consumption as a vision of capitalism—projected, for instance, in various "ethnographic" and audience-driven versions of cultural studies—is the sheerest ideology.

Similarly, in a *Primer for Everyday Life* (1991), Susan Willis maintains that the "contradictions of consumption are the contradictions of capitalism" and, consequently, that the fantastic democracy proposed by Marxist popular-culture critics like Fiske—what one might call a *commodity democracy*—simply reinforces the fundamental message of capitalism, the bottom line of which is to "say yes to everything."[67] According to Willis, the only way to *trans*form rather than *re*form a culture of the simulacrum is to confront, head on, the contradictions of capitalism and the commodity-form on which it is predicated. As in Spivak, the key to this social transformation is the concept of use-value, which unlike, say, the concept of sign-exchange-value in Baudrillard, provides a genuinely alternative as opposed to merely "resistant" practice of cultural politics.

With the ascension and recent theoretical hegemony of, among other things, a particularly weak strain of cultural politics, it is certainly difficult to deny the conceptual *and* rhetorical value of a non-facile notion of use-value as well as the related argument for a non-prescriptive form of socialized consumption. And to give credit where credit is due, Willis in particular—unlike all too many cultural critics on the academic Marxist left—appreciates the theoretical interest of both Adorno's and Baudrillard's work, which in its stress on, respectively, negative dialectics and symbolic exchange presents a vision of capitalism as a systemic totality even as it envisions the Other of capitalism as an impossible, utopian "elsewhere."

Yet despite her novel, Adornian reading of symbolic exchange, Willis, like Jameson, is ultimately unable to resist the lure of an almost strictly negative dialectics, or what I can only call the *seduction of negation*. Thus, if Willis challenges the "reader to resist reading prescriptive models of use-value"[68] in the essays collected in *A Primer for Everyday Life*, I challenge the reader to resist reading a palpable rhetoric of *dis*pleasure between the lines of the same essays. Perhaps the problem is a rhetorical one (though I dare say rhetoric remains a real, by no means separate, problem in Willis), but how else can one explain—in the wake of Benjamin and Barthes, Lefebvre and de Certeau, Bourdieu and Baudrillard, and, yes, Fiske and

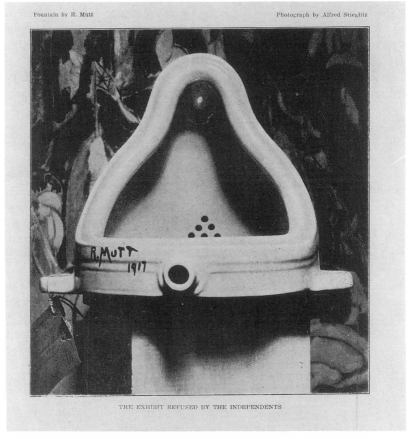

Fountain by R. Mutt   Photograph by Alfred Stieglitz

THE EXHIBIT REFUSED BY THE INDEPENDENTS

Figure 2.5 *"Madonna of the Bathroom":* Marcel Duchamp's *Fountain* (1917), photograph by Alfred Stieglitz (1917), silver gelatin print, $9^{5}/_{16}$ x 7 in., The Louise and Walter Arensberg Collection, Philadelphia Museum of Art.

Hebdige—the following claim: "We all make meanings with the commodities we use and bestow. But the meaning possibilities are already inscribed in the history of production and exchange."[69] Tell that to R. Mutt and his urinal![70]

Again, it is impossible to dispute the reality of that "spectacle of production" which has pervaded, and continues to pervade, our everyday lives. One has only to stroll down the aisle of any supermarket, as Willis invites us to do, to see that the display of exotic goods today is every bit as theatrical as a Madonna video. Still, recent work in social history and anthropology also indicates that the possible meanings of commodities are by no means exhausted by the history of production, and that the regimes and tournaments of value associated with what Arjun Appadurai calls the "dynamics of exchange" effectively deconstruct Willis's *a priori* invocation of the mode of production.[71] Indeed, for Appadurai, whose work derives from an unexpected convergence between Marx and Simmel, the link between value (Marx) and exchange (Simmel) affords a veritable politics, one that must be sought—at least in part—in the "political logic of consumption" (SLT 31).

Against, then, the excessively positivist conception of commodification that is entrenched in Marxism, Appadurai insists that a commodity is not simply "*any thing intended for exchange*" (SLT 9) but things that, "at a certain phase in their careers and in a particular context, meet the requirements of commodity candidacy" (SLT 16). The interest of this resolutely temporal approach is that, unlike certain classical accounts of commodity fetishism, it can persuasively account for the fact of *de*-commodification. As Appadurai puts it, things "move in *and* out of the commodity state," and "such movements can be slow or fast, reversible or terminal, normative or deviant" (SLT 13). In short, precisely because of its flexible understanding of commodification, Appadurai's state-specific, career-oriented conception of commodification goes a long way towards constructing a rhetoric of commodities responsive to the vagaries of value, in particular the hyperreal "body" of sign-value whose volatility is a direct function of the increasingly rapid flows of information associated with financial fetishism, the pure fetish form (Marx) of the present global debt/credit system.[72]

The point, of course, is not to lose sight of the fact that things *do* become commodities, and that to forget about this—about, that is to say, *surplus-value*—is to abandon in one stroke whatever critical force Marxism commands as a discursive practice. Hence the necessity of a determinate, albeit considered, return to the *problem* of production.

Return: Contradiction, Circulation, and the Production of Sign-Value

> The problem of commodification must not be considered in isolation or even regarded as the central problem in economics, but as the central structural problem of capitalist society in all its aspects.
>
> —Lukács, *History and Class Consciousness*

If it is imperative to attend to use- and exchange-value (as Willis and Appadurai, respectively, argue), it is equally important—as I have been arguing—to attend to the concept of sign-value. Arguably one way to get at the specificity of sign-value is to consider the significance of value per se, as diagrammed in Figure 2.6.

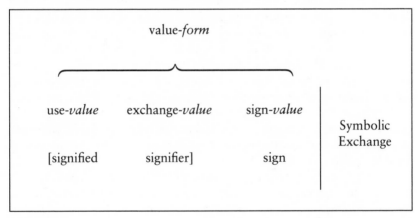

Figure 2.6

As the left hand of this diagram illustrates (i.e., non-Symbolic Exchange), the "real movement" of Baudrillard's model—such as it is—derives neither from consumption nor production but *simulation*, the so-called "*monopoly of the code*."[73] Indeed, the real driving force of the sign for Baudrillard is not so much sign-exchange-value as Symbolic Exchange, or what he calls after Bataille the sacrificial economy of true consummation—not, in other words, *consommativité* but *consumation* (the latter of which is, strictly speaking, beyond the sign).[74]

But if one brackets the question of Symbolic Exchange (as in Figure 2.6), the radicality of Baudrillard's "revolution of the object" begins to materialize, as in Figure 2.7 where the fundamental formula is: "sign-value is to symbolic exchange what exchange-value . . . is to

needs	use-*value*	exchange-*value*	sign-*value*
referent	[signified	signifier]	sign

Figure 2.7

use-value" (CPES 126). Here the referent or *content* of both classical bourgeois and Marxist political economy ("needs") is decisively bracketed, not unlike Symbolic Exchange, and only its *form*—its structural as opposed to functional character—remains.

Now, this radically non-, not to say anti-, naturalistic conception of political economy poses a number of problems, not the least of which is that it absolutely destroys—as opposed to, say, puts "under erasure"—the notion of need or utility. In fact, even as Baudrillard's emphasis on sign-value obscures the analytic specificity of use-value (which, as we have seen, both Spivak and Willis have been concerned to highlight), his semiurgic destruction of the notion of need—which recollects both Mauss and Bataille, but more Bataille than Mauss—courts the charge of *genetic* idealism (which, whatever its other flaws, Marxism cannot I think be accused of, insisting as it does on the original, irreducible "nature" of the material).

Still, to fully appreciate the force of Baudrillard's reconfiguration of value, it is necessary to understand a further transformation of his model of political economy, one where not only need but use-value and Symbolic Exchange are "expelled from the field of value" (CPES 128). The relevant formula here is "sign-value [is] to exchange-value what symbolic exchange is to use-value" (CPES 127).[75] The interest of the reconfiguration depicted in Figure 2.8—which involves a double, radical suppression of needs and use-value (as well as the utopian space of

Figure 2.8

Symbolic Exchange)[76]—is that it graphically articulates the internal movement of the Real, that history of rationalization or, for Marx, "real abstraction" which characterizes the logic of modernity (or, in this case, postmodernity). What we see here, in other words, is the emergence of a third order of representation, that phase of political economy where—as Baudrillard glosses Marx—even what is considered inalienable (love, knowledge, consciousness, etc.) "falls into the sphere of exchange-value" (MP 119). Or, as Julian Pefanis economically puts it, "production produces in order to produce production."[77]

Though no one, it seems to me, is more provocative on the topic of simulation than Baudrillard, the problem with his critique of use-value fetishism is that it is constitutively unable, for all its ingenuity, to explain the *production* of the sign—unless the above formulation ("production produces . . .")—counts as a necessary *and* sufficient explanation. In other words, if a strictly negative conception of consumption and commodification is, as it were, counterproductive, a critical-affirmative account of "commodity fetishism" must—if it is to function persuasively as *critique*—come to terms with that historical-materialist process which produces the *contradiction* between use-value and value as such (or, for Baudrillard, exchange- and sign-exchange-value), which process I have diagrammed in Figure 2.9. While this diagram is obviously only a figure for those concrete forms which constitute the contradictory and historically determined process of capitalist production, the force of this particular trope is that it does not simply reduce the *form* of use-*value*, as Baudrillard tends to do, to a "bad" equivalential logic or "simple formal mediation" (Marx).

Rather more to the point, there is a real—that is to say, substantial—epistemological stake here (as the dual character of use-value in the final diagram is intended to denote) inasmuch as use-value (without quotations) is itself a figure for need (*besoin*) or, more generally, that bio-material referent which is the real.[78] Put another way: if, on one hand, the relative bracketing (*encadrement*) of final consumption alludes to that which is, in one sense, beyond economics (hence its general-economic status), on the other hand, the *re*-insertion of the restricted, classical-Marxist economy of value within a general economy of "commodity fetishism"—one driven, as it were, by *Trieb* (Marx) or *désir* (Lacan)—marks an additional, critical stake.

As for this "perverse" reinsertion, it is important to note that the placement of the sign within the restricted political economy of commodity fetishism—a tactical gesture that explicitly reverses Baudrillard's strategic "inversion of the logic of value"[79]—accounts not only for that consumption which is productive (i.e., productive consumption) but for that site from which use-, exchange-, and sign-value can all be said to originate (i.e., production). The point of this particular, *political*-economic

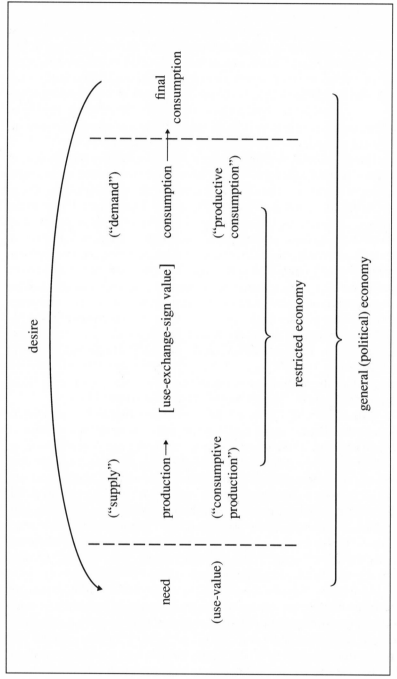

Figure 2.9

restriction is, I hope, obvious: in order to retain the concept of *surplus-value*, it is imperative to re-cite or "remember" the differentially weighted "point" of production, that *process* where exploitation happens.[80]

In fact, inasmuch as the above reinscription may seem like a not-so-subtle return to the classical-Marxist position on commodification, I would only reiterate the obvious: one needn't subscribe to Baudrillard's anarchist campaign against what he calls the total dictatorship of production[81] to realize—*pace* a certain reading of Marx—that the mode of production does not simply determine what Bourdieu calls the mode of consumption. Neither the concept of alienation nor exploitation negates—to offer a perfectly banal example—"the pleasure obtained from a television set."[82] Not to recognize the little truth of this truism—the dream-wish embodied in the commodity-body-sign—is to risk resurrecting, it seems to me, the sort of negative Frankenstein image hidden deep in the heart of classical Marxism and *re*-reified in the concept of reification.[83]

Such a counter-critique does not of course mean that we should pursue what Appadurai calls the political logic of consumption at the expense of a sustained reexamination of the mode of production. It is hopelessly regressive, it seems to me, to endlessly reproduce the argument for the "sovereignty" of consumption,[84] a one-dimensional argument that has been enshrined in classical political economy since at least Adam Smith ("Consumption is the sole end and purpose of all production").[85] Consumptivism of this sort, liberal or otherwise, is as unproductive as the most orthodox forms of productivism. Rather, in order to counter a drift towards an uncritical, utopianist sublation of the cultural contradictions of capitalism, one must continually and persistently reinscribe not only the concept of production but the concept of *contradiction*.[86]

While there are any number of seemingly insuperable contradictions that are at least as "old" as modernity itself (e.g., the conflict between the state and capital), the primary contradiction is ultimately not so much between consumption and production—as the final diagram (Figure 2.9), admittedly, suggests—as *between* the forces and relations of production, which may be rewritten as the antagonism between capital and labor, or most simply: profits and wages. If Ricardo recognized the significance of this opposition (if not its antagonistic character), it was left to Marx to point out that the result of the contradiction between the forces and relations of production—or, to adduce a structural as opposed to historical contrast, between concrete labor (relative value-form) and abstract labor (equivalent value-form)—is *surplus-value* and, consequently, capital formation and expansion, accumulation and reproduction.

Although Marx's critique of capitalism possesses, as has been noted, both a general and particular charge (respectively, class struggle and the proletariat as the historically privileged agent of revolutionary change), the same formulation also invites a different, less orthodox reading. To wit: if the contradiction between capital/labor and the production of surplus-value—especially as it is played out today in the egregious disjunction between First and Third World economies (as various dependency and cultural-imperialist theories attest)[87]—cannot be theorized away, the fact remains that "however opposed capital and labor may appear in the struggle of wage against profit," it is also always necessary—at least for capital to achieve *its* ends—for the laborer to "continue to buy and to continue to desire more goods" (MCMC 184). This, the so-called realization problem, is, as it were, *the* positive aspect of the problem of contradiction.[88]

Now, it may be entirely too much to hope that an absolute identity of interests will ever emerge between capital and labor (where, that is, capital produces only that which its "labor force as consumers demand[s] from it in the way of goods" [MCMC 184]). Still, if the dialectic between profits and wages constitutes, as Marx himself recognized, *the* precondition of production, the potential for some real balance, if not identity of interests, between the two is not some capitalist mirage, the "discreet charm" of bourgeois political economy, but a precondition of politics in general and "affirmative" politics in particular.

I hasten to add that even as the "constant fight for higher wages by members of the work-force cannot be reduced to a demand for the paypacket" but "must always imply a demand for the purchases represented by those wages" (i.e., wage goods [MCMC 188]), this implicit, structural demand must not be, it is clear, for just *any* goods.[89] In other words, if production for need or, more properly, need and desire vis-à-vis profit is to mean anything today, it must also reflect the demand for commodities that not only satisfy our desires, however defined,[90] but that do not imperil the planet and its already dwindling resources.[91]

Finally, if it is impossible to comprehend the commodity-body-sign without taking into account use- and exchange- as well as sign-value, it is equally impossible to formulate a critical-affirmative sense of "commodity fetishism" without coming to terms with the concept of *circulation*—with, that is to say, the various "moments" that constitute the circuit of capital:[92] production, distribution, exchange, and consumption. Indeed, it is only from the perspective of circulation in the general sense (to use my own schema as an object of critique) that the binary couple "production/ consumption" appears as the crude opposition that it is. So, in the *Grundrisse*, after explaining the dialectical relation between production and consumption, Marx writes: "Between the producer and the product, *distribution* steps in, determining by social laws his share in the world of products" (G 28).[93] If Marx himself associates distribution here with production, and exchange with consumption, he also insists—true to his dialectical method—that they are all members of one totality [*Totalität*], "different aspects of one unit" (G 33).

This sort of formulation may exude an unfashionably expressivist air, but its totalizing gesture is, it seems to me, something of a necessary risk today, now that theory—even some post-*Marxist* theory—is content to mime those centripetal forces of fragmentation and "schizophrenia," super-particularism and micro-differentiation, that have come to define postmodernity. In this sense, only a global perspective—one that recognizes not only that every theoretical position is as much an affirmative as a negative gesture but that the "little tactics" of theory are always in some sense complicit with the "great," geopolitical strategies of global capitalism[94]—only just such a total, general-economic perspective can begin to do social and not merely philosophical justice to the very real "fetish character of commodities."

Transit

That which withers in the age of mechanical reproduction is the aura of the work of art.

—Benjamin, "The Work of Art in the Age of Mechanical Reproduction"

Art (the work of art), confronted in modern times with the challenge of the commodity, does not, nor should it, look for rescue in a critical denial . . . but rather in outbidding the very formal and fetishized abstraction of commodities, under the enchantment of exchange value— becoming more commodity than commodity, since even farther from all use-value.

—Baudrillard, *Fatal Strategies*

(M)TV, The Art-Commodity in an Age of Electronic Reproduction

As it will I hope have become clear in the progress of this book, neither the *prima dialectica* of Hegel nor the negative dialectics of Adorno— bracing as the latter's astringent discourse is—is sufficiently dialectical when it comes to that contemporary cultural-political formation which is postmodernism. While it provides a useful corrective to what Eagleton calls the "patrician gloom of the Frankfurt School,"[1] neither Deleuze's neo-Nietzschean philosophy of double affirmation—of being and be- coming, the being of becoming and the becoming of being—nor Deleuze and Guattari's "schizoanalytic" program ultimately seems adequate to the contradictions of everyday life in late capitalism either. That their program, despite its estimable attention to what is surely one of the definitive traits of postmodernism, velocity, does not really speak to the deleterious effects of capital is, however, less a prohibitive judgment than an evaluation in the strong, Jamesonian sense of the term.

The concept of capital is decisive here because the turn in this book from the logic of negation/affirmation to that of "commodity fetishism" not only marks a shift from the philosophical to the cultural-economic register, it remarks as well the discourse from which the concept of capitalism derives its critical intelligibility: Marxism. Thus, if I have programmatically set Marcuse against Adorno, Foucault against Marcuse, and then—in the heart of this scenodrama—Baudrillard against Marx himself, it is in the interest of seeing what can still be done with a dialectical mode that is not governed simply or solely by an economic restriction (i.e., the "commodity law of value").

Just such a revision raises, however, a number of questions, the most important of which—at least in the context of postmodernism—is: What are the implications of a general theory of consumption and commodification for the work of art in an age of electronic reproduction? If the art-commodity is, as I indicated earlier, a perverse figure of the general economy of "commodity fetishism," another, working hypothesis of this book is that it also bears a necessary, determinate relation to the logic of capital and, equally importantly, to the mass electronic media. The former logic refers, of course, to late or transnational capitalism, while the latter refers to that process of postmodernization where, according to Jameson, the traditional fine arts are *mediatized*—where, that is to say, they "come to consciousness of themselves as various media within a mediatic system."[2]

As for specific media, in *Postmodernism, or, The Cultural Logic of Late Capitalism* Jameson makes the case that cinema is the "first distinctively mediatic art form" (P 68). In other words, cinema arguably constitutes something like the art-historical conditions of possibility of the emergent mediatic conceptuality, not simply the "ratio between the forms and media" but the way in which the "generic system" expresses the postmodern (P 300). Still, if film is in fact the first mediatic art-form, it is also becoming increasingly clear that television is now the dominant medium of postmodernism (in which case film itself has become, as it were, modernist, *late* modernist). The current cultural hegemony of television suggests, in fact, that the general economy of the art-commodity is deeply implicated in the whole question of televisuality.[3] It is with this televisual imperative in mind, then, that I turn to music television (i.e., MTV)[4] and, in particular, the academic, cultural-political appropriation of Madonna, or so-called "Madonna Studies."

Part III

> Live out your fantasies with me
> Touch my body
>
> —Madonna, "Into the Groove"

> This video alone [*Like a Virgin*], with its
> coruscating polarities of evil and innocence,
> would be enough to establish Madonna's
> artistic distinction for the next century.
>
> —Camille Paglia, "Madonna II: Venus
> of the Radio Waves"

The Case of "Madonna Studies"

Corpus Delicti: The Rise of Madonna Studies

In the chapter on video in *Postmodernism*, Jameson states that "thinking anything adequate about commercial television may well involve ignoring it and thinking about something else; in this instance, experimental video (or alternatively, that new form or genre called MTV, which I cannot deal with here)" (P 71).

True to his word, Jameson confines himself to experimental video, but despite the attendant disclaimer—"this is less a matter of mass versus elite culture than it is of controlled laboratory situations" (P 71)—the *de facto* valorization of video art in *Postmodernism* could itself be said to be driven by a certain modernist aesthetic. Indeed, since MTV has, at least as I read it, more in common with commercial television than video art as such, it is a "classic" example of the contemporary art-commodity, not least because, as E. Ann Kaplan among others has observed, it can be seen as one continuous commercial.[5]

More to the point perhaps, Jameson's decision not to take up MTV is especially surprising since MTV is the contemporary medium most associated in the popular imagination with postmodernism.[6]

Take, for instance, William Gibson, a writer about whom Jameson is unabashedly partial. For Gibson, the reality of MTV is well-nigh inescapable, though I think it is also fair to say that for all his vaunted postmodernist tendencies, Gibson is even less sanguine about music television than Jameson. Still, what else is that pervasive, *post*-postmodern medium referred to as "simstim" in Gibson's cyberpunk trilogy but some future mutation of MTV and, if Mona in *Mona Lisa Overdrive* (1988) is a reluctant "wannabe,"[7] who else is Angela Mitchell, *the* "simstim queen," but Madonna? Yet if there is a way in which MTV exemplifies postmodernism (postmodernism, as Daniel Harris says in a Swiftian spirit of overstatement, "*is* Madonna"[8]), in what follows I propose to read Madonna less as a trope of MTV or postmodernism than as a symptom or figure—a symptomatic *figure*, if you will—of contemporary media and cultural studies.

This proposition raises, of course, its own stubborn, methodological questions, such as: Why Madonna?

At least initially, I want to answer this question with another, equally reflexive question: Why not Madonna? That is to say, is there some sense in which Madonna is not, *a priori*, a valid object of study for contemporary cultural studies, not to mention *Kulturkritik*? Or is the problem less Madonna *per se* than the fact that so many academics are "working" on her, and far too many are far too celebratory?

To be frank, I am not especially interested either in defending the right of left critics to engage super-popular mass-cultural figures like Madonna (see Fiske), or in making an argument for that most vulgar of subjects, the fashion mode, as a necessary component of cultural studies (see Barthes). What I do want to do is re-pose and endeavor to answer the following question: What can Madonna tell us about the problem of affirmation? More specifically, if Madonna is the quintessential commodity-body-sign, what does the academic, cultural-political appropriation of her work say about contemporary consumption and commodification, that general economy of "perversion" I have reiterated here as postmodern "commodity fetishism"?

To begin with the negative position, I do not think it is too much to say that almost from the very beginning, the case against Madonna Studies has had the air of an all-American jeremiad about it. Here is Harris in the *Nation* (1992): "Just as members of the left often sentimentalize the proletariat, so academics have begun to sentimentalize popular culture by ascribing to it all sorts of admirable characteristics that it does not have—in particular, the potential to radicalize the huddled masses by providing typically quiescent MTV viewers with what is now fashionable to term a 'site of contention.' "[9] All the buzzwords are here—negatively inflected, of course: the left, academics, popular culture, the proletariat, the masses, MTV. The analogic of this passage— I hesitate to term it *critique*—is nonetheless illustrative: even as Harris tweaks the Old Left for its workerist sentimentality (this is post-Cold War rhetoric with a vengeance), he tars both "academics" *and* the "masses" with the same coarse brush. While the masses are huddled outside (and the MTV generation is inside watching MTV), left academics lounge around spinning ever-more-fashionable theories about the radicality of popular culture.

One such left academic is Kaplan who, with the publication of *Rocking around the Clock: Music Television, Postmodernism, & Consumer Culture* (1987), has been positively identified with the "Madonna Phenomenon." However, given the critical stress in Kaplan's work on, among other things, the site of production as opposed to contention, Harris might well have begun his survey of Madonna Studies with John Fiske, the only other "mass-media pundit" he favors with the word *scholar.* I'm thinking in particular of Fiske's "British Cultural Studies and Television," which appeared in the widely circulated anthology *Channels of Discourse* (1987). Though Fiske was by no means the first scholar to write on Madonna, his feminist-ethnographic reading of her was arguably the most visible and controversial at the time and, as such, can be said to represent the first moment of Madonna Studies.

Part of the historical and residual critical interest of Fiske's early reading of Madonna is that it rankled not only Harris but other left academics as well. The following passage from the conclusion to "British Cultural Studies and Television" is, I think, representative: "We must be able to understand how that bundle of meanings that we call 'Madonna' allows a *Playboy* reader to activate meanings of the 'compleat Boy Toy' at the same time a female fan sees her as sexy but not needing men, as being there 'all by herself.' "[10] According to Fiske, this polysemy on the part of the spectator constitutes the "third level of the intertextuality of television," what in *Television Culture* (1987) he calls the "tertiary text," or the texts that "viewers make out of their responses."[11]

If Fiske's position in "British Cultural Studies" appears to be dominated, as the above passage indicates, by the question of reception and consumption, this impression is confirmed in the first chapter of *Television Culture* where he somewhat off-handedly announces, *pace* Kaplan, that "this book is not concerned with television as an industrial practice or as a profit-making producer of commodities, though it is obviously both of these, but attempts to understand it from the perspective of its audience" (TC 13). Given this orientation, Fiske's project situates itself in direct contradistinction not only to the work of the Frankfurt School but, more recently and pointedly, Screen theory.[12] In fact, one of its overt aims is to contest—in the name of television and its viewers—"Screen theory's emphasis on the power of the text over the reader" (TC 74). This radical semiotic stress on reception and the "reader as the site of meaning" (TC 64) is reflected, appropriately enough, in his readings of specific televisual texts.

Now, inasmuch as Fiske's audience-oriented perspective openly challenges Kaplan's account of the "radical text,"[13] it's useful I think to compare their respective readings of Madonna's *Material Girl* (Mary Lambert, 1985).[14] Fiske's reading—which functions as one of the set pieces of "British Cultural Studies"—focuses on the video's representation of performance-as-parody: "Madonna knows she is putting on a performance. The fact that this knowingness is part of the performance enables the viewer to answer a different interpellation from that proposed by the dominant ideology, and thus to occupy a resisting subject position" (BCS 277). Fiske's model—which, as I noted above, represents a substantial departure from the sort of fixed subject-positioning associated with "high" Screen theory—could not be more different from that rather strict Lacanian-Althusserian model of spectatorship developed by Kaplan. Consider, for example, the last paragraph of *Rocking around the Clock*, which illustrates the difference between Fiske's and Kaplan's take on Madonna as well as their very different positions on (music) television itself:

> As is clear from this book, I have not addressed myself to the level of historical viewers. . . . MTV's postmodernist aspects may well be resisted or manipulated by such subjects in the viewing process. However this may be, evidence of specific spectator behavior in no way invalidates the theory of MTV as a postmodernist form in its dominant modes of production, consumption, and exhibition. (RC 158–59)

Kaplan's conclusion here, which unambiguously privileges the problem of production, consumption, and exhibition rather than, say, historical spectatorship or audience studies, itself echoes the book's opening sentence: "This book is concerned with rock videos as exhibited through Music Television—MTV—as an institution" (RC 1).

In sum, where Fiske is concerned with reception, Kaplan is concerned with the institution (i.e., production, consumption, exhibition);

where Fiske is interested in the "resisting," performative viewer, Kaplan is interested in the "hypothetical or model spectator"; where Fiske brackets the industrial aspects of television in order to attend to the power of the reader, Kaplan insists that spectatorship only makes sense "within the discussion of MTV as a commercial, popular institution, and as a specific televisual apparatus" (RC 1). Finally (to return to *Material Girl*), where Fiske's reading programmatically underscores the interrogative effects of self-parody, Madonna's control over the production of her image, "*her* ability to make *her own* meanings" out of the "symbolic systems available to her"—a productivity at the level of the signifier that is passed on to the viewer ("the emphasis on the making of the image allows, or even invites, an equivalent control by the reader over its reception" [BCS 279])—Kaplan's reading of *Material Girl* ultimately circles back to the site of production or, more generally, the complex, overdetermined relation among the sites of production, exhibition, and consumption:

> The analysis of "Material Girl" has shown the ambiguity of enunciative positions within the video that in turn is responsible for the ambiguous representation of the female image. The positioning of a video like "Material Girl," moreover, within the 24-hour flow on this commercial MTV channel, allows us to see that it is *this* sort of ambiguous image that appears frequently, as against any other possible female images, . . . which are only rarely cycled. (RC 127)

For Kaplan, the enunciative ambiguity of *Material Girl*—reflected, for Fiske, in the video's puns, parodic excess, and deconstructive mininarrative—cannot be understood outside the total music-video flow that virtually defines MTV (or, at last, *used* to define MTV).[15] In fact, given MTV's double industrial articulation, its commercial and promotional modes (i.e., both the merchandising of the music and the station itself), one might argue—as Kaplan does—that the site of consumption for MTV is relatively determined, so much so that the now manifestly unpopular lessons of Screen theory, not to mention the Frankfurt School itself, abruptly begin to reacquire some of their original force.

Certainly something like this logic of the "return of the repressed" animates Meaghan Morris's oft-cited counter-critique, "Banality in Cultural Studies" (1988) where, invoking Baudrillard as a point of reference for popular culture, Morris zeroes in on Fiske's "British Cultural Studies" in order to voice her irritation with certain recent developments in critical theory. Morris's tactic is to turn Baudrillard's own early

Frankfurt School sources against the British proponents of the politics of consumption: "In [the left-wing academic] analysis of everyday life, it seems to be criticism that actively strives to achieve 'banality,' rather than investing it *negatively* in the object of study."[16]

As this Adornian formulation hints, there are any number of problems, according to Morris, with Fiske's version of cultural studies. Not only does pop theory appear to replicate itself like any other mass-produced commodity, but severed from its original historical context (i.e., Thatcherism) and reproduced in quite different political cultures such as the United States and Australia, its critical force also "tends to disappear or mutate" (B 21). Moreover, though voxpop theory compulsively appeals to "the people" in order to buttress its arguments for what Fiske calls "semiotic democracy," the net effect of this operation (the *demos* is *ethnography*) is a particularly vicious hermeneutic circle insofar as the *demos* is both the "source of authority for a text and a figure of its own critical activity" (B 23).

So, in a scenario straight out of Gibson's *Mona Lisa Overdrive* (where Mona contemplates a poster of Angela Mitchell), Fiske in "British Cultural Studies" presents us with Lucy, a 14-year-old fan, on a Madonna poster: "She's tarty and seductive . . . but it looks alright when she does it" (BCS 273). This response confirms—after, of course, the appropriate commentary ("we can note a number of points here . . .")— Fiske's interpretation of Madonna as well as his own populist enterprise. In other words, what is effaced here—in the process of citation, translation, and identification of ostensibly raw but, in fact, pre-cooked ethno-semiological data—are those discursive strategies that Fiske mobilizes in his ethnographic work, not to mention those "invisible" but by no means negligible institutional sites which precondition the so-called tertiary text.

More simply, although Fiske encourages Lucy to voice her opinion, he never recognizes what Morris calls the "double play of transference": "Lucy tells him her pleasure in Madonna: but what is his pleasure in Lucy's?" (B 22). It may be, of course, that Lucy's interests contradict those of the "dominant patriarchy," as Fiske's reading insists; however, if the formal language of Madonna's texts in fact speak *to* and *for* girl fans like Lucy, one would imagine that it is important to understand not only how the *Playboy* reader's interests are served by the same texts but how the sites of reception at work here—both the dominant and subcultural as well as Fiske's own scholastic-ethnographic one—articulate with those rather different sites from which the Madonna commodity-body-sign issues in the "first" instance (i.e., the site of production).

I will turn to the issue of production in a moment, but the gender implications of Morris's critique of Fiske suggest that a more nuanced ethnographic approach to the problem of Madonna might be the answer. Lisa Lewis's *Gender Politics and MTV: Voicing the Difference* (1990), which followed on the heels of Fiske and Kaplan's books, in fact promises as much, examining as it does the emergent discourse of female adolescence on MTV and, in particular, the "historical intersection between female labor, female politics, and consumption practice."[17] Yet if Lewis's argument for the semiosis of access and discovery[18] represents a necessary response to those cultural critics who have been "reluctant to consider areas of consumption as sites of cultural production" (classical cultural criticism typically expresses, she adds, "an aversion to all forms of consumer culture" [GP 198]), her gender-inflected analysis of consumption and commodification also tends to attribute entirely too much agency to her female adolescent fans, as if fandom were unconstrained by, say, access and class, *class* access. To revise Morris on Fiske: "In [Lewis's] text, [women] have . . . an indominable capacity to 'negotiate' readings, generate new interpretations, and to remake the materials of culture" (B 23).

Given just such "generous" assumptions about reception, however, Lewis can argue that Kaplan's stress on the site of exhibition (i.e., MTV's continuous 24-hour flow) not only renders "engagement with individual 'alternative' texts impossible"—a position essentially at odds, according to Lewis, with the practice of fandom—but that Kaplan's "overarching reliance on 'postmodern' critique" hinders her understanding of the problem of signification or, more simply, "the creation of meanings by interested viewers" (GP 216). The primary source for this viewer-dominant position is—surprise!—John Fiske (GP 217). In sum, though Lewis recognizes that commercial-ideological imperatives pose problems for the "*production* of subjective voices" (GP 219, emphasis mine), her voxpop theory is predicated, like Fiske's, on an insufficiently critical reading of reception *and* commodification.

The differences between Lewis's and Kaplan's position on MTV are telling in this context. Unlike Lewis, Kaplan explicitly foregrounds her position of enunciation, *à la* Morris, self-incriminating as this discursive gesture might be. (Kaplan's knowledge of contemporary music is rudimentary at best, embarrassingly non-existent at worst.) So, in "Why Write a Book about MTV," the introduction to *Rocking around the Clock*, Kaplan writes: "In the 1970s I dropped out to become an adult, only vaguely keeping track of punk, new wave and heavy metal—largely through my daughter" (RC 6). Despite this generational gap, though, MTV intrigued Kaplan as an object of study because of its similarity to, and difference from, her own formative adolescent cultures: the "politicized," *pre*-Beatles British youth cultures of the early 1960s. And make no mistake about it: compared to the proto-youth cultures of London in the early 1960s,[19] MTV for Kaplan is a "full blown, heavily commercialized youth *phenomenon*" (RC 6, emphasis mine): cool, phallic, parodic—in a word, *non*-oppositional.

Which raises an intriguing question (one that Shelagh Young first posed in "Whose Gaze Is It Anyway?" [1989]):[20] Given the disjunction between Lewis's sympathetic and Kaplan's oppositional view of MTV, could it be that the generational difference between the two explains, in part, their opposing views of this particular "institution"? This generational difference, even antagonism, is played out in their respective readings of Madonna's *Open Your Heart* (Jean-Baptiste Mondrino, 1986).[21] Where Lewis argues that Madonna in *Open Your Heart* embodies the sexual and economic power of the new, postmodern woman, Kaplan situates this video—the last one she addresses in *Rocking around the Clock*—within what she calls the "circulation of the image and its ties to consumption" (RC 157).[22]

Now, if this negative coding of consumption as advertising is consonant with a certain classical Marxism, a position that fundamentally differentiates Kaplan from a younger generation of American feminists who, like Lewis, have stopped worrying about popular culture and learned to love it, her Lacanian reading of *Open Your Heart* is anything but orthodox, as the following passage testifies: "MTV, more than other television, may be said to be *about* consumption. It evokes a kind of hypnotic trance in which the spectator is suspended in a state of unsatisfied desire but forever under the illusion of *imminent* satisfaction through some kind of purchase" (RC 12). MTV's lure for Kaplan is, it is clear, a specifically televisual one; unlike the pre-Oedipality of film, which ostensibly mimics the dream state, MTV is decidedly *post*-Oedipal: splintered, shattered subjects, we consume ad-segment after ad-segment in order to satisfy our finally insatiable desire for the phallus.

While Kaplan's Freudo-Marxian account of MTV would appear to offer a theory of "commodity fetishism" along the lines I sketched at the end of Part Two, upon closer inspection, her model of consumption and spectatorship is not only hypothetical in the pejorative sense, but is itself transfixed (*medusée*, as Baudrillard would say) by the sublime ideology of the phallus. Bluntly, if Kaplan's reading of MTV is plainly materialist (though Lacanian psychoanalysis hardly seems capable of articulating the medium-specific differences between cinema and television), it is not—for all its Althusserianism—properly *historical*.

Similarly, for all its supposed ethnographic interest, Fiske's super-positive spin on reception and the popular economy all too often seems like the mere inverse of Kaplan at her most determinist. There is no doubt that the commodity is at least double-voiced—as Fiske, citing Lewis on Madonna wannabes, claims (TC 262)—but it is another question altogether whether there are parallel but separate economies (one financial, one cultural) and, even more problematically, whether the "cultural economy drives the financial in a dialectic force that counters the power of capital" (TC 326).

In retrospect, of course (and in partial defense of Fiske), it also needs to be said that the high phase of cultural populism was itself the product of a determinate historical moment. Indeed, it's worth recollecting that in Great Britain and the United States in the 1980s—from, say, 1983 to 1987 (and either despite, or perhaps because of, Thatcherism and Reaganism)—there was a palpable sense of intellectual liberation in the air, an "immense sigh of relief," as McGuigan puts it, "at finally being let off the 'hook' of puritanical critique."[23] The left cultural critic was free—free at last!—to enjoy mass-popular culture instead of being compelled to "expose the dire workings of the system and its dreadful ideologies."[24] From this perspective, then, there was no doubt something salutary about even the most uncritical, celebratory excesses of cultural studies, excesses associated in both the elite and popular media with that ultimate sign of academic excess, Madonna Studies itself.

Madonna Overdrive: The Star Commodity-Body-Sign

With her sensorium expertly modulated by Piper Hill, her first stims are greeted with unprecedented enthusiasm. Her global audience is entranced by her freshness, her vigor, the delightfully ingenuous way in which she seems to discover her glamorous life as if for the first time.

—William Gibson, *Mona Lisa Overdrive*

I looked out at a wide expanse of night sky, saw the stars, and felt a sense of wonder . . . In one sudden, miraculous moment Madonna appears in and across the whole sky. She was a projection, an apparition, a Madonna in the flesh and in person all at the same time.

—Nancy, from *I Dream of Madonna*

> There are Amish kids in Pennsylvania who
> know about Madonna.
>
> —Robert Bork, "Sex and Hollywood: What
> Should the Government's Role Be?"

In 1992, with the simultaneous appearance of *Sex* and *Erotica*, the Madonna phenomenon went into complete overdrive. One sign of this cyberblitz was the opening sequence of Tarantino's *Reservoir Dogs* (1992) where, improbably enough, a motley crew of would-be bank robbers partake in a knowing, post-prandial discussion of Madonna's music videos.

Another sign was the publication of the first critical collection on Madonna, *The Madonna Connection: Representational Politics, Subcultural Identities, and Cultural Theory* (1992).[25] According to the editor, Cathy Schwichtenberg, Madonna's work is a paradigm case that offers a particularly convenient opportunity to "engage in the negotiation of cultural *business* at that busy intersection" between politics and popular culture (MC 4, emphasis mine). Hence the blurb from *Vanity Fair* that graces the back cover of the paperback edition: "Even academics are doing a brisk trade in Madonnaology."

However, if connection is the key term in the book's title (business aside for the moment), what is ultimately at stake in any discussion of Madonna's impact, according to Schwichtenberg, is the politics of representation (MC 2). By politics, Schwichtenberg is referring not so much to public policy or political science as to what has been called—since the *Tel Quel* days at least—the politics of the signifier. Schwichtenberg acknowledges in her gloss of "subcultural identities" that the politics of the signifier functions "within the larger purview of late capitalism" (MC 3), but she maintains that Madonna's various texts "may well present the conditions for the coalescence and mobilization of identities yet to be pacified by commodity culture" (MC 3).

While one has to wonder whether any identity, parodic or otherwise, can be said to be constituted before or outside the logic of capital (there are no unpacified bodies, to paraphrase Foucault, in the arena of late, transnational capitalism), the concept of the commodity-body-sign is arguably one "economic" way to examine the second phase of Madonna Studies (1988–1992), the transitional, sometimes tumultuous period from *Like a Prayer* to *Sex* and *Erotica*.

Body

It's no doubt a gross understatement to say that, for good or ill, Madonna mobilizes the discourse of the body. Thus, one of the ironies of the "new" politics of the signifier, "Madonna politics" included, is that resistance—as Susan Bordo argues—"is imagined as the refusal to em-*body any* positioned subjectivity at all" (MC 281, initial emphasis mine). The net result of this grand refusal is what one might call the *glissement* of the body politic, where the body as well as whatever politics one might derive from even a strategically punctual agent is subjected to an extraordinary, and extraordinarily withering, discursive charge. As the above formulation is meant to underscore (body politic), this discursivization of the corporeal represents, in turn, a radical *de-*materialization of the political.

Before I turn to the issue of the body in the Madonna (star) commodity-body-sign, I would therefore like to post the following question: Given the value of the deconstructive critique of the classical representational subject (and it is clear that one cannot underestimate the significance of this critique for subaltern and subcultural constitu-encies), what can "representational politics" possibly mean if there is *no body* left to represent?

One way to anchor or button down the *glissement* of the body (politic) is, as I intimated in Part Two, to think the concept-metaphor of the commodity-body-sign.[26] My working assumption here is that, in some sense, to some degree, every body is a commodity-sign today inasmuch as there is no way to wholly escape the ubiquitous codes of postmodern capitalist culture, a proposition that is especially true, it seems to me, of spectacular star bodies such as Madonna's. Moreover, though it may be a perverse assertion (albeit one not unfamiliar to Freud), I think it is safe to say that the body of Madonna is at once esoteric and obscene, normal and pathological. It is, in a word, repre-sentative. That is, the body of Madonna is a dream of and for the *polis*, screening as it does those collective and sometimes not so republican desires and fantasies that fuel the national Imaginary.[27]

The body of Madonna is also, as I will argue a little later in this segment, a figure or trope for an international world order that may be neither new nor benign. Which is simply to say that this particular commodity-body travels, as does the theory that cannot, now, be disas-sociated from it. In this sense, the body of Madonna—which, as *The Madonna Connection* makes clear, comprises Madonna's *corpus* in the widest, telecommunicational sense and therefore remains irreducible to "Madonna's body" (the *propre* is not appropriate here)—this "body" is indeed a paradigmatic site for cultural studies. To say this, though—to say that the body of Madonna is a paradigm case for the study of culture—is by no means to guarantee, in advance, its politicality, which of course remains very much to be determined.

The body—especially when it is articulated with the sign and commodity—is, however, one determinate instance, even if only a negative one. Hence, in her essay on Madonna, Susan Bordo contends, *pace* Lewis, that in *Open Your Heart* the "female body is offered to the viewer purely as a spectacle, an object of sight, a visual commodity to be consumed" (MC 287). Indeed, Bordo's reading of *Open Your Heart* openly contests the politics of the signifier espoused by other Madonna critics:[28]

> The video's postmodern conceits . . . facilitate rather than deconstruct the presentation of Madonna's body as an object of display. For in the absence of a coherent critical position *on* the images, the individual images themselves become preeminent, hypnotic, fixating. . . . Ultimately, this video is entirely about Madonna's body, the narrative context virtually irrelevant, an excuse to showcase the physical achievements of the star, a video centerfold. (MC 287)

For Bordo, any estimation of Madonna's *Open Your Heart*—in particular, the ostensibly empowered "female" gaze—must critically account for the normalizing power of the socio-cultural gaze and, equally importantly, the "sadly continuing social realities of dominance and subordination" (MC 289).

Bordo's essay—the subtitle of which is "Effacements of Postmodern Culture"—usefully locates Madonna's body within a more general culture of the body, one that relentlessly subjects women's bodies to certain repressive regimes of physical beauty; equally clearly, her essay also performs its own not-so-subtle effacements of both the Material Girl and postmodern culture. Thus, with respect to the materiality of Madonna's body, Bordo's valorization of the early, voluptuous Madonna substantially downplays the embodied historicity of the later, leaner Madonna. How else can one explain the following dictum: "Madonna's new body has no material history; it conceals its praxis, it does not reveal its pain" (MC 286)? While the "new" Madonna—post *Open Your Heart*, say—may conform more to the canons of contemporary female beauty than the "old" Madonna, one might well argue the exact opposite: that Madonna has in fact helped *construct* a new, muscular body-image for women—a butch figure, if you will.[29]

There is no question of substantiality here (in the classical, rationalist-idealist sense that Judith Butler has been at pains to problematize).[30] If there were, the body of Madonna would merely signify, as Bordo says, a "new inscription of mind/body dualism" (MC 288), a postmodern twist on a now very old Cartesianism. At the same time, it seems to me that, *pace* Bordo, we do not actually have to see the concrete labor that went into Madonna's physical transformation (though just such a "baring of the device" would satisfy some of the conditions for the Marxist-Brechtian determination of aesthetic use-value), since if the endlessly circulated shots of Madonna exercising were not enough, the postmodern ideal-typical body lives and dies by the truism "no pain, no gain." Put another way, just as one can change history, so too can one change the body; however (and this is, I take it, the crucial proviso), it is not only a painstaking, if not painful, *process*, but the possibilities of transformation are always subject to determinate, structural—which is to say, *material*—limits.

In addition (to take up the question of postmodern culture), postmodernism cannot, I think, be flatly described as what Bordo calls postmodern conversation: "celebration of 'difference' . . . along with a rush to protect difference from its homogenizing abuses" (MC 276). While this description captures one, popular-academic aspect of postmodernism, it is difficult to square such a negative, one-sided characterization of the postmodern with the dialectical and pro-totality reading represented by someone like Jameson. In short, neither Madonna nor postmodernism in general is quite as simple as Bordo implies; in fact, if *The Madonna Connection* is any indication (and for all its unevenness, I think it is), the readings which constitute this collection and within which Bordo's own essay must, in part, be situated testify that both Madonna and postmodernism are deeply contradictory phenomena very much open to interpretation.

Consider, for example, Cindy Patton's essay "Embodying Subaltern Memory," which focuses on the urban Latino and African-American gay subcultures featured in *Vogue* (David Fincher, 1990). Although there is a sense in which even Patton's essay forecloses on the problematic character of Madonna's appropriation of (to cite *The Madonna Connection*) "subcultural identities,"[31] its thesis remains—as I noted in the introduction—a distinctly provocative one, involving as it does not only dance, a subject that is notoriously recalcitrant to theoretical analysis, but that embattled majority: white middle-class heterosexuals. According to Patton, when white middle-class heterosexuals are dancing to "Vogue" at clubs, they are "performing, however *non*-cognitively, the kinesthesia that *embodies* the problematics of race and gender from the perspective of subalterns" (MC 86, emphasis mine). Given the controversial nature of this claim, including and especially its bracketing of cognition, Patton's reading concludes, appropriately enough, on a qualified note: "If *Vogue* cannot tell us from whence it came, that is

because the *lieux de memoire* [sites of memory] of voguing are not in
a time or place but of the body" (MC 99).

However, the real interest of "Embodying Subaltern Memory," at
least for me (which is to say, within the context of this book's argument), is the way it periodically works the negative, as in the following
emblematic passage where Patton's critique of deconstruction marks a
moment of resistance against her own appropriation of the deconstructive
politics of the signifier:

> Admonished to free ourselves from a painful world by "let[ting]
> your body move to the music," *Vogue* provides a stylistic
> paradigm for freedom of movement. This paradigm elides the
> sources of repression that the dance means to deconstruct
> because these sources are disassociated from the particularities
> of a culture of resistance. The moves of voguing deconstruct
> gender and race, but *Vogue* makes it difficult to recall why
> such a deconstruction might be desirable. (MC 98)

Here, Patton's historical sense, her stubborn recollection of the *Un/Lust*
of a particular past—the Houses of Vogue alluded to in Malcolm
McClaren's "Deep in Vogue" (1989) and, more remotely, pre-Stonewall
homosexual culture and, more remotely still, the "interwar diaspora
that facilitated the Harlem Renaissance" (MC 88)—this act of recollection engenders its own kind of kinesthesia, fleshing out those signifiers
of subalternity that Madonna's *Vogue* telegraphically *re*-appropriates.

Precisely because of its negative dialectics, then, Patton's examination of the intricate play of race and sex-gender in Madonna's videos
distinguishes her work from that done in the first flush of Madonna
Studies (which tended to theorize from unexamined predicates about
white heterosexuality) as well as other essays in *The Madonna Connection* (which tend to be either too negative or too affirmative). In fact,
with respect to the latter collection, one might venture that the absence
of a dialectically derived moment of negativity in the various contribu-
tors' account of the politics of the signifier is ultimately what makes
their affirmation of the Material Girl seem so facile and celebratory or,
in a word, *immaterial*.

Sign

If Patton's "Embodying Subaltern Memory" engages the heterosexual
body from the perspective of homosexuality, her recollective reading of
the body in dance is also situated in terms of "message-transfer notions

of consumption" (hence the stress on the signifier vis-à-vis the signified or referent) as well as, more generally, the sort of ideology critique associated with Marxist cultural studies. Indeed, since *Ideologiekritik*— unlike Patton's own preferred mode, postmodern rhetorical critique— "almost inevitably require[s] critique of 'negative' images and replacement by 'positive' ones" (MC 85)—it is necessary, according to Patton, to abandon conventional arguments about cooptation in order to understand how critique exists "within the very surface of the proper of culture" (MC 83).

Accordingly, where *Vogue* for some critics is "parasitic" on gay Afro-Latino culture, for Patton the video's mass-cultural *re*-circulation of everyday critiques of the dominant culture makes these critiques more, not less, accessible. *Vogue*, in other words, is less an instance of cooptation or appropriation *per se* than pastiche, where pastiche—though seemingly reformist or retrostylistic—is a species of gender trouble, a tactic of passing which performatively re-mixes the codes of masculinity and femininity. In short, a mainstream popular-cultural text like *Vogue* may well commodify site-specific, subaltern discourses, but it also simultaneously solicits the "meaning of difference" and, in so doing, connects the video to "earlier, 'queer' meanings of modern homosexuality" (MC 87).

While Patton is careful, unlike a number of proponents of the politics of the signifier, to delimit the subversive effects of pastiche and rhetorical critique, "Embodying Subaltern Memory" also constructs a loaded, binary opposition between Marxism and postmodernism or, more precisely, between Marxist ideology critique (–) and postmodern rhetorical criticism (+). Moreover, true to this antinomic logic, the commodity appears in Patton's essay in a classically negative light. The net effect is an asymmetrical account of production and consumption, as if commodification had no necessary, internal relation to subalternity (and vice versa).

Admittedly, given Marxism's historical lack of interest in issues of gender and sexuality, to broach the issue of "commodity fetishism" in this particular context may well be construed as an analytical regression—moving, as Kaplan says, "from postmodernism back to Marxism" (MC 160). On the other hand, given the location of Madonna's work within the capital-intensive, horizontally integrated nexus of film/music/video production, it also strikes me as critically irresponsible to talk about the oppositionality of Madonna's politics without at some point engaging the *question* of the commodity.

To insist, however, on the commodity in the commodity-body-sign is by no means to demand a negative, ultra-critical determination of either *Vogue* or Madonna's work in general. As Lauren Berlant and Elizabeth Freeman show in "Queer Nationality," Queer Nation's parodies of mainstream advertisements—say, changing the *P* in the New York GAP series to a *Y*—slyly exploit the queerness of the commodities that heterosexual culture both produces and consumes, thereby making queer good the old-fashioned, all-American way by "making goods queer."[32] In other words, if there is a politics of the signifier, there is a politics of the commodity-body as well, as evidenced by Queer Nation's reinscription of the homophobic Bart Simpson tee-shirt which reads "Back off, faggot!"[33] With its counter-discursive retort, "Get used to it, dude!," the queered Bart Simpson tee-shirt—complete with earring, pink-triangle button, and QN tee-shirt (a meta-ad *en abîme*)—flags the body (politic), graphically demonstrating that the "commodity is a central means by which individuals tap into the collective experience of public desire" (QN 164).

The queered Bart Simpson tee-shirt is, it seems to me, an exemplary instance of the "perverse" political economy of "commodity fetishism," but the added significance of Bart's new and revised "commodity identity" is that it is a "generic body stamped with Queer Nation's own trademarked aesthetic," a civil-social determination that allows other consumers to publicly identify themselves as members of a queer nation (QN 164). In fact, in just this civil-social sense, Berlant and Freeman's reading of Queer Nation supplements Patton's reading of *Vogue*'s dequeening of the gay drag subculture documented in Jenny Livingstone's *Paris Is Burning* (1992): where Patton asserts that "postmodernity can have no utopia" (MC 98), Berlant and Freeman maintain, echoing the author of the *Passagen-werk*, that Queer Nation's "corporate strategy" links the "utopian promises of the commodity with those of the nation" (QN 164). Here, one might say—in a scenario straight out of some queer postmodern cartoon—Benjamin meets Bart Simpson.

Something of the same spirit or *esprit* would appear to inform Schwichtenberg's own contribution to *The Madonna Connection*, "Madonna's Postmodern Feminism," which argues that Madonna's fluid persona and simulation aesthetic should be understood as "hallmarks of a postmodern commodity culture where modernist notions of authenticity surrender to postmodern fabrication" (MC 130), a disingenuous figuration that reveals a "potential political core at the heart of play" (MC 135). One effect of this putatively coalitional rather than foundational politics, according to Schwichtenberg, is that it permits one to envisage a form of feminism that is not alien to lesbianism (where, for instance, Madonna's political stylistics deconstruct the sort of identity politics associated with straight feminism). In fact, what for certain critics like Bordo remains a minus about postmodernism (simulation, fragmentation, fetishization, etc.) is, according to Schwichtenberg, a definite plus for lesbians since it allows them to "move from the margin to the center" (MC 141).

Postmodern to the core, *Justify My Love* (Jean-Baptiste Mondrino, 1990) is exemplary in this respect, crossing as it does Madonna with Mapplethorpe or, to echo Schwichtenberg's analysis, Foucault with Butler (where the latter conjunction marks a double cognitive dissonance, as in the couple "gay/lesbianism"). Hence the politial promise of postmodern feminism, or lesbian postmodernism, which constructs itself under the sign of linguistic mutability, the play of figuration and fabrication, displacement and destabilization.

However, if Schwichtenberg's essay persuasively counters Bordo's one-dimensional critique of postmodernism, it also tends to elide, like Bordo's essay, those racial signifiers that are an integral part of *Justify My Love* and Madonna's work in general,[34] presenting a simple, black-and-white affirmation that belies Madonna's own *significance*, whether as body, commodity, or sign. Bluntly, Schwichtenberg's reading of *Justify My Love* never really justifies itself since it never really questions its wholly affirmative position on Madonna—unlike, say, Greta Gaard's "The Laugh of Madonna" (which activates both a radical lesbian feminist voice *and* "les-bi-gay-trans activist" one)[35] or Lisa Henderson's "Madonna and the Politics of Queer Sex," which returns again and again to Madonna's privileged, albeit ambivalent, position vis-à-vis queer culture.

Henderson's reading of *Justify My Love* provides an especially interesting contrast to Schwichtenberg's, since Henderson is not unfamiliar with what Schwichtenberg calls the "artifice of gender"—the "playful *and* painful liminalities of lesbian and gay life" (MC 109, emphasis mine). As this doubly double locution italicizes, Henderson remains alert to the very real ambivalence of Madonna's body politic, which is at once liberatory and regressive, progressive and reactionary. Indeed, the political instability, not to say volatility, of this particular dialectic (which is bound to disturb politically correct critics, and which is rather different than the one valorized by Schwichtenberg), goes a long way, I think, towards explaining Madonna's tremendous popular appeal. On one hand, one can argue, as Henderson does, that the sexual-gender ambiguity of *Justify My Love* is what makes this particular mass-cultural product available to lesbian (and gay) appropriation; on the other hand, if one reads against the grain of this against-the-grain reading, a strategy that problematizes any affirmative reading of Madonna, some of the troubling pain of gender trouble begins to surface:

Many of *Justify My Love*'s sexual gestures depend on dominance and subordination for their effect, overturning the
standard of mutuality in much feminist and humanist rethinking of sexual relationships. For some viewers, such
images are likely to evoke not erotic choices but real-life
sexual coercion and brutality, the experience of huge num-
bers of girls and women in the United States and abroad.
(MC 112)

As for the so-called lesbian scene in *Justify My Love*, Henderson observes that although we cannot be certain that Madonna does *not* kiss
a woman, such ambiguity is finally just that—ambiguous, and ambiguity—as a number of critics of deconstruction have pointed out—has its
limits: "In a pop-cultural universe that makes heterosex abundant and
abundantly clear, allusions to homosex are nice but not enough.
Postmodernism's playful indeterminacy becomes gay activism's short
shrift" (MC 113).

Though Henderson proceeds to synthesize this moment of negativity in the next section of her reading, "Articulating Sex" (where she
argues for an *anti*-anti-porn position on *Justify My Love*), her conclusion—tellingly titled "Ambivalent Articulations"—returns to the above,
determinate negation, asking in the process some very hard questions
about Madonna, such as: "How grateful are lesbian and gay people
supposed to be?" (MC 123). As Henderson remarks, many gays and
lesbians will recognize, say, the Mapplethorpe in *Justify My Love* or the
Harlem drag culture in *Vogue*; however, most members of her mainstream, heterosexual audience will not, and more to the point, Madonna herself "has not gone out of her way to credit (or remunerate)
her sources" (MC 123). Finally, while Schwichtenberg is content to cite
Butler ("the deconstruction of identity is not the deconstruction of
politics"),[36] Henderson entertains the possibility that "multi-Madonna"
is less a matter of political multi-discursivity than a multiple market
approach—that is to say, "less designed for deconstruction than pop
idol diversification" (MC 123).

Such an economic-corporate evaluation does not, needless to say,
negate Madonna as such. It does, however, suggest that, confronted
with the inspired simulacra thrown up by super-popular performers like
Madonna, it may well be necessary to cross Butler or Baudrillard with
someone like Gramsci, since the sort of institutional structures that his
work endeavored to articulate are remarkably immune to seduction and
simulation (and, for that matter, to be fair to Patton, ideology critique
as well). Put another, more emphatic way: if the politics of the signifier

in fact *supplements* rather than complements identity politics (with the full force of the Derridian reading of the *supplément*), the politics of the signifier remains, strictly speaking, supplementary.

An anecdote ("Truth is where you find it"): In 1990 Madonna, to her credit, promoted the civic virtues of voting in her controversial "Rock the Vote" spot on MTV. Alas, it turns out that she wasn't even registered to vote when she made the commercial.[37] My point here is that there are politics and there are politics, and whatever one might want to say about "Madonna politics"—which, like the "body" of Madonna, cannot be reduced to Madonna's personal politics—the politics of the signifier is not, for all its necessity, sufficient. The danger, or so it seems to me, is somehow thinking that it is or might be.

Commodity

When it comes to the commodity, Madonna Studies has not, for the most part, been especially interested. This is rather ironic, to radically understate the matter, since both the street and elite take on Madonna has been that she is merely in it "for the money."

There are, however, notable exceptions. For instance, in "Madonna Politics," the follow-up essay to her work on Madonna in *Rocking around the Clock*, E. Ann Kaplan wonders, if only rhetorically, whether the politics of the signifier can help us "analyze Madonna as commodity" (MC 161). While one might dialectically reverse this question and ask, as I have, whether the commodity-body can help us analyze the Madonna sign, Kaplan—unlike, say, Patton—is willing to seriously entertain the theoretical use-value of ideology critique. In fact, Kaplan advances the classical-Marxist argument about the effacement of labor-power to which Bordo's essay only alludes: "The Madonna image embodies the supreme example of commodity fetishism in that the address to the spectator works to conceal the operations of labor . . . that underlie its production and display" (MC 161).

However, if Kaplan adopts what she herself calls the "repression theory" of Marxism, her ensuing defense of Madonna suggests that something in fact is being repressed here, and that something is, paradoxically enough, the commodity. Thus, with respect to whether or not Madonna is in collusion for her own gain with an oppressive late capitalism, Kaplan offers a host of arguments in defense of her: that Madonna has "consistently supported gay and lesbian sex" (MC 161); that Madonna has been "using her wealth and power for socially conscious ends" (safe sex, AIDS research, etc. [MC 161]); that Madonna, like Mapplethorpe, is not only an avant-garde artist but one who attacks censorship (e.g., *Justify My Love* [MC 161]); and, finally, that Madonna is "sensitive" to the critique of consumer capitalism (MC 161). (Madonna's reply to Forrest Sawyer on "Nightline"—"You want me to advertise some of my button-pushing products?" [MC 161]—is the attendant evidence for the last claim.)

Now, most of these claims are, I think, true enough, and obviously say something about Madonna and her politics. Still, Kaplan's defense does not quite speak, as she would have us believe, to the question of the commodity. With respect to the second of the above points, for instance, it is quite possible, even imperative, to adopt a quite "vulgar" position: that Madonna's philanthropism, however admirable, can in no way be construed as anticapitalist, since neither philanthropy nor sensitivity, state-of-the-art aesthetics nor free-speech advocacy, constitutes, necessarily, a critique of capital.

Kaplan is rather closer to the truth when she abandons what is ultimately an extremely weak, *ex tempore* defense of Madonna's anticapitalism and admits that Madonna "*construct[s]* herself as merely making use of consumption economies that she did not create and for which she is not responsible" (MC 162, emphasis mine). Unlike the above claims, Kaplan's recourse here to the word *construct* underlines the sort of ethical stakes that frequently get lost in performance theories of subjectivity. No one of course is personally responsible for capitalism, just as no one person is responsible for the institution of sexism or racism. But such *carte blanche* excuses will hardly do for Madonna (or, for that matter, anyone else), as Kaplan herself is perfectly aware. Thus, when push comes to shove (when, that is, she is about to conclude her argument), the repressed returns, and Kaplan concedes the obvious: that Madonna has never really addressed the material effects of her stardom (MC 162).

This particular issue or problem—what I call the *star* commodity-body-sign—is addressed in *The Madonna Connection*, if only in the last instance. Indeed, in the final part of the collection, which is titled "The Political Economy of Postmodernism: Madonna as Star Commodity," David Tetzlaff unapologetically tenders the sort of orthodox Marxist argument against Madonna that Kaplan merely parodies: "Postmodernism applies commodity fetishism to aesthetics, emptying the use-value of symbols in the search for exchange-value, but it also aestheticizes the realm of commodities, turning economic exchange into spectacle for mass consumption" (MC 248). Within this particular political-*economic* context, the text of Madonna produces, according to Tetzlaff, quite specific metatextual effects.

Specifically, Madonna's postmodern feminism as well as her phenomenal popularity should be read, according to Tetzlaff, as an instance of the "historical shift from patriarchy to capitalism as the dominant discourse for middle-class women" (MC 250). This feminist/post-Fordist address is not, however, without its very real downside. In other words, if Madonna's politics of the signifier is ultimately dependent on the specific social and cultural location of the consumer-spectator, what works for, say, white bourgeois North American women will not necessarily work for other, less privileged women. There, one might say— at the margin or periphery—the economic imperatives of postmodern capitalism have not compelled the patriarchy to unlearn its "old," but still brutally productive, ways. One can therefore wonder, as Tetzlaff pointedly does, how free Madonna herself would be for self-actualization if she were economically tied to the "historically rooted struggles of the subaltern groups who populate her videos" (MC 259).[38]

Unfortunately, in order to ground this "subaltern" critique (which, I might add, seems to be absolutely beyond someone like Camille Paglia),[39] Tetzlaff rounds up the usual suspects: capitalism, postmodernism, and, somewhat surprisingly, feminism itself. Thus, with respect to feminism and postmodernism, Tetzlaff contends that Madonna is not only a screen for the big business of late capitalism, her image changing chameleon-like with the seasonal cycles of the fashion mode, but the sort of postmodern, semiotic-rich figures she trades in don't, for all their manifest impact, "signify anything at all" (MC 256). So much, one might say, for popular-cultural, not to mention gender or queer, studies. As for feminism, the Madonna phenomenon represents merely yet another, albeit feminized, moment in the history of capital, since Madonna's goal, according to Tetzlaff, is not resistance but consumption, not subversion but self-promotion. Hence the following simple—and given Tetzlaff's *pro forma* reading of commodity fetishism—super-negative determination: Madonna "is the commodity" (MC 257).

And yet, if, as Tetzlaff asserts, Madonna "poses no threat to the established economic order" (but then, one must ask, What artist does?), her commodity status is not therefore obvious. In other words, Madonna, or so it seems to me, is not simply a commodity nor, Daniel Harris's hyperbolic formulation aside ("Madonna is postmodernism"), is she equivalent in any real sense with postmodernism or, for that matter, feminism.

Accordingly, Tetzlaff's identification of feminism as post-feminist capitalism (where, that is, "economic terms dominate sexual representations" [MC 251]) threatens not only to dissolve the semi-autonomy of the category of sex/gender but to underestimate the by no means residual power of the patriarchy. Capitalism may not be able, it is true, "to afford the old forms of sexism anymore" (MC 250), but sexism and capitalism, not to mention racism, are by no means structurally symmetrical phenomena (except in the loosest homological sense). Rather more to the point, such "macro" social formations are rather more heterogeneous than Tetzlaff's analysis suggests, subject as they are to the law of uneven development. To intimate otherwise, as Tetzlaff does— even in the interests of a overtly liberatory project (the "liberation of the masses" [MC 262])—is, it seems to me, to hail the worst sort of universalism.

In short, if Tetzlaff's reading of the Madonna commodity addresses the issue of capital, it also faithfully—which is to say, all too literally—reproduces the classic cultural-industrial critique of affirmative culture. The result is a sub rosa moralism:

> Madonna's conscious self-commodification may be the primary trait for which she is admired by her mainstream audience. This is a frightening indication of how deeply late capitalist values have been absorbed into our popular culture. Commodity values are more precious than human values. Our culture validates success no matter what is sacrificed to achieve it. (MC 258)

While it is true that there is a distinct ethical charge to Marx, even to the later Marx (*pace* certain analytical-structuralist Marxists), the above critique merely repeats the abstract, monolithic protest against reification associated with classical Marxism, as if the sort of commodity values *embodied* in popular-cultural star-signs like Madonna were absolutely divorced from "human values."

Unlike Tetzlaff's "Metatextual Girl," which employs a restricted, strictly negative concept of the commodity (and whose cynical rhetoric tends to negate whatever criticality the essay may be said to possess), Greg Seigworth's work draws on Barry King's performance theory of stardom in order to situate Madonna as a unique—that is to say, *specific*—commodity within the general site of commodity-exchange.[40] At once labor in process and the product of labor (MC 295), Madonna functions for Seigworth as a body-sign as well as a star-commodity, or *star* commodity-body-sign.

Now, the materiality and specificity of star-commodities may not give us the sort of "insight into the nature of labor power in general" (MC 295) that King's and Seigworth's work promises, but making connections between the spheres of consumption and production of which the commodity-body is one material sign does foreground the various economies that subtend star-driven texts such as Madonna's.[41] In fact, *if* critics are to avoid becoming star-struck (a real occupational hazard, this), it is important to examine not only the production/consumption of the commodity-body-sign, as I argued at the end of Part Two, but distribution/exhibition and, more generally, circulation as well.

Of course, even to begin to talk about the circulation of star-commodities today is to broach the subject of international capital and those multinational corporations that daily conduct its flow. Which is simply to say that Madonna's (global) corporate identity, however occluded, cannot be separated out from her politics.[42] Therefore, with respect to production ("The star system is first of all production," as Edgar Morin says),[43] it is crucial to keep a number of economic facts in mind: first, that Madonna's 1992 deal with Time Warner was worth in excess of $60 million,[44] and, second, that this capital deployment was only one very small part of this parent company's accumulated capital at the time. Indeed, in this cultural-industrial context, it's worth noting that, as of Spring 1992 (when Madonna signed her deal), Time Warner was not only one of the top seventy-five companies in the Forbes 500, with assets in the double-digit billions ($24,900 million, to be exact),[45] but one of six record companies that currently dominate the global record business (MC 306).

It is also I think worth noting that Madonna is herself a corporation, and a rather diverse one at that, as the following litany of companies suggests: Music Tours Inc., Slutco (video production), Webo Girl (music publishing), Boy Toy Inc. (music and record royalties), Siren Films (film and video production), and, last but certainly not least, Maverick.[46] Though this corporate-economic aspect of Madonna's multi-faceted persona is difficult to determine with any real precision (as she is especially secretive when it comes to financial matters—"her lips are sealed," as one article puts it), it remains a determinate, if by no means simply negative, part of her *identity*.[47] (Capital, for all its postmodern liquidity, maintains a remarkable degree of perdurability.)

Again, let me be clear about the import of such a determinate negation: if it is necessary to situate the Madonna star commodity-body-sign within an industrial context—if only to get some sense, however crude, of her cultural exchange-value—this *re*-materialization does not obviate either her use- or sign-value. In other words, if on one hand, it's obvious that the individual art-commodity—say, that corpus which is Madonna—is both implicated in, and exceeds, the logic of political economy, on the other hand, it's equally obvious that in certain contexts (for instance, contemporary Anglophone cultural studies), a working understanding of the commodity can introduce, as Brecht knew, a necessary crudeness.[48] Without it—without, that is, some sense of "commodity fetishism" (understood in the "perverse," general-economic sense that I have argued for here)—cultural studies almost inevitably becomes culturalist.[49]

Body of Evidence: The Fatality of Madonna Studies

> "It's a Madonna pap smear. . . . I know it's kind of disgusting, but it's like . . . getting to know the real Madonna."
>
> —Pap Smear Pusher, *Slacker*

> The scandal of *Sex* is the scandal of S/M. . . . The critics bay for [Madonna's] blood: a woman who takes sex and money into her own hands must—sooner or later—bare her breasts to the knife.
>
> —Anne McClintock, "Maid to Order"

If 1992—the year in which, in the wake of *Sex* and *Erotica*, Madonna referred to herself as a revolutionary—marked the high or, depending on your perspective, low point of Madonna's career (or what I think of here as her second phase), 1993 looked at the moment very much like the "Beginning of the End."[50] This was not, needless to say, the first time that Madonna's demise had been predicted—hence the banality, at least in this case, of the "fatal" prognosticative impulse that is the real message of the Warholian maxim about fame.

Madonna, however, seemed to have nine lives, mutating as fast as media culture itself, outpacing the postmodern Fates at every turn of the course. As *Newsweek* aptly put it, stealing from the ultimate "art" of appropriation, advertising: "Like the Energizer Bunny, [Madonna] just keeps going."[51] And yet, covering Madonna's 1993 "Girlie Show" (in which Madonna traded Gaulthier for Dolce & Gabbana, mixing Dietrich with Doolittle, *Trapeze* with *Singin' in the Rain*, big-top Las Vegas with Broadway's Big White Way), even *Newsweek*'s relatively upbeat report concluded on a downbeat note: "Then again, buzzards are circling the bunny these days."[52]

While this gloomy scenario merely confirms the boom and bust mentality that drives both postmodernism and late capitalism (in particular, the pop culture industries), *Newsweek*'s Energizer-bunny trope is not without its ironic truth, as if in the transition from the *Playboy*-cum-Boy Toy sexuality of the early Madonna to the retro-chic, tongue-in-cheek erotica of the "Girlie Show" (the latter of which could be said to have prefigured both *Showgirls* [1995] and *Striptease* [1996]), Madonna had somehow been reduced in the process to a fuzzy, Pepto-Bismol automaton, more parodic than provocative. Rather more to the point, it was as if a "body of evidence" had finally accumulated and the attendant mass-cultural verdict had come in, definitive as the Roman *pollice verso*: Madonna was not simply guilty of bad taste and worse morals but, the ultimate rap for a superstar, she was now defunct, banal, passé.

In this sense, Madonna's real crime was not so much her "shocking" vulgarity or increasingly radical, polymorphous display of sexuality, but as Andrew Ferguson observed, citing Büchner on the death of Danton, her longevity.[53] Of course, this is arguably the fate of all pop-cultural revolutionaries, especially self-styled ones such as Madonna: "Icons come, icons go."[54] Or, as Madonna herself sardonically put it in the song "Human Nature" (1995): "Did I stay too long?"

Although Madonna's sudden decline was no doubt a result, at least in part, of the increasingly delirious rate of obsolescence that virtually defines pop-cultural celebrity, her fall cannot be fully understood outside that political culture which she both embodied and refracted.[55] The year 1992 is crucial in this respect, since if Madonna was the "perfect symbol for Reagan-era America"—"materialistic, blond as a Hollywood fantasy, adept at creating a career through photo opportunities,"[56] she was also something of an MTV Robespierre, periodically flaming the discursive hegemony of the Reagan-Bush regime. Which is simply to say that Madonna's rise coincided with a specific historical moment marked by—both in Britain and America—"the emergence of the 'New Right' and its advocacy of 'traditional family values,' "[57] and that if her work up to and including 1992 was not revolutionary in the classical-political sense, it nonetheless mobilized a series of popular signs than ran distinctly counter to the dominant political discourse of the time. What we are talking about here, in other words, is the desire of the body politic, or *political* desire.[58]

For all her controversiality, however (or, more probably, precisely because of it), Madonna's career in this period paid handsome, not to say astonomical, material dividends (to accent the *commodity* in the commodity-body-sign), though her notoriety also exacted, one imagines, a certain price or "pound of flesh." Consider, for instance, Madonna's 1994 appearance on the David Letterman show, when after the very public travails of 1992–93, she "acted out" the mass media trashing she had received during the previous year by effectively telling everybody to "fuck off." Then, less than six months later, she did an almost complete about-face, simultaneously renouncing her "bad girl" image and announcing her desire for kids and a man—"like Robert Redford in *The Way We Were.*"[59]

"Madonna's records," Simon Frith has remarked, are "soundtracks to her life" (M 89), and *Bedtime Stories* (1994), her first recording since *Erotica*, captures the above moment in all its moody ambivalence. There are still echoes of the old in-your-face bravado ("I'm not your bitch/ Don't hang your shit on me") and the halycon dance-music days of "Into the Groove" ("get up on the dance floor/Keep movin,' keep groovin' "), but despite new takes on old personae ("I'm not an angel"—cf. "Angel" [1985]) and the occasional hard-won note of optimism ("Here's my story: no risk, no glory"), the message is as clear as the wailing saxophone in "Sanctuary" (the title of which was equally indicative).

But if the subtext of *Bedtime Stories*—epitomized by the frank invitation of the title track "Bedtime Story" ("Let's get unconscious")— seems to be more about Thanatos than the regenerative powers of Eros, the video version of "Secret" also suggests a departure from the various vicissitudes of the death drive—repression and loss, anger and aggression—registered so vividly on *Bedtime Stories*. In fact, given Madonna's announcement in May 1996 that she was finally pregnant, *Secret* appears in retrospect to be less about a "cleansing rebirth"[60] than maternity-as-rebirth.

It is on just this regenerative note—one visually tied in *Secret* to the issue of race—that it is useful to turn to the academic response to Madonna's career since 1992: to return, that is, to the post-*Sex*, pre-"Madonna" Madonna. The most striking and symptomatic reading of this moment of Madonna Studies—what I think of here as the third phase—is bell hooks's "Power to the Pussy" (1993), which not unlike Kobena Mercer's diptych on Mapplethorpe, "Reading Racial Fetishism" (1993), represents an implicit *reprise* of her own, earlier essay, "Madonna: Plantation Mistress or Soul Sister?" (1992).[61]

Part of the continuing interest of the Mercer for me—in addition to its examination of racial fetishism—is his enunciation of himself as a desiring subject.[62] Hence, reviewing his initial, programmatic take on Mapplethorpe's photographs of black male nudes, he acknowledges that his anger at the stereotypical racial and sexual representation of black masculinity in, say, *Man in Polyester Suit* (1980) may have been the expression of a certain envy on his part, which was an effect, in turn, of an "imagined rivalry over some idealized and unattainable object of

homosexual desire" (RRF 320). Mercer's conclusion—a rhetorically
qualified but suggestive one—is that this critical aggressivity effectively
obscured his own narcissistic investment in the anxious pleasures which
Mapplethorpe's texts make available to white *and* black (gay) (male)
spectators.

The context is obviously different in the case of hooks's reading
of Madonna (since, among other things, Mapplethorpe's mediatic engagement with black culture, "art" or avant-garde photography, is rather
more restricted than Madonna's), but as in Mercer's initial interpretation of Mapplethorpe, hooks's "Madonna: Plantation Mistress or Soul
Sister?" is suffused with the negative, imaginary-laden language of
aggressivity.[63] The difference between the two Madonna essays is that
in the first, exploratory piece, hooks also discloses the other, affirmative
aspect of ambivalence—which is to say, *her* own envy and desire: "Many
of the black women I spoke with expressed intense disgust and hatred
of Madonna. Most did not respond to my cautious attempts to suggest
that underlying these negative feelings might lurk feelings of envy, and
dare I say it, desire" (MPM 219). For hooks, it is precisely because
Madonna's work embodies a powerful desire for those traits which are
the "quintessential markers of racial aesthetic superiority" that she has
"so much in common with black women"—in particular, those who
"suffer from internalized racism" (MPM 219).[64]

And yet, if in the first essay on Madonna hooks recognizes the
ambivalent play of (commodity) fetishism, the way desire is entangled
with disgust, envy with anger, the bulk of her reading is nonetheless
devoted to strenuously resisting her own dreadful fascination with "being" and/or "having" Madonna. In other words, if envy and desire are
tropes of identification and seduction respectively, in the final analysis
hooks opts for *critique* and its political-theoretical synonyms: opposition, transgression, "critical self-interrogation" (MPM 226). Moreover,
true to the oppositional logic of *Ideologiekritik*, critique is emphatically
opposed to both seduction and affirmation.[65]

Accordingly, hooks concedes that although she admires Madonna
because she has created a "cultural space where she can invent and
reinvent herself and receive public *affirmation*" (MPM 218, emphasis
mine), "when the chips are down," Madonna's affirmation of black
culture conceals "acts of racist aggression" (MPM 220). Bluntly (if this
were not blunt enough), Madonna opportunistically colonizes and exploits, commodifies and appropriates, black cultural experience. Given
this rhetoric of appropriation and commodification,[66] hooks's essay concludes, not so surprisingly, with a caveat not for the consumer but the
"artist": to wit, only when Madonna is able to intimately understand

the politics of domination and submission (and, consequently, discover a "deeper connection with oppositional black culture"), only then will she be able to "create new and different cultural productions, work that will be truly transgressive—acts of resistance that transform rather than simply seduce" (MPM 226).[67]

Now, it is no doubt too simple to say that hooks's essay on Madonna is a classic instance of an "instinct" (here envy or desire) undergoing a reversal into its opposite or, more specifically yet, a reversal of content (from, as it were, desire to disgust, seduction to resistance),[68] but such a reading does I think suggest some of the vicissitudes that attend the complex play of desire and identification in hooks's *critique*.[69] Indeed, some such psychosexual dynamic can be said to inform the general (political) economy of "commodity fetishism." At stake is not only the dialectical relation between production and consumption but, more generally, that between negation and affirmation or, to echo hooks's own terminology, critique and seduction.

This dialectic, at once libidinal and political-economic, rematerializes with something of the force of the repressed in hooks's slightly later essay on Madonna, "Power to the Pussy: We Don't Wannabe Dicks in Drag" (1993),[70] the aggressively slangy title of which—compared at least to the classic, antithetical balance of the earlier essay[71]—points to a certain hyper-cathexis. Before I examine hooks's reconsideration of Madonna, though, I would only reiterate what I hope has become clear in the course of this book: that the Madonna commodity-body-sign is not simply, or only, a commodity-fetish but a figure or sign, a *symptom*. Indeed, it is in just this overdetermined sense that one can speak of Madonna as an *hypericon*, a dialectical image that is not merely a "particular sign for something" (say, reification) but a "figure that symbolizes the process of figuration itself."[72] The additional theoretical interest of this particular concept-metaphor—Madonna-as-hypericon—is that it may be expanded, as Thomas Kemple explains, to include the commodification of the imagination (or the *art*-commodity), the production of commodities as images (or the commodity-body-*sign*), and the specularization of all culture (as in the postmodern society of the spectacle [RMW 177]).

More to the point of hooks's critique, if the exemplary figure of commodity fetishism for Marx is the "black Madonna," a *matrix figure* that structures the relations not only between images and things but between things and social practices (RMW 187), the black Madonna, true to the "perverse," general-economic character of "commodity fetishism," reveals a fundamental ambivalence, one that is reflected in, among other things, the Christian folklore tradition of the "wise prostitute" (RMW 180).

I will return to the issue of prostitution below as it relates to one, mass-popular figuration of Madonna (i.e., Madonna as slut), but it is not insignificant, I think, that hooks's "Power to the Pussy" begins with an autobiographical account of her first peregrination to Europe and, more specifically, her first pilgrimage to the shrine of the black Madonna (PP 65). Though I cannot do justice here to the textual and structural richness of hooks's preface, I do want to note that the "primitive" space of the black Madonna—a trope of Europe itself, or at least a certain Bohemian image of it (Europe, that is to say, as a "place of artistic and cultural freedom")[73]—this sacred space is also, for hooks, a place of *jouissance*: "to be with her was to be in the place of ecstasy" (PP 66). The place of the black Madonna is, in other words, a space of fantasy, a fantasmatic space where, paradoxically enough, identification yields to desire—to ecstasy or *jouissance*.[74]

The problem for hooks with this ecstatic moment of communion—where the black Madonna signifies not simply a utopian figure of Europe but a more cosmopolitan vision of "home" itself, of the "divine" artistic community that hooks dreamed about as a child during "Sunday morning church service" (PP 65)—is that it in no way alters the "politics of domination outside, in the space of the real" (PP 66). While a momentary sanctuary of sorts, the fantasmatic is absolutely divorced, according to hooks, from the real world and its politics. As she plaintively says in the conclusion to her reminiscence on the black Madonna: "None of us could remain there" (PP 66).

Appropriately enough, given the home-and-away structure of hooks's preface to "Power to the Pussy," it does not end on the above, strictly speaking, mournful note,[75] but circles back to the originary pain associated for her with home:

> My journey ended. I did not return home to become a Bohemian artist. My creative work, painting and writing, was pushed to the background as I worked hard to succeed in the academy, to become something I never wanted to be. To this day I feel imprisoned in the academic world as I felt in the world of my growing up. And I still cling to the dream of a radical visionary artistic community that can sustain and nurture creativity. (PP 66)

The mass-cultural iconicity of Madonna recollects, it is clear, hooks's ecstatic experience of the black Madonna as well as, rather more problematically, her continuing, if painfully unrequited, dream of a radical artistic community.

Indeed, it is as if Madonna for hooks were merely the sign or *objet petit a* of some profound absence, some loss or lack. This, at least, is how I understand hooks's comment that she was initially less "into" Madonna's music than her presence: "Her image, like that of the black Madonna, evoked a sense of promise and possibility, a vision of freedom; feminist in that she was daring to transgress sexist boundaries; Bohemian in that she was an adventurer, a risk taker; daring in that she presented a complex non-static ever-changing subjectivity" (PP 67).

hooks's representation here of the early Madonna is a strikingly progressive one—Madonna, as it were, before the fall: "a symbol of *unrepressed* female creativity and power—sexy, seductive, serious, and strong" (PP 67, emphasis mine). This is Madonna the miraculous, a transcendental wish-image that perfectly embodies *jouissance*: coming to power, coming to cultural fulfillment (PP 67).[76] In fact, for hooks, the early Madonna—young, hip, feminist—was not only the utopian antithesis, like the black Madonna, of the "heartbreaking estrangement" associated for her with the racially segregated South, but a beacon or guiding light for other young women "confined" like her in the academy (where the American academy is itself a punishing space of repression and discipline [PP 67]).[77]

As hooks's negative take on the academy indicates, the institutional and autobiographical conditions of possibility of hooks's "Power to the Pussy" are pervasively marked by the figure, at once racial and sexual, of *repression*. The question that therefore arises, especially in light of hooks's own earlier, rather severe critique of Madonna, is: What exactly is it about the early Madonna that was so "miraculous," so much so that she could function for hooks as a general sign of unrepressed presence? Put another way, if the later Madonna (*Sex*, the *Vanity Fair* "little-girl sex kitten layout," etc.)[78] elicits feelings of betrayal and loss, what is the difference between the two Madonnas that engenders such intense "collective lament" (PP 67)?

hooks's major premise in "Power to the Pussy" is that the "subversive," super-politicized subject-position which she associates with the early Madonna—"her opposition to conformist fixed identity"—abruptly disappeared (PP 69). Gone was the shifting radical subjectivity and sexual aggressiveness that once seemed so intoxicating and liberating; here instead—laid out for the "*mass* patriarchal gaze" in the Mylar-bound pages of *Sex*[79]—is mere cultural hedonism and shallow exhibitionism (PP 68, 69). Furthermore, where the early, younger Madonna was a sign of "feminist promise and power" (PP 67), the later, older (but by no means wiser) Madonna has steadfastly refused to enter "mature womanhood" like her feminist sisters and has endeavored in-

stead to sustain a perpetually youthful image. This particular image—
a "little-girl-on-the-playground sex symbol" (PP 68)—is, according to
hooks, neither avant-garde nor cool, transgressive nor hip. It is, quite
simply, bad—aesthetically *and* politically.

In addition to this general stricture, the minor premises of hooks's
critique, which emerge most clearly in her reading of *Sex*, pivot on the
following four issues: (1) Madonna's appropriation of homoerotic imagery, (2) her representation of S/M, (3) her recourse to racially charged
imagery (PP 75), and (4) her violence and cruelty towards women (PP
76). Thus, with respect to Madonna's exploitative use of gay imagery,
hooks invokes the figure of the white imperialist, echoing in the process
the title of her own earlier essay, "Madonna: Plantation Mistress or
Soul Sister?": "Mirroring the role of plantation overseer in a slave-
based economy, Madonna surveys the landscape of sexual hedonism,
her 'gay' freedom, her territory of the other, her jungle" (PP 73). Later
in the same essay, hooks reaccentuates the racial implications of this
post-colonial conceit, commenting that when Madonna occupies the
"wilderness of black culture," she assumes the "mantle of the white
colonial adventurer" (PP 77).

Madonna, it is clear, is not the fabulous, transgressive icon she
once was for hooks: if, once upon a time, she was the American popular-cultural equivalent of the black Madonna, now, disgraced, retrogres-
sive, she is the ultimate embodiment of racial and sexual imperialism,
colonialism incarnate, predatory, territorial, her adventurism a black
mask for white skin-trade. But what, one wonders, is driving this per-
nicious exploitation of gay and black modes of representation?

Since hooks's critique is tied, as I noted earlier, to issues of consumption and production, Madonna's precipitous fall from grace would
appear to be a function of her craven capitulation to capital. Indeed,
though hooks allows—in one of the rare, affirmative moments of "Power
to the Pussy"—that Madonna's mass marketing of homoerotic imagery
in *Sex* may have a "disruptive challenging impact" (PP 71), she maintains that the only difference between *Sex* and traditional pornography
is that Madonna's iconic, superstar status allows her to access a much
larger audience—a "mass audience" (PP 70). The bottom line, as it
were, is that "Madonna is really only a link in the marketing chain that
exploits representations of sexuality and the body for profit" (PP 70).

hooks's emphasis here on marketing is presumably a reference to
late or post-Fordist capitalism (where the accent is on, say, marketing
and publicity as opposed to manufacturing),[80] but as the earlier passage
about a slave-based economy, however provocative, suggests, her com-
pulsive-repetitive invocation of capitalism in "Power to the Pussy" tends

to be reflexive and generic. Marx's somewhat narrow understanding of the "slave mode of production" aside, late or transnational capitalism is reduced, for instance, to a market economy, which "cannibalistic" economy is linked in turn to consumption—to, in particular, the consumption of pornography.[81] Indeed, not only does hooks's frequent, pejorative recourse to the word *mass* align her reading of Madonna with the classic left critique of mass culture (where, for instance, mass consumption is the mirror of mass production), pornography itself functions for hooks as something of a master trope of capitalism and its mass-consumptive effects.

The real interest of hooks's "Power to the Pussy," though, has less to do with its economics—the way in which its critique of consumption serves as a diacritical complement to her critique of production—than the essay's symptomatic character or "structure of feeling." The critical question here, one that hooks's own essay raises in its rhetorical insistence on the language of longing,[82] is: What is the relation between (black) (female) pleasure—or joy-as-*jouissance*—and popular culture?[83]

I'm thinking here not only of "Power to the Pussy" but the opening paragraph of hooks's first essay on Madonna where she reflects on Madonna's envy of black culture: "The thing about envy is that it is always ready to destroy, erase, take over, and *consume* the desired object" (MPM 218, emphasis mine).[84] This determination of envy as consumption—which is not, it is obvious, without its polemical effect (especially in the context of race)—recurs in "Power to the Pussy" where hooks invokes, in typically pleonastic fashion, the "consuming voyeuristic pornographic gaze" (PP 72). Thus, about the lesbian *ménage à trois* in *Sex*, hooks writes: "Since . . . the literate reader of [Madonna's] opening remarks knows that we are not really seeing documentary photos but a carefully constructed sexual stage, we can never forget that our gaze is directed, controlled. We have paid for our right to look, just as Madonna has paid the two women to appear with her" (PP 72).

The problem with pornography, then (and hooks's critique here is conventional enough), is that we have to pay to consume it—or, more colloquially, *we have to pay for it.* In other words (to flip the above voyeuristic scenario), "Madonna's exhibitionism is . . . [simply] an economic strategy" (M143).[85] Just such a "base" economic determination raises, however, some very basic, albeit vexed, questions about voyeurism and exhibitionism (as well as, more generally, consumption and production, not to mention *the* pornographic gaze). Carol Queen, for example, queries: What about the (lesbian) "consumer who *wants* an album full of pictures of Madonna naked?" (M 143). Or, better yet, what about "having *Sex* for money?" (M 143).

Though hooks's complaint about the staged, pay-per-view aspect of *Sex* could be said to miss at least part of the point of the book, since as Queen contends, its camp, over-the-top theatricality is precisely all about "fetish sex" (M 153),[86] for hooks *Sex*, precisely because of its stereotypical sexual representations, constitutes the "highest expression of capitalist patriarchal pornographic power" (PP 72). Still, the most serious problem with *Sex*, according to hooks, is not so much its aesthetic quality (which is inferior—at least for the "literate reader") or even its humdrum deployment of voyeurism-exhibitionism as Madonna's "dangerous" remarks on S/M, remarks that signal a complete "break with feminist thinking" (PP 74).

Here is Madonna-as-Dita:

> "I think for the most part if women are in an abusive relationship and they know it and they stay in it, they must be digging it. I suppose some people might think that's an irresponsible statement. I'm sure there are lots of women in abusive relationships who don't want to be, who are trapped economically; they have all these kids and they have to deal with it. But I have friends who have money and are educated and they stay in abusive relationships, so they must be getting something out of it."[87]

Madonna, it is obvious, is "no expert on domestic violence" (PP 74). Rather more seriously, the above monologue on S/M confuses, as hooks argues, "heterosexual violence against women with consensual sadomasochism" (PP 74), a conflation that does not do nearly enough justice to the difference between fantasy and reality.

Still, if it true that Madonna's remarks mix S/M with domestic violence (since, as Pat Califia maintains, they do not adequately account for the "social forces that can shape [women's] ability to even imagine that [they] have choices, let alone give or withhold consent" (M 176), hooks's own feminist, anticapitalist reading of sadomasochism as negotiation—"the antithesis of competitive struggle" (PP 74)—also fails to account for the complex libidinal economics of S/M.[88] That is to say, hooks's utopian claim that S/M is the "antithesis of competitive struggle" misrecognizes what one might call the "real" force of sadomasochism, its *symbolic* power, where—as Madonna's comments about class intimate—S/M is, in part, the libidinal sublimation of the economic vicissitudes of late capitalism.[89] This, for me, is the real "dirty little secret" of Madonna's "reactionary" remarks on S/M: that just as late capitalism cannot be understood apart from the vicissitudes of sadomasochism, so the practice of S/M is part and parcel of the general (political) economy of "commodity fetishism."

On a more general note, I would only add that with respect to hooks's critical program, it is not enough simply to identify the symptom, say the identificatory play of positive and negative images in Madonna's work.[90] Nor, given the perversely demanding, roller-coaster loop-de-loops of desire, is it enough merely to go through or traverse the fantasy: say, one's, even my own, anxiety- and pleasure-ridden desire *for* Madonna. Rather, having identified the drive which befalls any and every act of identification, the point is not so much to identify *with* the symptom as to continue to elucidate the distance *between* identification and desire: to maintain, as it were, a "thin line between love and hate."[91]

I want to turn now, as promised, to the issue of prostitution since, more so than sadomasochism, it has historically functioned as one of the most powerful and pervasive metaphors of the intimate/extimate relation between capitalism and sexuality and is, as such, a classic instance of the *commodity*-body.[92] As a supplement of sorts to the hooks, it is useful to begin with Margery Metzstein's reading of *Sex*, "Signed, Sealed, and Delivered" (1993), which not only tackles the problem of sadomasochism (like "Power to the Pussy," though rather more simplistically), but the issue of prostitution as well.

The pretext of Metzstein's critique is the following exchange in *Sex*:

Doctor: Have you ever been mistaken for a prostitute?

Dita: Everytime anyone reviews anything I do, I'm mistaken for a prostitute.

Commenting on this fictional exchange (Dita is Madonna's *nom de plume* in *Sex*),[93] Metzstein writes: "If prostitution is defined by someone who sells themselves for money, or someone who degrades themselves by *publicity*, then this is the correct word to describe Madonna" (DM 97, emphasis mine). Having issued this moral-categorical judgment, Metzstein volunteers the following autobiographical anecdote in order to "suture" her reading of Madonna-as-prostitute:

When my daughter and her friends were looking through *Sex*, my eleven-year-old son walked into her bedroom and caught a glimpse of the contents. He started to cry. Later, when I asked why he was crying he said: *She doesn't need to show herself like that. She's got lots of money already. She just wants to be popular. She's a sad, sad person.* He realized, even if we adults do not—with our sophisticated theoretical rationalizations—that this book is an insult which degrades Madonna, and humiliates women. (DM 97)

This is an astonishing scenario, to say the least: Metzstein's daughter and her friends are perusing *Sex* in the daughter's bedroom (presumably with Metzstein's permission) when her pre-teen son catches a glimpse of the contents and begins to cry.

The moral of this socio-sexual scenario? In a startling variation on Freud's primal scene, the eleven-year-old *boy* not only interrupts what is arguably a feminine scene of instruction but, by crying (and thereby "acting out" the author's moral repressed), shames his mother, his daughter, and her friends, all of whom have been "caught looking."[94] For the author-mother at least (interestingly enough, we do not hear from the daughter or her friends), rationalization swiftly gives way to revulsion, blindness to insight: "If this kind of analysis is open to the charge of pessimism then at least I'm in good company. I wept with my son because I recognized my own reaction which had previously been buried under layers of accommodation" (DM 98).[95]

There are any number of questions that immediately come to mind given the reactive nature of Metzstein's analysis, such as: What does it mean that the son is the agent of his mother's "feminist" catharsis (rather than, say, Madonna)? The irony here—and I do not think one has to be especially sophisticated, theoretically speaking, to realize this—is that in the above scene of pathos, the son effectively stands in not only for the doctor (and the sorts of medical-juridical sex-power-knowledge that this figure is classically associated with) but the father himself.

While one can imagine other, more optimistic, even utopian scenarios (where, for instance, Madonna is the agent of enlightenment via the good bad book *Sex*—*à la* the black Madonna as wise prostitute), Madonna cannot assume this propadeutic role since, for Metzstein, she is always only a "fallen," morally corrupt woman. But if Madonna "doesn't need to show herself" as she does in *Sex* (since, as Metzstein's son says, she's already "got lots of money"), why in fact *does* she do it? The answer, plain and simple, is greed—which of course makes Madonna the worse kind of prostitute: she sells herself not because she has to (Madonna, alas, is no working-class girl) but because she *likes* to.

As I observed earlier, Madonna's prostitution also conveys a larger, cultural-political message. Citing the *Dialectic of Enlightenment*, Metzstein observes that a "culture which can easily accommodate its own degradation is terminally ill" (DM 97). The problem, according to Metzstein (who invokes yet another classic trope of capital, that of the vampire),[96] is that mass culture "feeds off both icons and consumers" (DM 97). In other words, both Madonna and her target audience, having succumbed to the "sad," sick dynamic of the culture industry (which is at once degraded and degrading), are coactive "participants in a process which impoverishes all and creates the promise of fulfillment which can never be delivered" (DM 97). In short, mass culture—which is driven by technology (which in turn is controlled by capital [DM 97])—never really delivers on its meretricious come-ons or "promissory notes."[97]

Like Keith Tester's reading of the Clash in *Media, Culture, and Morality* (which I discuss in the introduction), Metzstein's moralizing analysis of the political-economic conditions of possibility of Madonna's *Sex* represents an especially uncritical appropriation of Adorno and Horkheimer's critique of mass culture;[98] however, the interest of this critical-ideological analysis is that unlike Tester's, it articulates, even if only negatively, the extraordinary libidinal charge that underwrites the political economy of late capitalism. Thus, of the above, unfulfilling and impoverishing cultural-industrial dynamic, Metzstein writes: "*Sex* is the perfect metaphor for this process because everyone is being fucked, including those who think they are doing the fucking" (DM 97). In fact, since Madonna, according to Metzstein, is as much a pawn of capital as her audiences (DM 97), sadomasochism is an even better, more specific metaphor for the vampiric relation between icon and audience in mass culture because it perfectly captures the "violence caused to the spirit of the, willing or unwilling, participants" (DM 97).

Whether or not one believes, as I do, that Metzstein's critique of mass culture does its own sort of violence to contemporary mass media *texts* such as the Madonna commodity-body-sign, it is worth noting, I think, that the photograph that accompanies the conclusion to Metzstein's essay in *Deconstructing Madonna* (1993) is not without a certain, deconstructive irony. The illustration is the well-known 1991 Meisel photograph of Madonna with her hands on top of her braided platinum-blonde head, her paisley fuck-me pants unzipped, her muscular-shadowed back bare to us and embossed like a back-stage pass with the following message: "ALL ACCESS."[99] Question: Am I the only one who thinks there is something radically democratic about this particular promotional image?[100]

Though such a reading would appear to confirm the Lacanian determination of the signifier (where the letter, *pace* Derrida, always eventually arrives at its destination), I mention the illustration not simply as a visual counterpoint to Metzstein's contrary argument (which is an excellent example, however unintentional, of the severity of the cultural super-ego) but as illustrative, albeit anecdotal, evidence that Madonna's body is a determinate signifier of contemporary public culture—of, that is to say, postmodern *publicity*. This particular aspect or effect of the Madonna commodity-body-sign—publicity as prostitution—is, of course, a significant part of her image, as the following, dissenting opinion attests. Echoing the sentiments of Metzstein's son, Steve Allen—yes, Steve Allen ("prominent star of American stage, movies and TV for over a half a century")—writes: "[Madonna] is a mega-millionaire and indeed at present is probably making so much money she herself doesn't have an accurate accounting of it. She has, therefore, no excuse whatever for deciding to become a public slut."[101]

According to Allen, there is one simple reason why Madonna "made a conscious, calculated decision to debase herself": "the big money."[102] Madonna, in other words, is not simply a public slut, but as Metzstein's reading insinuates, a rich one as well. The irony of this sort of argument (which is nothing if not self-righteous) is summed up by Kirsten Marthe Lentz, who comments that when it comes to Madonna, "suddenly everybody is a critic of capitalism" (M 163).

But what exactly does it mean to say that Madonna is a "corporation in the form of flesh" (*Vanity Fair)* or, as I prefer to think of it (with a nod to Lauren Berlant by way of Billy Idol), "flesh for national fantasy"?

If, as Lentz puts it, "Madonna *sells* sex" (M 164), her corpus can be said to signify sex incorporated, a *public* corporation that flamboyantly combines the "sexual 'greed' we associate with sixties sexual liberation" with the "economic greed we associate with present day corporate culture" (M 164). The net result of this historical hybridity is a rich, " 'sexually liberated' prostitute who loves her work" (M 164). Given the current cultural-political climate where, as it were, PC reigns on the left and the PMRC on the right, what could be more perverse?

A monster of the American imaginary, a postmodern embodiment of Lady Liberty (which itself represents a perversion of sorts of Delacroix's *Liberté*),[103] Madonna possesses all the sex-appeal Benjamin attributed to the commodity but with that enigmatic something extra, the X in sex (*plus-de-jouir*), which is the definition of fetishism. Which is to say that even as Madonna guilelessly defaces what is left of public culture, the so-called phantom or post-enlightenment public sphere (as Allen puts it, "Madonna scrawls graffiti on the national dialogue"),[104] she also gives face, like Warhol himself, to the libidinal economics of American-style capitalism.[105]

There is something distinctly odd, then, about reading Madonna's libertinism through the émigré lens of Adorno and Horkheimer, as Metzstein does. At the same time, if contemporary cultural criticism has tended—as John Champagne argues—to reject the tradition associated with the Frankfurt School of discovering in the texts of mass culture "only the most disturbing and debilitating cultural and political tendencies,"[106] to reverse this trend and explore the way popular culture resists the dominant hegemony, or—a slightly more sophisticated version of the same strategy—to read popular culture as a "site of contradictory ideologies," hardly seems dialectically equal to the task at hand.[107] Given this aporia or impasse, the reflexive reinvocation of classical critical theory—as in Metzstein's ostensibly conclusive recourse in her reading of *Sex* to the "Culture Industry" chapter of the *Dialectic of Enlightenment*—suggests that, for all its banality, Madonna Studies is not without its fatal dimension.

This element of fatality receives something like its consummate expression in Douglas Kellner's essay in *Media Culture* (1995), "Madonna, Fashion, and Image," which given his own early critical investment in the Frankfurt School (in particular, Marcuse),[108] implicitly dramatizes the fatality of Madonna Studies. Focusing on "shifts in [Madonna's] musical production, her deployment of fashion and sexuality, and the construction of her image" (MFI 268), Kellner demarcates three distinct periods in Madonna's career: (1) Madonna I: the Boy Toy (from, say, the dance music of "Lucky Star" [1983] and "Holiday" [1983] to the topicality and classic-realist narrativity of "Papa Don't Preach" [1986]); (2) Madonna II: Who's That Girl? (from the screwball highjinks of *Who's That Girl* [1987][109] to the gender-bending and pop German Expressionism of *Express Yourself* [1989]); and (3) Madonna III: Blonde Ambition (from the sadomasochistic panache of *Justify My Love* [1990] to the soft-core pornography of the "Girlie Show" [1993]).

Kellner's main thesis is that "although 'Madonna' is a site of genuine contradiction that must be articulated and appraised" to adequately calculate her textual effects (MFI 263), she merely reinforces the norms of a consumer society and, in doing so, "promotes the possibilities of a new commodity 'self' through consumption and the products of the fashion industry" (MFI 263). Madonna, to cite the author of *Postmodernism and Islam* (1993), is the "supreme product of the consumerist culture."[110] Or, to sample Kellner himself, Madonna is the "epitome of *banal* consumerism run rampant in media culture" (MFI 263, emphasis mine).

The answer to the above, methodological question of contradiction—where contradiction is, as we have seen, the rallying cry of post-

Marxist, post-Frankfurt School cultural studies—is, according to Kellner, to pay more attention to "political economy and the production of culture" (MFI 269). In other words, in order to grasp that sublime, elusive object of ideology which is Madonna, it is necessary to interrogate the "conditions under which the multiplicity of discourses on Madonna, and contradictory readings and evaluations, are produced" (MFI 262). More synoptically, if Madonna is all about consumerism (where the theoretical version of this ideological discourse is textual analysis and reception studies), the key to this phenomenon is production, the political-*economic* conditions of textual consumption.

Now, as I suggested earlier, this unequivocally *anti*-banal position is not without a fatal element. For instance, though the analytical focus in Kellner's essay is ostensibly on style and fashion, iconic images and superstar identities or, more generally, what he calls, *à la* Warhol, the image factory,[111] the real focus turns out to be not so much the "image" as the factory—in other words, not so much the (star) body-sign as the commodity. The net effect of this rhetorical displacement is what one might call pop-modernist ideology critique, where the significance of the Madonna commodity-body is less a function of the forces of the Fordist mode of production (as in the classic Frankfurt School critique of the culture *industry*) as post-Fordist image production, the *way* that media culture "sells cultural commodities to audiences" (MFI 285).

To be fair, Kellner's emphasis on post-Fordist production makes a lot of critical sense at the moment, especially in the larger context of, as I've argued above, publicity or postmodern celebrity culture; however, valuable as this circumscribed approach is, the economics of fatality nonetheless manifests itself in the micrological effects of rhetorical inflection, as in the following representative sentence: "Madonna's success is *largely* a marketing success, and her music, videos, other products, and image are triumphs of extremely successful production and marketing strategies" (MFI 269, emphasis mine). In sum, Madonna— "one of the greatest PR machines in history" (MFI 268)—is a publicity stunt.

But if Madonna is largely a story about publicity and marketing, the right connections and production strategies, what's art got to do with it?

Discussing the desire of students of popular culture to understand Madonna's enormous popularity, Kellner insists that her works can be "read *either* as works of art, *or* analyzed as commodities that shrewdly exploit markets" (MFI 281, emphasis mine). With this conventional critical-ideological opposition firmly in place, Kellner then argues that although Madonna "embodies postmodern themes and aesthetic strat-

egies" (e.g., "camp, irony, and humor" [MFI 281]), in the final analysis
her work is "more modernist than postmodernist (where the latter
aesthetic mode is characterized by "shock, spectacle, and theatricality"
[MFI 283]). Indeed, precisely because she is positioned *between* the
modern and postmodern, Madonna's corpus is an instance *par excellence* of what Kellner calls pop modernist aesthetics or, more simply,
pop modernism (MFI 294, note 13).

The meta-irony of this reading—which is, as it were, more modernist than postmodernist—is reflected in the comparison between
Madonna and Laurie Anderson that Kellner uses to clinch his argument. Kellner admits near the end of his analysis that Anderson is an
avant-garde performance artist and Madonna the reigning queen of pop
(so the comparison is ultimately, as he says, "between two rather different species of culture" [MFI 290]). However, the more serious problem, it seems to me, is that this comparison presupposes an *a priori*,
"modernist" distinction between avant-garde and pop culture. More
specifically, if Kellner's neologism "pop modernism" usefully points up
the uneven development and effects of mass media texts, it does so only
by neglecting the way media culture is itself comprised of both art *and*
commerce.

But the real fatality of Kellner's reading can be seen in "The
Madonna Contradiction Machine," the aptly titled conclusion to his
chapter on Madonna, where after citing hooks's "Madonna: Plantation
Mistress or Soul Sister?" he repeats his thesis ("Madonna is a site of
genuine contradiction") only to make the following anticlimatic, not to
say banal assertion: "Madonna calls herself an artistic revolutionary
and celebrates modernist subversion, yet her work is circulated in the
commodity form of popular music and music videos, which are, after
all, at bottom, advertisements for the songs" (MFI 292). The super-
banality of this position is that it reflexively *re*-circulates one of the
foundational clichés of mass-cultural criticism—that popular music is
merely a commodity-form—as if it were critical news. STOP THE
PRESSES: Madonna's music is circulated via the commodity-form! As
for Kellner's all-too-symptomatic grace note about music videos, a rhetorical question should suffice at this point: Can one really say—to take
an especially loaded example—that Madonna's "Make a Wish" (1989)
is, at bottom, *only* an advertisement?[112]

Coda

> We may affirm absolutely that *nothing great in the World* has been accomplished without *passion.* . . .
>
> —Hegel, *Lectures on the Philosophy of History*

> The utopia of the qualitative—the things which through their differences and uniqueness cannot be absorbed into the prevalent exchange relationships—take refuge under capitalism in the traits of fetishism. But . . . no happiness without fetishism.
>
> —Adorno, *Minima Moralia*

While the commodity circuit—understood in the narrow, restricted-economic sense as the "money form" of value—is clearly the "best model for understanding the circuit of capital,"[1] it is not necessarily the best model, as Part Two of this book argues, for understanding that sign which is the *art*-commodity. For contemporary capitalism in its broadest sense—for, that is to say, the commodity-body-*sign*—it is equally important to work what Spivak after Marx calls the "total or expanded form of value,"[2] or what I have elaborated here as the general (political) economy of "commodity fetishism." For if the rise of the new social movements and attendant politics of difference has taught us anything,[3] it is that the commodity-form and whatever politics one might deduce from it are subject to the incommensurability of the "particular," in particular the kinks and quirks associated with the aesthetic.

Indeed, the specific use-value of Madonna Studies is that, not unlike the "outlaw" discourse of aesthetic judgment, it illustrates the perverse oscillation in contemporary cultural criticism between negation and affirmation, production and consumption, the politics of disidentification and the imperatives of the political-economic.[4] This dialectic also dramatizes the fetishism at the heart of the commodity-form,[5] where the commodity-body is signified not simply by individual consumer-spectators in all their sovereign excess but by various social formations in all their ambivalence, desires, and identifications. Madonna Studies in the broadest sense—which includes all those who love Madonna as well as those who love to hate her, those who want to hit as well as those who want to kiss her[6]—is one such "perverse" social formation.

As for Madonna, dire predictions about her imminent demise—as her performance in, among other things, *Evita* demonstrates (1996)— are ultimately just as banal as fateful, laudatory allegories about her miraculous rise to stardom.

History, not unlike the art-commodity itself, tends to elude the predestination of both classical dialectics and political orthodoxy—something of a liberating thought-image (*Denkbild*) in these censorious times. While it is doubtful that Adorno, Jacob to Benjamin's new-fangled angel,[7] would have appreciated Madonna's aesthetically variable and politically indeterminate corpus, his untimely meditations on the preponderance of the object are a timely reminder not only of the deadliness of doxa in all its forms but the incalculable, unforeseen effects of the art-commodity.

Finally, if the zig-zag history of Madonna Studies says anything about the future of critical theory (and, of course, I think it does), it is that its continuing viability, even validity, will depend on a certain interdisciplinary improvisation where, among other things, "affirmative" cultural studies will have to seriously confront the sometime fatal axioms of *Ideologiekritik* just as *Kulturkritik*—not unlike the later, post-expatriate Adorno[8]—will have to critically come to terms with its own negative-dialectical banalities. Simply put, cultural studies will have to mine the chiasmus that constitutes its present discursive and historical conditions of possibility—and, hopefully, to a beat you can dance to.

Notes

Triptik

1. See Michel Foucault, "Nietzsche, Genealogy, History," *Language, Counter-Memory, Practice*, trans. Donald F. Bouchard (Ithaca, NY: Cornell University Press, 1977), pp. 139–64.

2. Meaghan Morris, "Banality in Cultural Studies," in *What Is Cultural Studies?*, ed. John Storey (London: Arnold, 1996), p. 157.

3. Roland Barthes, *The Pleasure of the Text*, trans. Richard Miller (New York: Hill and Wang, 1975), p. ix.

4. Ibid., p. 3.

5. Jürgen Habermas, "The Entwinement of Myth and Enlightenment," *The Philosophical Discourse of Modernity*, trans. Frederick Lawrence (Cambridge, MA: MIT Press, 1990), p. 128.

6. Guy Debord, "The Commodity as Spectacle," *The Society of the Spectacle* (Detroit, MI: Black and Red, 1983), p. 35.

7. Jean Baudrillard, "The Concept of Labor," *The Mirror of Production*, trans. Mark Poster (St. Louis, MO: Telos Press, 1975), p. 31.

Introduction

1. Andrew Blake, "Madonna the Musician," in *Deconstructing Madonna*, ed. Fran Lloyd (London: B. T. Batsford, 1993), p. 17.

2. Ibid., p. 17.

3. See Theodor Adorno, written with the assistance of George Simpson, "On Popular Music," in *On Record*, ed. Simon Frith and Andrew Goodwin (New York: Pantheon, 1990), p. 310. For a restatement, see also "Popular Music," in *Introduction to the Sociology of Music*, trans. E. B. Ashton (New York: Seabury Press, 1976), pp. 21–38.

4. For an example of Adorno's economistic position on music, see the postscript to *Introduction to the Sociology of Music* where he argues that the task of "musical sociology" is the "exploration and analysis of the economic base of music" (p. 222). See also "Perennial Fashion—Jazz": "The paradoxical immortality of jazz has its roots in the economy" (*Prisms*, trans. Samuel and Shierry Weber [Cambridge, MA: MIT Press, 1986], p. 124).

5. A pointed example because Lauper's music in the mid 1980s—I'm thinking in particular of *She's So Unusual* (Portrait, 1989)—provided, especially within the male-dominated context of MTV, alternative representations of femininity. On Lauper see, for instance, Gillian G. Gaar, *She's a Rebel: The History of Women in Rock & Roll* (Seattle: Seal Press, 1992), pp. 329–32. In this context, see also Simon Frith's discussion of race with respect to popular music in "The Cultural Study of Popular Music," in *Cultural Studies* ("*White boys just want to have fun*"), ed. Lawrence Grossberg, Cary Nelson, and Paula A. Treichler (New York: Routledge, 1992), p. 181. As Frith notes, the model of (white) men having fun together is, of course, the "gay club and gay disco," both of which have had a "determinative influence on British pop culture" (p. 181). See note 36 below.

6. Blake, "Madonna the Musician," p. 17.

7. While the title of the chapter on popular music in the German edition of the *Introduction to the Sociology of Music* is "light music" (*leichte Musik*), what Adorno calls "serious music" in the English-version essay on popular music is referred to in the *Introduction to the Sociology of Music* as the "higher music," a hierarchical determination that is reinforced by Adorno's recourse in the same essay to the disparaging term *Unterhaltungsmusik*.

8. For a recent reading of Adorno on mass culture, see Peter Uwe Hohendahl, "Reading Mass Culture," in *Prismatic Thought: Theodor W. Adorno* (Lincoln, NE: University of Nebraska Press, 1995), pp. 119–48. For an excellent overview of the "mass culture debate," one that situates the Frankfurt School's position with respect to not only conservative critics such as Nietzsche, Arnold, Spengler, Leavis, and Eliot but "mandarin optimists" (Bell, Berelson, and Shils), "cultural relativists" (Bryson, Gans, Lynes, and Riesman), and "aesthetic pluralists" (Denney, Kouwenhoven, and Seldes), see Eugene Lunn, "The Frankfurt School in the Development of the Mass Culture Debate," in *The Aesthetics of the Critical Theorists*, ed. Ronald Roblin (Lewiston, NY: Edwin Mellen Press, 1990), pp. 26–84. See also Dominic Strinati's "Mass Culture and Popular Culture," which is especially good on Dwight MacDonald, in *An Introduction to Theories of Popular Culture* (New York: Routledge, 1995), pp. 2–50. On the MacDonald, see in particular "Masscult & Midcult," in *Against the American Grain* (New York: Random House, 1962), pp. 3–75.

9. See Adorno's preface to *The Philosophy of Modern Music*, trans. Anne G. Mitchell and Wesley V. Blomster (New York: Seabury Press, 1973), p. xi.

10. Here I can second Lawrence Grossberg whose "studies of rock" emphasize the importance of "affect" in contemporary cultural studies; see "Theory, Politics, Passion," the introduction to *We Gotta Get Out of This Place: Popular Conservatism and Postmodern Culture* (New York: Routledge, 1992), pp. 2–30.

11. Walter Benjamin, "The Work of Art in the Age of Mechanical Reproduction," in *Illuminations*, ed. Hannah Arendt, trans. Harry Zohn (New York: Shocken, 1969), p. 240.

12. See the letter from Benjamin to Adorno (December 9, 1938 [Paris]), trans. Harry Zohn, in *Aesthetics and Politics*, trans. ed. Ronald Taylor (London: Verso, 1988 [1977]), p. 140.

13. Rodolphe Gasché, "Objective Diversions: On Some Kantian Themes in Benjamin's 'The Work of Art in the Age of Mechanical Reproduction,'" in *Walter Benjamin's Philosophy: Destruction and Experience*, ed. Andrew Benjamin and Peter Osborne (New York: Routledge, 1994), pp. 183–204.

14. Letter from Adorno to Benjamin (March 18, 1936 [London]), *Aesthetics and Politics*, p. 123. The simple reason for Adorno's argument against Benjamin's theory of distraction: "in communist society work will be organized in such a way that people will no longer be so tired and so stultified that they need distraction" (AP 123). Given the hopelessly utopian tenor of Adorno's position here, I am tempted to counter with an "ontological" claim: that whatever social arrangements prevail in the future, "people" will always need to be distracted (i.e., "People [will] want to have fun").

15. Adorno, "On the Fetish Character in Music and the Regression of Listening," in *The Essential Frankfurt School Reader*, ed. Andrew Arato and Eike Gebhardt (New York: Urizen Books, 1978), pp. 170–299.

16. For one of the most recent, and best, discussions of Adorno's "critique of jazz," see James M. Harding, "Adorno, Ellison, and the Critique of Jazz," *Cultural Critique* 31 (Fall 1995), pp. 129–58. Working from a premise about the "duplicity" or "double life of jazz," Harding makes the novel claim that "Adorno's most vociferous attacks on the commercial jazz industry are contemporaneously as well as philosophically in harmony with the temperament of bebop" (p. 147). The question then becomes, What are the cultural-political limits of—oxymoron of oxymorons—the Adornian bebop position? Or, more simply, what about Satchmo? Harding's conclusion: "Insofar as jazz has maintained a double life, . . . it is most readily to be found in the forging of a space which is simultaneously commercial and aesthetically interesting" (p. 153). On, *inter alia*, Satchmo's handkerchief, see Andrew Ross's "Hip, and the Long Front of Color" where, like Harding, he argues for popular music's capacity to "transmit, disseminate, and render 'black' meanings *precisely because of*, and not in spite of, its industrial forms of production, distribution, and consumption" (*No Respect: Intellectuals and Popular Culture* [New York: Routledge, 1989], p. 71).

17. As Andrew Ross chronicles in "Hip, and the Long Front of Color": "Through the medium of radio and the jukebox, and in huge dancehalls . . . , the formation of a popular taste for jazz in the thirties lay more in its capacity to move and animate bodies than to create an appreciative, listening audience" (*No Respect*, 75). In response to this "dance excitement," even Artie Shaw referred to jitterbugs as "morons" (p. 75). Finally, it should be noted that R&B—and, consequently, R&R—"was music to move to, and it did not invite anything like the cool, disconnected response that the danceless bebop and most jazz culture had gone out of its way to encourage" (p. 96). For an excellent, historically informed discussion of the distinction between "hot" jazz and "sweet" dance music, see William Howland Kenney, "Historical Context and the Definition of Jazz," in *Jazz among the Discourses*, ed. Krin Gabbard (Durham: Duke University Press, 1995), pp. 100–16.

18. On Adorno's reading of the musical avant-garde, see the chapter of the same title in *Introduction to the Sociology of Music*, pp. 178–93. On Adorno's understanding of music in general, see—among the growing body of literature in English—Martin Jay, "Culture as Manipulation; Culture as Redemption," *Adorno* (Cambridge, MA: Harvard University Press, 1984), pp. 111–60; Rose Rosengard Subotnik, *Developing Variations: Style and Ideology in Western Music* (Minneapolis: University of Minnesota Press, 1991); David Roberts, *Art and Enlightenment: Aesthetic Theory after Adorno* (Lincoln: University of Nebraska Press, 1991).

19. This, I take it, is the gist of the editors' remark in the presentation to the Adorno-Benjamin correspondence that the "only form to approximate to a fertile aesthetic distraction has been rock, because of its use relationship to dance" (Rodney Livingstone, Perry Anderson, and Francis Mulhern, "Presentation III," *Aesthetics and Politics*, p. 108).

20. W. F. Haug, *Critique of Commodity Aesthetics*, trans. Robert Buck (Minneapolis, MN: University of Minnesota Press, 1986), p. 30.

21. See Andrew Goodwin, *Dancing in the Distraction Factory: Music Television and Popular Culture* (Minneapolis: University of Minnesota Press, 1992), pp. 68–71.

22. Cindy Patton, "Embodying Subaltern Memory," in *The Madonna Connection: Representational Politics, Subcultural Identities, and Cultural Theory*, ed. Cathy Schwichtenberg (Boulder: Westview Press, 1993), pp. 81–105. On dance subcultures, see Sarah Thornton, *Club Cultures: Music, Media, and Subcultural Capital* (Hanover: University Press of New England, 1996).

23. On commodity fetishism as what he calls "eternization," see Kenneth Mark Harris, *The Film Fetish* (New York: Peter Lang, 1992), pp. 6–8.

24. Adorno and Max Horkheimer, "The Importance of the Body" ("Notes and Drafts"), *Dialectic of Enlightenment*, trans. John Cumming (New York: Continuum, 1987), pp. 231–36.

25. For a thoughtful reading of Adorno's position on pleasure and the *promesse de bonheur*, see Fredric Jameson, "Mass Culture as Big Business," *Late Marxism: Adorno, or, The Persistence of the Dialectic* (New York: Verso, 1990), pp. 139–47. See also note 34 below.

26. On the issue of asceticism, Jay writes: "Although [Adorno] always remained skeptical of the possibilities of achieving real gratification in the present society, a wariness that often gave his writings an ascetic aura, he wholeheartedly endorsed the demand for its ultimate realization" (*Adorno*, 88). In this, what Jay calls Adorno's hope for the "somatic prefiguration of a more generalized future happiness" (p. 113), Adorno differs from both Montaigne and Montaigne's other, Pascal (with whom he nonetheless shares a disdain for diversion); unlike Pascal, "Adorno did not identify man's highest state with spiritual salvation; rather, he contended that it was genuine corporeal gratification that was denied by the culture industry" (*Adorno*, 121).

27. Adorno, "A Word for Morality," *Minima Moralia: Reflections from Damaged Life*, trans. E. F. N. Jephcott (New York: Verso, 1987 [1974]), p. 97.

28. See, in general, Donald Lowe, *The Body in Late-Capitalist USA* (Durham: Duke University Press, 1995).

29. For a superb discussion of the issue of phantasmagoria in Benjamin (as well as Adorno's response), see "Benjamin's Marxisms" and "*Le Diable à Paris*: Benjamin's Phantasmagoria," in Margaret Cohen, *Profane Illuminations: Walter Benjamin and the Paris of Surrealist Revolution* (Berkeley: University of California Press, 1993), pp. 17–55 and 217–59 respectively. I might add that Cohen's sense of "critical phantasmagoria" (p. 259) is very close to my critical-affirmative sense of "commodity fetishism."

30. See Lowe who argues that the "late-capitalist commodity. . . is a *semiotic hybrid* in an expanded, accelerated terrain of production and consumption" (*The Body in Late-Capitalist USA*, 72).

31. It is difficult, it seems to me, to underestimate the significance of the affinity between Benjamin and Adorno on the issue of use-value (which Adorno repeats late in the same letter [AP 113]), since it suggests a radically progressive understanding of the commodity-form. See note 33 below.

32. For this point, see Adorno's *Introduction to the Sociology of Music*, p. 22. See also John Frow, who points to the "impossibility either of espousing, in any simple way, the norms of high culture, in so far as this represents that exercise of distinction which works to exclude those not possessed of cultural capital; or, on the other hand, of espousing, in any simple way, the norms of 'popular' culture to the extent that this involves, for the possessors of cultural capital, a fantasy of otherness and a politically dubious will to speak on behalf of this Imaginary Other" ("Economies of Value," *Cultural Studies and Cultural Value* [Oxford, UK: Clarendon Press, 1995], 159).

33. Indeed, Adorno criticized the original Baudelaire texts—which he effectively rejected for publication in the *Zeitschrift für Sozialforschung*—precisely because of what he referred to as Benjamin's "anthropological materialism" (AP 105). In this regard, Adorno's theoretical mantra might well be said to be: *mediation, mediation, mediation*!

34. With respect to the question of the body and sexuality, one must nonetheless acknowledge Adorno's extraordinary, counter-Enlightenment critique of Freud in *Minima Moralia*, titled, appropriately enough, "This Side of the Pleasure Principle": "Reason is for [Freud] a mere superstructure, not—as official philosophy maintains—on account of his psychologism, which has penetrated deeply enough into the historical moment of truth, but rather because he rejects the end, remote to meaning, impervious to reason, which alone could prove the means, reason, to be reasonable: *pleasure*" (p. 61, emphasis mine). Hence this utopian Adorno: "He alone who could situate utopia in blind somatic pleasure, which satisfying the ultimate intention, is intentionless, has a stable and valid idea of truth" (MM 61).

35. Adorno, "Cultural Criticism and Society," *Prisms*, p. 33.

36. The question of gender, not to mention homosexuality, is a crucial aspect of Adorno's position on both mass and popular culture. See, among other things, Andreas Huyssen, "Mass Culture as Woman: Modernism's Other," in *Studies in Entertainment*, ed. Tania Modleski (Bloomington: Indiana University Press, 1986), pp. 188–207; Patrice Petro, "Modernity and Mass Culture in Weimar: Contours of a Discourse on Sexuality in Early Theories of Perception and Reception," *New German Critique* 40 (Spring 1987), pp. 115–46; Sabine Wilke, " 'Torn Halves of an Integral Freedom': Adorno's and Benjamin's Readings of Mass Culture," *The Aesthetics of the Critical Theorists*, pp. 124–46; and Barbara Engh, "Adorno and the Sirens: Tele-Phono-Graphic Bodies," in *Embodied Voices: Representing Female Vocality in Western Culture*, ed. Leslie Dunn and Nancy A. Jones (Cambridge, UK: Cambridge University Press, 1994), pp. 120–35. See also note 48 below.

37. The relation between Brecht and Benjamin, not to mention Adorno and Lukács, is of course a complicated one. I would only note here that the issue of liquidation in Adorno's epistolary critique of Benjamin is frequently linked to Brecht or, more precisely, to Adorno's anxiety about Brecht's undue influence on Benjamin. How else can one explain the, for me, amazing passage near the end of the following letter from Adorno to Benjamin (March 18, 1936 [London]): "I feel that our theoretical disagreement is not really a discord between us but rather, that it is my task to hold your arm steady until the sun of Brecht has once more sunk into exotic waters" (AP 126)?

38. For a reading of Titian's *Flaying of Marsyas* in the context of cultural studies, see Fred Inglis, "Art or Culture?" in *Cultural Studies* (Cambridge, MA: Blackwell, 1993), pp. 196–98.

39. I am referring of course to Penelope Spheeris's documentary on the Los Angeles punk scene in the late 1970s, *Decline of Western Civilization* (1981).

40. Adorno, *Introduction to the Sociology of Music*, p. 225.

41. The German is: *"Die Wahrheit ist der Bacchantische Taumel, worin alle Gestalten trunken sind"* (G. W. F. Hegel, *Texts and Commentary*, ed. and trans. Walter Kaufmann [Notre Dame: University of Notre Dame Press, 1986], p. 70).

42. Roland Barthes, *Mythologies*, trans. Annette Lavers (New York: Farrar, Straus, & Giroux, 1990 [1972]), p. 157.

43. Ibid., 159.

44. In retrospect, of course, Adorno's position is perfectly understandable, even commendable: given the aestheticization of politics in Nazi ideology, art—*if* it was to retain any "measure" of autonomy and, *a fortiori*, criticality— had to remain detached from both commerce and politics. However, for the theoretical price that Adorno later had to pay for his theory of *totale Verblendungszusammenhang*, which he developed during the "authoritarian" era of Nazism, Stalinism, and the emerging Cold War, see Richard Wolin, "Mimesis, Utopia, and Renunciation," *The Terms of Cultural Criticism* (New York: Columbia University Press, 1992), p. 76.

45. Rick Rylance, "Mythography: Structuralist Analysis and Popular Culture," *Roland Barthes* (Hemel Hempstead, UK: Harvester Wheatsheaf, 1994), 46.

46. Barthes, *Mythologies*, pp. 88–90.

47. For these citations, see Rylance, *Roland Barthes*, pp. 49, 51, and 63 respectively. Rylance observes—and here one thinks of West Germany in the 1950s—that the "subject matter of [*Mythologies*] is diverse, but the collection is probably best seen as a sardonic panorama of French culture during a period of crucial change, particularly the dramatic shift towards consumer-oriented 'modernisation' which had parallels across Western Europe during the postwar boom" (p. 43).

48. Space prevents me from exploring the question of homosexuality in Adorno; as a provocation, see, however, "Tough Baby" in *Minima Moralia* ("Totalitarianism and homosexuality belong together"), p. 46.

49. Benjamin himself was less favorably inclined to what he called "acoustic" as opposed to "optic" media; see, for example, his reply to Adorno in *Aesthetics and Politics*, p. 125.

50. For the most recent and rigorous critique of Hegelian dialectics that is also informed by Marxism (though decidedly critical of both Marxist dialectics and, more generally, Marxist philosophy), see Roy Bhaskar's *Dialectic: The*

Pulse of Freedom (London: Verso, 1993), in particular "Marxian Dialectic I" and "II," pp. 344–47 and 348–53 respectively. Against what he calls the "neo-positivism of analytical Marxism, the neo-Kantianism of Habermasian communicative action theory, and the neo-Nietzscheanism of post-Marxism," Bhaskar argues for a "dialectical critical realism" (*Dialectic*, p. 352).

51. Arkady Plotnitsky, *In the Shadow of Hegel: Complementarity, History, and the Unconscious* (Gainesville, FL: University Press of Florida, 1993), p. 10.

52. See, in particular, the chapter "Matrices" in Plotnitsky's *In the Shadow of Hegel*, p. 17; see also, in general, Plotnitsky, "Radical Alterity: Materialism, History, and the Unconscious," in *Reconfigurations: Critical Theory and General Economy* (Gainesville, FL: University Press of Florida, 1993), pp. 245–95.

53. According to Plotnitsky, Marxism has lost the theoretical battle to, specifically, Nietzsche as well as "other forces in play . . . in the wake of Nietzsche": i.e., Freud, Foucault, Deleuze, and Derrida (R 256). I might add that if one were in fact to pursue a reading of Marxism along the lines that Plotnitsky's work suggests, one would eventually have to deal with the limits of what Bhaskar calls the "neo-Nietzscheanism of post-Marxism" (*Dialectic*, p. 352).

54. To put it in dialectical terms: if, on one hand, there can be no such thing, *stricto sensu*, as Marxian political economy, on the other hand, an exaggerated emphasis on the rigor of general economy can produce a form of theoretical *rigor mortis*, as in Plotnitsky's near-obsessive need to make super-fine, and generally negative, judgments about the relative general-economic character of this or that discourse. Put another way, it is not at all self-evident that a general economy "can relate theory and politics more richly than a restricted economy" (R 22), an assertion that Plotnitsky repeats a number of times but never really justifies. One of the explicit aims of this book, however, has been to examine the critical and political implications of a general economy for Marxism, while another, related aim has been to illustrate how a general (political) economy of "commodity fetishism" provides a "richer" understanding of the relation between certain contemporary social issues (e.g., sex-gender) and particular cultural-political phenomena (e.g., Madonna Studies).

55. For a representative collection of responses, see Robin Blackburn, ed., *After the Fall: The Failure of Communism and the Future of Socialism* (London: Verso, 1991).

56. See Slavoj Žižek's reading of *Vertigo* in "Sublimation and the Fall of the Object," *Looking Awry: An Introduction to Jacques Lacan through Popular Culture* (Cambridge, MA: MIT Press, 1994), pp. 83–87.

57. For a more autobiographical take on what Ronald Aronson calls the "burden of mourning," see his preface to *After Marxism* (New York: Guilford Press, 1995), pp. vii–ix. For an autopsy of sorts, see Frank E. Manuel, *A*

Requiem for Karl Marx (Cambridge, MA: Harvard University Press, 1995), in particular "Vicissitudes of an Icon" (227–40).

58. Jacques Derrida, *Specters of Marx: The State of Debt, the Work of Mourning, and the New International,* trans. Peggy Kamuf (New York: Routledge, 1994), pp. 51–52.

59. The critical work of affirmation is therefore to be distinguished from (to take two relatively random examples) the "affirmative postmodernism of cultural studies" described by Ben Agger in *Cultural Studies and Critical Theory* (Washington, DC: Falmer Press, 1992) as well as from Donald Morton and Mas'ud Zavarzadeh's rather grand refusal to offer "any 'affirmative' view" in their *Theory, (Post)Modernity, Opposition: An "Other" Introduction to Literary and Cultural Studies* (Washington, DC: Maisonneuve Press, 1991).

60. Bernd Magnus and Stephen Cullenberg, "Introduction," *Whither Marxism?: Global Crises in International Perspective,* ed. Magnus and Cullenberg (New York: Routledge, 1995), p. xi.

61. I am alluding here to the early great Sex Pistols' song, "No Future," which was later recorded and retitled—against, I might add, John Lydon's strenuous objections—as "God Save the Queen," on *Never Mind the Bollocks* (Virgin Records, 1977).

62. It is important, I believe, not to dismiss the recent profusion of work on fetishism as merely a function of intellectual fashion, since there is no fashion, as it were, without fetishism (and vice versa). On this particular topic, see Valerie Steele, *Fetish: Fashion, Sex, and Power* (New York: Oxford University Press, 1996).

63. William Pietz, "The Problem of the Fetish, I," *Res* 9 (Spring 1985), pp. 6–7. See also Pietz, "The Problem of the Fetish, II," *Res* 13 (Spring 1987), pp. 23–45. On the twentieth-century Dutch merchants who mined the Gold and Slave coasts circa 1642 (which was also the "high moment of Dutch still life"), see Hal Foster, "The Art of Fetishism: Notes on Dutch Still Life," in *Fetishism as Cultural Discourse,* ed. Emily Apter and Pietz (Ithaca, NY: Cornell University Press, 1993), pp. 251–65.

64. On the subject of "female fetishism" (to invoke only one critical discourse), see, after, *inter alia,* Schor and Kofman, Gaylyn Studlar's *In The Realm of Pleasure: Von Sternberg, Dietrich, and the Masochistic Aesthetic* (Urbana, IL: University of Illinois Press, 1988), pp. 45–47. See also Elizabeth A. Grosz's "Lesbian Fetishism," in "Queer Theory: Lesbian and Gay Sexualities," *differences* 3, No. 2 (Summer 1991), pp. 39–54; Grosz's critique of Teresa de Lauretis in "Labors of Love: Analyzing Perverse Desire," in *Space, Time, and Perversion: Essays on the Politics of Bodies* (New York: Routledge, 1995), pp. 155–71; and Heather Findlay's "Freud's 'Fetishism' and the Lesbian Dildo Debates," in *Out in Culture: Gay, Lesbian, and Queer Essays on Popular Culture,* ed. Corey K. Creekmur and Alexander Doty (Durham: Duke Univer-

sity Press, 1995), pp. 325–42. For a related argument, see Tania Modleski's "Lethal Bodies" where she articulates what, after Barthes, one might call a "scrupulous fetishism." For the Modleski, see *Feminism without Women: Culture and Criticism in a "Postfeminist" Age* (New York: Routledge, 1991), pp. 135–63; on the Barthes ("scrupulous fetishist"), see "Upon Leaving the Movie Theatre," in *Cinematographic Apparatus: Selected Writings*, ed. Theresa Hak Kyung Cha (New York: Tanem Press, 1980), p. 3. Finally, see in general Emily Apter's *Feminizing the Fetish: Psychoanalysis and Narrative Obsession in Turn-of-the-Century France* (Ithaca: Cornell University Press, 1991) and Lorraine Gamman and Merja Makinen's *Female Fetishism* (New York: New York University Press, 1994). With respect to the last text, I might add that if there are in fact "three types of fetishism" (anthropological, commodity, and sexual), the accent in this book is decidedly on *commodity* fetishism, though unlike Gamman and Makinen, I am less interested in sorting out the various forms of fetishism than in exploring their constellatory inter-articulation.

65. Homi Bhabha, "The Other Question," *The Location of Culture* (New York: Routledge, 1994), pp. 76–77. For my sense of Bhabha's work, see Aijaz Ahmad's "Literary Theory and 'Third World Literature,' " *In Theory: Classes, Nations, Literatures* (London: Verso, 1992), pp. 43–72, esp. 68–69.

66. See Bhabha, "Articulating the Archaic," *The Location of Culture*, p. 132.

67. See, for example, "Signs Taken for Wonders" where Bhabha cites Victor Smirnoff to the effect that the "separateness of the fetish" is what allows the subject to "make use of it in his own way and establish it in an order of things that frees it from any subordination" (LC 120). On hybridity, see, in general, Robert C. Young, *Colonial Desire: Hybridity in Theory, Culture and Race* (New York: Routledge, 1995).

68. Kobena Mercer, "Reading Racial Fetishism: The Photographs of Robert Mapplethorpe," in *Fetishism as Cultural Discourse*, pp. 307–29. For the location of this essay within the context of Mercer's other work, see also *Welcome to the Jungle: New Positions in Black Cultural Studies* (New York: Routledge, 1994). On racial fetishism, see Gail Ching-Liang Low, *White Skin/Black Masks: Representation and Colonialism* (New York: Routledge, 1996), pp. 221–26.

69. To wit: in the second part of "Reading Racial Fetishism," Mercer situates himself vis-à-vis Mapplethorpe's photographs as a gay black male spectator who is "already inside its intertextual field," narcissistically implicated in a graphic economy of eros and aggressivity that the text "makes available not only for white spectators but for black spectators as well" (RRF 320). From this site-specific position, Mercer argues that "what is experienced in the *reception* of Mapplethorpe's text as its characteristic 'shock' effect betrays a radical *unfixing* that upsets and disrupts the spectator's horizon of expectations" (RRF 323, initial emphasis mine). The net effect of this perspectival shift for Mercer is that once Mapplethorpe's work is repositioned as an "avant-garde practice located in the specific historical milieu of an urban gay male subculture" (RRF 322), it

can be read as a "subversive deconstruction" of ethnocentrism. In other words, given this condition of reception, Mapplethorpe's black male nudes become, strictly speaking, "undecidable" (RRF 320).

70. To suggest that Mercer's essay is symptomatic is not, however, to claim that it is programmatic, since if the emphasis in the second part of "Reading Racial Fetishism" falls on the "author-function" (Foucault) as opposed to the author or text (or, more generally, production studies), Mercer's revision also retains—unlike, for instance, most work in American cultural studies—an explanatory role for class.

71. See, in general, Stuart Hall, *The Hard Road to Renewal: Thatcherism and the Crisis of the Left* (London: Verso, 1988).

72. See Frank Mort, "The Politics of Consumption" (1988), in *New Times: The Changing Face of Politics in the 1990s*, ed. Stuart Hall and Martin Jacques (London: Lawrence & Wishart, 1989), pp. 160–72. On consumption and masculinity, see also Mort's recent work, in particular *Cultures of Consumption: Masculinities and Social Space in Late Twentieth-Century Britain* (New York: Routledge, 1996).

73. Jim McGuigan, *Cultural Populism* (New York: Routledge, 1992), p. 4.

74. Hall, "The Culture Gap," *Hard Road to Renewal*, p. 215.

75. For some sense of this historical context, see McGuigan, "From Hegemony Theory to the New Revisionism," *Cultural Populism*, pp. 70–71. The British feminist responses were Diana Simmonds in *Marxism Today* (October 1985), Judith Williamson in the *New Socialist* (October 1985), and Sheryl Garratt in *Women's Review* (March 1986).

76. John Fiske, "Shopping for Pleasure," *Reading the Popular* (Boston: Unwin Hyman, 1989), pp. 16–17. For a rather more nuanced understanding of consumption, see Fiske's cultural account of racial protests in the sphere of consumption—what he calls "radical shopping" (i.e., looting)—in "Los Angeles: A Tale of Three Videos," *Media Matters: Everyday Culture and Political Change* (Minneapolis: University of Minnesota Press, 1994), pp. 125–90, especially the segment titled "Latasha Harlins and Soon Ja Du: Consuming Race" (159–69).

77. Michael Bérubé, "Pop Goes the Academy: Cult Studies Fight the Power," *Public Access: Literary Theory and American Cultural Politics* (New York: Verso, 1994), p. 150.

78. Ibid., p. 150.

79. Tricia Rose, "Soul Sonic Forces," *Black Noise: Rap Music and Black Culture in Contemporary America* (Hanover, NH: University Press of New England, 1994), pp. 55. For a more informal take on this position—in particular, the issue of "contradictory" vs. "regressive" cultural forces—see Rose's response

in "A Symposium on Popular Culture and Political Correctness," *Social Text* 36 (Fall 1993), pp. 16–22.

80. Paul Smith, *Clint Eastwood: A Cultural Production* (Minneapolis: University of Minnesota Press, 1994), pp. xv–xvi. For a review essay that takes a different, rather more psychoanalytic tack, see my "Lust, Fantasy, Male Hysteria: *Clint Eastwood* (Un-) Bound," *Minnesota Review* 43/44 (November 1995), pp. 150–63.

81. Jostein Gripsrud, "The Frankfurt School Revisited," *The Dynasty Years: Hollywood Television and Critical Media Studies* (New York: Routledge, 1995), pp. 5–8.

82. Ibid., p. 18.

83. For instance, Gripsrud remarks *à la* Bernard Gendron that Adorno's work on popular music is especially problematic as it elides the differences between text and artefact—as, for instance, in Adorno's comparison of pop records to mass-produced cars (*The Dynasty Years*, p. 7). For the Adorno, see, for example, "Perennial Fashion—Jazz": "[Jazz's] vitality is difficult to take seriously in the face of the assembly line procedure that is standardized down to its most minute deviations" (124). See also MacDonald, who tends to parrot Adorno's position on mass culture, as in the following passage from "Masscult & Midcult": "Those who consume Masscult might as well be eating ice-cream sodas, while those who fabricate it are no more expressing themselves than are the 'stylists' who design the latest atrocity from Detroit" (p. 5).

For the Gendron, which argues that the assembly line is an "inappropriate model for the production of texts as universals" (p. 28), see "Theodor Adorno Meets the Cadillacs," in *Studies in Entertainment: Critical Approaches to Mass Culture*, ed. Tania Modleski (Bloomington, IN: Indiana University Press, 1986), pp. 18–36.

84. Keith Tester, *Media, Culture, and Morality* (New York: Routledge, 1994), 3. The reference to cretinism is, alas, not an isolated phenomenon in the book; rather, it's a leitmotif of sorts: e.g., "Adorno himself sees the fans of astrology as people who, basically, have been rendered cretinous by the intellectual division of labour in modern social arrangements" (MCM 51); "For Adorno, the culture industry does not just reduce high art to the lower by asking only of its financial worth; it actually trivializes and makes cretinous absolutely all cultural activities and production" (MCM 41).

85. See the letter from Adorno to Benjamin (November 10, 1938 [New York]), in *Aesthetics and Politics*, p. 129. For a restatement with respect to Marxism as well as a rather withering critique of Benjamin's "tributes" to Marx in the Arcades project, see also *Aesthetics and Politics*, p. 130.

86. "A television set is fetishized when I talk about its wonderful sound reproduction but forget that it might well have been made by poor slum dwellers from the Third World" (*Media, Culture, and Morality*, p. 76).

87. For a more original and sympathetic use of Adorno with respect to punk, see Greil Marcus, *Lipstick Traces: A Secret History of the 20th Century* (Cambridge, MA: Harvard University Press, 1989), pp. 68–77.

88. Tester also asserts, in parenthesis, that a "similar story of the take-over of the initial rebelliousness of punk by the culture industry can be *extracted* from Savage 1991" (MCM 43, emphasis mine). If my own use of Savage does not sufficiently indicate my differences with Tester's reading of *England's Dreaming*, the above use of the word *extract* perhaps suggests the sort of interpetative violence Tester does to Savage's thick-descriptive and unusually balanced interpretation of the Clash. For the Savage, see *England's Dreaming: Anarchy, Sex Pistols, Punk Music, and Beyond* (New York: St. Martin's, 1992), p. 488. See also my "Punk Pedagogy, or Performing Contradiction: The Risk and Rewards of (Anti-) Transference," in *Review of Education/Pedagogy/Cultural Studies* 16, No. 1 (1994), pp. 57–67; reprinted in *Education and Cultural Studies: Toward a Performative Practice*, ed. Henry Giroux and Patrick Shannon (New York: Routledge, 1997), pp. 259–70.

89. In this context, it is important I think to note—as Savage does—that "punk groups seem to have been fantastically naive about the [music] industry" (ED 304). He continues: "Concerning their ideas about freedom and autonomy, this naivety seems both *willful and magnificent*" (ED 304). As Joe Strummer put it: "We were completely in the dark. . . . What did we know about record companies and contracts?" (ED 304). In other words: ignorance, even complicity, is one thing, "selling out" another. Not so incidentally, the above logic can be heard, as it were, in the difference between the Clash's "Remote Control" (which CBS released as a single against the group's wishes in 1977) and "Complete Control," which not only featured Lee Perry as producer but is a hymn, like "White Man in Hammersmith Palais," to "punk autonomy at its moment of eclipse" (ED 399). On "Complete Control," see also Neil Nehring, "Theorizing Authoritarian Culture," *Flowers in the Dustbin: Culture, Anarchy, and Postwar England* (Ann Arbor, MI: University of Michigan Press, 1993), p. 89.

90. For the Adorno ("out-and-out romanticization"), see his letter to Benjamin, in *Aesthetics and Politics*, p. 123. Bérubé captures the difficulty of this position in his review of *Cultural Studies* (1992): "Ten years hence, people may be heard saying things like 'I only care about early cultural studies—you know, before *Cultural Studies* came out,' in roughly the same manner people profess enthusiasm for early Clash, early Hüsker Du, early Lemonheads, before all those guys sold out" (*Public Access*, 146).

91. On the ambiguous address of "White Riot" (CBS, 1977), see, for example, Hebdige, *Subculture: The Meaning of Style* (New York: Routledge, 1991), p. 29; and Savage, *England's Dreaming*, p. 235. As Savage comments, "any fascist ambiguity in Punk [as, for example, in "White Riot"] was fueled by the way that style had bled rock dry of all black influences: one way to overcome any taint of white supremacy was to affirm visible links with reggae" (ED 398).

92. On the homosocial worldview of the Clash, see Simon Reynolds and Joy Press, "Brothers in Arms: Combat Rock and Other Stories for Boys," in *The Sex Revolts: Gender, Rebellion, and Rock 'n' Roll* (Cambridge, MA: Harvard University Press), p. 67. On punk and queer culture, see Matias Viegener, " 'The Only Haircut That Makes Sense Anymore': Queer Subcultures and Gay Resistance," in *Queer Looks*, ed. Martha Gever, et. al. (NY: Routledge, 1993), pp. 116–33.

93. On the Clash and reggae (audible as early as the cover of Junior Murvin's "Police & Thieves" on *The Clash*), see Hebdige, "Boredom in Babylon," *Subculture*, pp. 27–29; Savage, *England's Dreaming*, pp. 237–38; and, more generally, Iain Chambers, "The Release from Obscurity: Black Music, 1966–1976," *Urban Rhythms: Pop Music and Popular Culture* (New York: St. Martin's, 1983), pp. 150–74.

94. My musical taste and opinions aside, see, for example, Savage's entry for *Combat Rock* in the "Discography" (ED 567). As for the Tester, I say if you want to *hear* a more interesting, because complicated, narrative about money and rebellion, listen—again—to *Combat Rock* (1982), then decide for yourself whether the Clash's *music* after 1978—including *Cut the Crap* (1985)—is a textbook illustration of what happens to "music as soon as it has been taken up by the culture industry" (MCM 44).

Part One

1. G. W. F. Hegel, *Hegel: Texts and Commentary*, trans. Walter Kaufmann (Notre Dame, IN: University of Notre Dame Press, 1987 [1977]), p. 30.

2. I'm thinking here of the ladder trope—very much *not* in the spirit of Wittgenstein—in the preface to the *Phenomenology*: "the individual has the right to demand that science should at least furnish him with a ladder to this [phenomenological] standpoint" (PS 40).

3. *Science of Logic*, trans. A. V. Miller (New York: Humanities Press, 1976), p. 28. Translations emended. For the original, see *Wissenschaft der Logik*, 2 vols., ed. George Lasson (Hamburg: Felix Meiner, 1963). In terms of the extensive literature on the *Logic*, I would only cite *Hegel and His Critics*, ed. William Desmond (Albany: State University of New York Press, 1989), particularly Walter Zimmerli's "Is Hegel's Logic a Logic?" which reviews recent, influential German readings of the *Logik*.

4. There is a "good" and "bad" dialectic even in Kant: thus, in the *Critique of Pure Reason*, the bad is the dialectic or logic of mere appearance, while the good is the transcendental dialectic, the latter of which constitutes a critique of the above "dialectical *Schein*" (*Hegel: Texts and Commentary*, 167). Of course, if Kant revises Plato, Hegel's objective logic revises, in turn, Plato's sophistic dialectic as well as Kant's transcendental one.

5. Hegel, *Lectures on the History of Philosophy*, cited by Lucio Colletti, *Marxism and Hegel*, trans. Lawrence Garner (London: New Left Books, 1973), p. 28.

6. For a thorough critique of the Hegelian logic that defines history as the development and unfolding of the Absolute and absolutely self-conscious Spirit, see, in general, Arkady Plotnitsky, *In the Shadow of Hegel* (Gainesville, FL: University Press of Florida, 1993).

7. "What Adorno called positivism is very precisely what we now call postmodernism, only at a more primitive stage" (Fredric Jameson, "Adorno in the Postmodern," *Late Marxism* [London: Verso, 1990], 249).

8. Again, for a reading of Hegel that goes very much against the grain of the interpretation advanced here, see Žižek's *Sublime Object of Ideology* (London: Verso, 1989) and, in particular, *For They Know Not What They Do* (London: Verso, 1991). See also note 9 below.

9. See my " 'Going through the Fantasy': Screening Slavoj Žižek," *South Atlantic Quarterly* (forthcoming: Spring 1998).

10. Theodor W. Adorno, *Negative Dialectics*, trans. E. B. Ashton (New York: Seabury Press, 1973), p. 17. *Negative Dialektik* (Frankfurt: Suhrkamp, 1975).

11. On determinate negation, see Lambert Zuidervaart, *Adorno's Aesthetic Theory: The Redemption of Illusion* (Cambridge, MA: MIT Press, 1991), pp. 55–57.

12. On the constellation, see—for instance—Susan Buck-Morss, "Constellations," *Origin of Negative Dialectics: Theodor Adorno, Walter Benjamin, and the Frankfurt Institute* (New York: Free Press, 1975), pp. 90–95.

13. See Patrick McHugh's "Ecstasy and Exile: Cultural Theory between Heidegger and Adorno," *Cultural Critique* 25 (Fall 1993), pp. 121–52.

14. See, in this context, Stanley Aronowitz's "Tensions of Critical Theory: Is Negative Dialectics All There Is?," in *Postmodernism and Social Theory*, ed. Steven Seidman and David Wagner (Cambridge, MA: Blackwell, 1992), pp. 289–321.

15. On Derrida/Adorno, see Martin Jay, *Adorno* (Cambridge, MA: Harvard University Press, 1984), p. 21; Rainer Nägele, "The Scene of the Other: Theodor W. Adorno's Negative Dialectic in the Context of Poststructuralism," in *Postmodernism and Politics*, ed. Jonathan Arac (Minneapolis: University of Minnesota Press, 1986), pp. 91–111; Jürgen Habermas, *The Philosophical Discourse of Modernity* (Cambridge, MA: MIT Press, 1990), pp. 185–90. For dissenting opinions, see Jameson, *Late Marxism*, pp. 9–10; Peter Dews, "Adorno, Poststructuralism, and the Critique of Identity," in *The Problems of Modernity: Adorno and Benjamin*, ed. Andrew Benjamin (London:

Routledge, 1989), pp. 15–18; and, most recently, Asha Varadharajan, "Rethinking the Object," *Exotic Parodies: Subjectivity in Adorno, Spivak, and Said* (Minneapolis: University of Minnesota Press, 1995), pp. 20–33.

16. Jacques Derrida, *Positions*, trans. Alan Bass (Chicago: University of Chicago Press, 1982), p. 96. See also Derrida's interview with Imre Salusinsky, in *Criticism in Society* (New York: Methuen, 1987), p. 20.

17. Adorno, *Minima Moralia*, trans. E. F. N. Jephcott (London: Verso, 1987), p. 247.

18. See Eugene Lunn, *Marxism and Modernism: An Historical Study of Lukács, Brecht, Benjamin and Adorno* (Berkeley: University of California Press, 1982), p. 216.

19. For an aphoristic instance of this strain in Adorno, see "Olet" in *Minima Moralia*: "In Europe the pre-bourgeois past survives in the shame felt at being paid for personal services or favors. The new continent knows nothing of this" (p. 195).

20. See, for example, Jameson's "Baleful Enchantments of the Concept" where he argues that Adorno and Horkheimer's convergence theory represents a comment on the nascent media technology's impact on the public spheres of the USA and Germany as well as, more generally, a comment on the "indissociability of the Culture Industry and fascism" or, more specifically, "American mass democracy" and the "Nazi interregnum" (LM 140).

21. Such is the opening gambit of Adorno's "Culture Industry Reconsidered," trans. Anson G. Rabinbach, *New German Critique* 6 (Fall 1975), p. 12.

22. Adorno, *In Search of Wagner*, trans. Rodney Livingstone (London: New Left Books, 1981), p. 107.

23. Adorno and Max Horkheimer, "The Culture Industry: Enlightenment as Mass Deception," *Dialectic of Enlightenment*, trans. John Cumming (New York: Continuum, 1987), p. 126.

24. See, for instance, Marsha Kinder, *Playing with Power in Movies, Television, and Video Games: From Muppet Babies to Mutant Ninja Turtles* (Berkeley: University of California Press, 1991), in particular "Saturday Morning Television" (39–86).

25. On the "cult of technology" (*Technikkult*) which swept Berlin during the "stabilizing phase of the Weimar Republic" and which influenced Kracauer, Brecht, and Benjamin (but alienated the Viennese Adorno), see Huyssen, "Introduction to Adorno," *New German Critique* 6 (Fall 1975), pp. 2–11.

26. Adorno, "Culture Industry Reconsidered," *New German Critique* 6, p. 12.

27. Huyssen, "Adorno in Reverse," *After the Great Divide: Modernism, Mass Culture, Postmodernism* (Bloomington: Indiana University Press, 1986), p. 22.

28. See Huyssen's "Politics of Identification: 'Holocaust' and West German Drama," in *After the Great Divide*, pp. 94–114.

29. Habermas, "Political Experience and the Renewal of Marxist Theory," *Autonomy and Solidarity: Interviews*, ed. Peter Dews (London: Verso, 1986), p. 90.

30. Along just these lines, see Žižek's Lacanian-Hegelian reading of the *Grundrisse* in, *inter alia, Tarrying with the Negative: Kant, Hegel, and the Critique of Ideology* (Durham, NC: Duke University Press, 1993), pp. 25–27.

31. Habermas, *Autonomy and Solidarity*, p. 108.

32. On Nietzsche and Adorno (-Horkheimer), see Habermas, "The Entwinement of Myth and Enlightenment," in *The Philosophical Discourse of Modernity*, pp. 106–30. See also Gillian Rose, *The Melancholy Science: An Introduction to the Thought of Theodor W. Adorno* (New York: Columbia University Press, 1978), pp. 17–26.

33. So, in the "Introduction" to *Modernism and Hegemony*, Neil Larsen states that the "logic of Adornian critique is finally to invert, rather than collapse, being and consciousness in the manner of the classical idealist systems: a melancholized Hegelianism" ([Minneapolis: University of Minnesota Press, 1990], p. xxv).

34. Friedrich Nietzsche, *Ecce Homo*, trans. Walter Kaufmann (New York: Vintage, 1969), p. 271.

35. Cornel West, "Interview with Cornel West," interviewed by Anders Stephanson, in *Universal Abandon?: The Politics of Postmodernism*, ed. Andrew Ross (Minneapolis: University of Minnesota Press, 1988), p. 275.

36. Michel Foucault, preface to Gilles Deleuze and Félix Guattari, *Anti-Oedipus: Capitalism and Schizophrenia*, trans. Robert Hurley et al. (Minneapolis: University of Minnesota Press, 1985), p. xiii.

37. Deleuze, *Nietzsche and Philosophy*, trans. Hugh Tomlinson (Minneapolis: University of Minnesota Press, 1983), p. 8. *Nietzsche et la philosophie* (Paris: Presses Universitaires de France, 1973). My reading of Deleuze/Nietzsche is indebted to Ronald Bogue's "Deleuze's Nietzsche," *Deleuze and Guattari* (London: Routledge, 1989), pp. 15–34.

38. See Hegel, "Remark: The Expression 'To Sublate,' " in *The Science of Logic*, pp. 106–08.

39. Deleuze, *Spinoza: Practical Philosophy*, trans. Robert Hurley (San Francisco: City Lights, 1988), p. 96.

40. On the binary logic of the root tree, see, for instance, Deleuze and Guattari's introduction to *A Thousand Plateaus*: "Aborescent systems are hierarchial systems with centers of signification and subjectification, central automata like organized memories" (trans. Brian Massumi [Minneapolis: University of Minnesota Press, 1987], p. 17).

41. Jameson, "Marxism and Historicism," in *The Ideologies of Theory: Syntax of History*, Vol. 2 (Minneapolis: University of Minnesota Press, 1988), p. 160.

42. For a positive reading of Deleuze and Guattari, see Alice Jardine, "Thinking the Unrepresentable: The Displacement of Difference," *Gynesis: Configurations of Women and Modernity* (Ithaca, NY: Cornell University Press, 1985), p. 133. See also Paul Patton, "Marxism and Beyond: Strategies of Reterritorialization," in *Marxism and the Interpretation of Culture*, ed. Cary Nelson and Lawrence Grossberg (Urbana, IL: University of Illinois Press, 1988), p. 123; for a critique, see, in the same volume, Belden Fields's response to the Patton (151–54). On Deleuze and Guattari's understanding of capitalism as a "quasicause" with an attendant "double axiomatic" (worker/capitalist and commodity/consumer), see Brian Massumi, "Monstrosity," *A User's Guide to Capitalism and Schizophrenia* (Cambridge, MA: MIT Press, 1992), pp. 126–41.

43. See Todd May's "Difference and Unity in Gilles Deleuze," where he poses the problem of "total affirmation" (*Gilles Deleuze and the Theatre of Philosophy*, ed. Constantin V. Boundas and Dorothea Olkowski [New York: Routledge, 1994], p. 38).

44. While Deleuze's work on Nietzsche is, I believe, the more originary gesture of affirmation (after Nietzsche, of course), see also François Lyotard's early work, in particular *Libidinal Economy*, trans. Iain Hamilton Grant (Bloomington, IN: Indiana University Press, 1993). For an especially cogent reading of the last, see Peter Dews, "From Perception to Desire," *Logics of Disintegration: Post-Structuralist Thought and the Claims of Critical Theory* (New York: Verso, 1989), pp. 109–43. See also Christa Burger, "Modernity as Postmodernity," especially "On Lyotard's 'Affirmative' Aesthetics," in *Modernity and Identity*, ed. Scott Lash and Jonathan Friedman (Cambridge, MA: Blackwell, 1992), pp. 73–93.

45. One instance of this essentialization is Deleuze and Guattari's notion of "the becoming woman" (*le devenir femme*) in *A Thousand Plateaus*, a concept-metaphor that is the key to all the other becomings. Specifically, if "the becoming woman" is *the* point-sign or master signifier of "the future" (*l'avenir*) of man and therefore a category with some claim to generality, one might well inquire whether women in all their cultural-historical specificity will not have been *aufgehoben* in the process. Put another way: one does not have to subscribe to an idealist-positivist notion of woman to wonder about Deleuze and Guattari's valorization of the Overwoman, predicated as it appears to be on a

residual essentialism. See Jardine, "Becoming a Body without Organs: Gilles Deleuze and His Brothers," *Gynesis*, p. 217. For a complementary analysis, see Rosi Braidotti, "Deleuze and the Becoming-Minority of Women," in *Patterns of Dissonance: A Study of Women in Contemporary Philosophy*, trans. Elizabeth Guild (New York: Routledge, 1991), pp. 108–27. For a sympathetic but not uncritical reading that engages both Jardine and Braidotti (as well as Irigaray), see Elizabeth Grosz's work, in particular "Intensities and Flows," in *Volatile Bodies: Toward a Corporeal Feminism* (Bloomington, IN: Indiana University Press, 1994), pp. 160–83.

46. Judith Butler, "Deleuze: From Slave Morality to Productive Desire," *Subjects of Desire: Reflections on Twentieth-Century France* (New York: Columbia University Press, 1987), p. 216. For a related argument, see Butler, "Arguing with the Real," *Bodies That Matter: On the Discursive Limits of "Sex"* (New York: Routledge, 1993), pp. 187–222.

47. See, for instance, "The Body without Organs" and "November 28, 1947: How to Make Yourself a Body without Organs," in *Anti-Oedipus* and *A Thousand Plateaus* respectively, pp. 9–16 and 149–66. See also Deleuze and Claire Parnet, *Dialogues*, trans. Hugh Tomlinson and Barbara Habberjam (New York: Columbia University Press, 1987), pp. 91–95.

48. See Gayatri Spivak, "Can the Subaltern Speak?" in *Marxism and the Interpretation of Culture*, p. 289. For a more affirmative take on *Anti-Oedipus* for postcolonial studies, see Robert C. Young, "Colonialism and the Desiring Machine," *Colonial Desire: Hybridity in Theory, Culture, and Race* (New York: Routledge, 1995), pp. 166–74; and "Decolonizing the Map," in *The Post-Colonial Reader*, ed. Bill Ashcroft, Gareth Griffiths, and Helen Tiffin (London: Routledge, 1995), pp. 407–11.

49. On peripheral Fordism and "primitive" or "bloody Taylorization," see Alain Lipietz, *Mirages and Miracles: The Crises of Global Fordism*, trans. David Macey (London: Verso, 1987), p. 189. The intensive regime of accumulation that is, or was, dominant in the postwar period in the so-called North—that is to say, Fordism—was of course centered upon, as Lipietz argues, mass consumption (p. 15). As Michel Aglietta writes in *A Theory of Capitalist Regulation*: "The social revolutions through which capitalism succeeded in producing the characteristic mode of consumption of the wage-earning class, and in integrating this mode of consumption into the conditions of production, are the chief elements needed to explain the great disturbances of the first half of the 20th century and the exceptional growth that followed the Second World War" (trans. David Fernbach [London: New Left Books, 1979], p. 25).

50. On Adorno and Deleuze and Guattari, see Joanna Hodge, "Feminism and Postmodernism: Misleading Divisions Imposed by the Opposition between Modernism and Postmodernism," *The Problems of Modernity*, p. 110.

Part Two

1. Gayatri Spivak, "Scattered Speculations on the Question of Value," *In Other Worlds* (New York: Methuen, 1987), p. 162. On this aspect of Spivak's work, see Rey Chow, "Ethics after Idealism," *Diacritics* 23, 1 (Spring 1993), pp. 3–22. On the question of value, see also Spivak's "Limits and Openings of Marx in Derrida," *Outside in the Teaching Machine* (New York: Routledge, 1993), pp. 97–119.

2. Fredric Jameson, *"Culture," Postmodernism, or, The Cultural Logic of Late Capitalism* (Durham, NC: Duke University Press, 1991), p. 47.

3. Andreas Huyssen, "Mapping the Postmodern," *After the Great Divide* (Bloomington, IN: Indiana University Press, 1986), p. 200.

4. Ibid., pp. 220–21.

5. "By means . . . of the value relation expressed in our equation, the bodily form of commodity B becomes the value form of commodity A, or the body of commodity B acts as a mirror to the value of commodity A." In Marx, *Capital: A Critical Analysis of Capitalist Production* (London 1887), ed. Friedrich Engels and trans. Samuel Moore and Edward Aveling, in Marx and Engels, *Gesamtausgabe*, MEGA II/9 (Berlin: Dietz Verlag, 1990), p. 27. For the German, see *Das Kapital. Kritik der Politischen Ökonomie* (Hamburg 1883), Vol. 1, MEGA II/8 (Berlin: Dietz Verlag, 1989).

For a very different understanding and use of the term commodity-body, see Leo Braudy, "Hostages of the Eye: The Body as Commodity," *The Frenzy of Renown: Fame and Its History* (New York: Oxford University Press, 1986), pp. 566–83. In this context, see also Robert Goldman, in particular "Commodity Fetishism," in *Reading Ads Socially* (New York: Routledge, 1992), pp. 130–54. I would only add that although I share Goldman's understanding of the *commodity-sign*, my critical-affirmative sense of this term (which also comprises the "body" of use-value) differs substantially from his astute but in many ways classically negative critique.

6. Herbert Marcuse, "The Affirmative Character of Culture," in *Negations: Essays in Critical Theory*, trans. Jeremy J. Shapiro (Boston: Beacon Press, 1968), p. 95.

7. For the argument that " 'culture' can no longer be conceived as a Grand Hotel" (i.e., "a totalizable system that somehow orchestrates all cultural production and reception according to one master system" [xiii]), see Jim Collins's *Uncommon Cultures: Popular Culture and Postmodernism* (New York: Routledge, 1989), pp. 1–17. See also James Naremore and Patrick Brantlinger, "Introduction: Six Artistic Cultures," in *Modernity and Mass Culture*, ed. Naremore and Brantlinger (Bloomington: Indiana University Press, 1991), pp. 1–23.

8. Marcuse, *An Essay on Liberation* (Boston: Beacon Press, 1969), p. 11.

9. See, for example, Douglas Kellner, "Critique of Marcuse's Aesthetics," in *Herbert Marcuse and the Crisis of Marxism* (Berkeley: University of California Press, 1984), pp. 357–62.

10. Michel Foucault, *Discipline and Punish: The Birth of the Prison,* trans. Alan Sheridan (New York: Vintage, 1979), pp. 137–38.

11. For an instance of this influence, see *Discipline and Punish*, note 2, p. 309 ("the body of the condemned").

12. Foucault, *The History of Sexuality*, Vol. 1, trans. Robert Hurley (New York: Vintage, 1980), p. 114.

13. For example, in "Body/Power" (1975), Foucault muses: "As regards Marxism, I'm not one of those who try to elicit the effects of power at the level of ideology. Indeed I wonder whether, before one poses the question of ideology, it wouldn't be more materialist to study first the question of the body and the effects of power on it" (*Power and Knowledge: Selected Interviews and Other Writings, 1972–1977*, trans. Colin Gordon et al. [New York: Pantheon, 1980], p. 58).

14. Sigmund Freud, "Unsuitable Substitutes for the Sexual Object," *Three Essays on the Theory of Sexuality*, trans. James Strachey (London: The Hogarth Press, 1962), p. 19.

15. Freud, "Fetishism," *Collected Papers* (1888–1938), Vol. 5, trans. Joan Riviere and ed. James Strachey (London: The Hogarth Press, 1953), p. 201. "Fetischismus," *Psychologie des Unbewußten*, in *Studienausgabe* 3 (Frankfurt am Main: S. Fischer Verlag, 1975), pp. 379–88.

16. In "A Denial of Difference: Theories of Cinematic Identification" (1982), Anne Friedberg argues that "fetishism is a relation incurred by the anxiety of sexual difference" (in *Psychoanalysis and Cinema*, ed. E. Ann Kaplan [New York: Routledge, 1990], p. 40). For the Kaja Silverman ("primary castration"), see "Lost Objects and Mistaken Subjects: A Prologue," in *The Acoustic Mirror: The Female Voice in Psychoanalysis and Cinema* (Bloomington, IN: Indiana University Press, 1988), pp. 1–41.

17. Linda Williams, "Fetishism and Hard Core: Marx, Freud, and the 'Money Shot,' " *Hard Core: Power, Pleasure, and the "Frenzy of the Visible"* (Berkeley, CA: University of California Press, 1989), pp. 93–119. On, in particular, the clitoris vis-à-vis the penis (as well as "penis envy"), see E. L. McCallum, "How to Do Things with Fetishism," *differences* 7, No. 3 (Fall 1995), pp. 24–49.

18. For a similar sentiment, see the introduction to Judith Butler's *Bodies That Matter: On the Discursive Limits of "Sex"* (New York: Routledge, 1993), p. 22.

19. Jean Baudrillard, "Fetishism and Ideology," in *For a Critique of the Political Economy of the Sign*, trans. Charles Levin (St. Louis: Telos, 1981), pp. 88–101; "Fétichisme et idéologie: la réduction sémiologique," *Pour une critique de l'économie politique du signe* (Paris: Gallimard, 1972), pp. 95–113. I presuppose here Bataille and Derrida, in particular the latter's "From Restricted to General Economy: A Hegelianism without Reserve" (trans. Alan Bass, *Writing and Difference* [Chicago: University of Chicago Press, 1978], pp. 251–77). Commenting on Hegel by way of Bataille, Derrida writes: "the phenomenology of the mind . . . corresponds to a restricted economy: restricted to commercial values, . . . limited to the meaning and the established value of objects, and to their *circulation*. The *circularity* of absolute knowldge could dominate . . . only this circulation, only the *circuit of reproductive consumption*" (p. 271). On general economy, see Arkady Plotnitsky's *In the Shadow of Hegel: Complementarity, History, and the Unconscious* (Gainesville, FL: University Press of Florida, 1993) and *Reconfigurations: Critical Theory and General Economy* (Gainesville: University Press of Florida, 1993). For a more detailed discussion of this issue—what I call a general (political) economy of "commodity fetishism"—see the introduction to this book.

20. Marx himself explicitly invokes the notion of perversion: "All forms of society, in so far as they reach the stage of commodity-production and money circulation, take part in this perversion" (i.e., commodity fetishism) ("Trinity Formula," *Capital: A Critique of Political Economy*, Vol. 3, ed. Frederick Engels and trans. anonymous [New York: International, 1967], pp. 826–27). On perversion and social theory, see Joel Whitebook, *Perversion and Utopia: A Study in Psychoanalysis and Theory* (Cambridge, MA: MIT Press, 1995).

21. My retention of the standard translation here ("queer"), however poor, is intentional. Thus, one of the effects of the reinscription of commodity fetishism as a general (political) economy of "commodity fetishism" is that it opens onto the question of sexual perversion in particular and, in general, a problematic that articulates both money and sexuality. On the last, see Jonathan Dollimore's "Sexual Perversion: Pathology to Politics," in *Sexual Dissidence: Augustine to Wilde, Freud to Foucault* (Oxford, UK: Oxford University Press, 1991), pp. 169–230. I have also been productively provoked by the following remarks by Michael Warner: "gay culture is anything but external to the advanced capitalism that many on the left are so eager to disavow. Post-Stonewall urban gay men reek of the commodity. We give off the smell of capitalism in rut, and therefore demand a more dialectical view of capitalism than many people have imagination for" ("Introduction," *Fear of a Queer Planet: Queer Politics and Social Theory*, ed. Warner [Minneapolis: University of Minnesota Press, 1993], p. xxxi, note 28).

22. Walter Benjamin, "The Paris of the Second Empire in Baudelaire," *Charles Baudelaire: A Lyric Poet in the Era of High Capitalism*, trans. Harry Zohn (London: New Left Books, 1973), p. 5.

23. Jean-Joseph Goux, "Numismatics," *Symbolic Economies: After Marx and Freud*, trans. Jennifer Curtiss Gage (Ithaca, NY: Cornell University Press, 1990), p. 33. I should note that to invoke Goux here is not to accept, without qualification, the structural homologism so insistent in, say, *Freud, Marx: Économie et symbolique* (1973); for a critique, see Robert D'Amico, "The Economic and Symbolic in Culture," in *Marx and Philosophy of Culture* (Gainesville, FL: University Presses of Florida, 1981), pp. 31–43.

24. Goux, *Symbolic Economies*, p. 33.

25. Jack Amariglio and Antonio Callari put it this way in "Marxian Value Theory and the Problem of the Subject: The Role of Commodity Fetishism": "The non-determinist view [of commodity fetishism] treats this concept as a sign—a strategically located sign—that the relations between economic and noneconomic processes are neither unproblematic nor unidirectional" (in *Fetishism as Cultural Discourse*, ed. Emily Apter and William Pietz [Ithaca, NY: Cornell University Press, 1993], p. 202).

26. For the best discussion of the body-image with respect to late capitalism, see Donald Lowe, *The Body in Late-Capitalist USA* (Durham, NC: Duke University Press, 1995).

27. Christian Metz, "Disavowal, Fetishism," in *The Imaginary Signifier*, trans. Celia Britton et al. (Bloomington, IN: Indiana University Press, 1982), p. 71.

28. For a provocative argument about, among other things, the umbilical cord as the repressed or suppressed origin of fetishism, see Marcia Ian, "Being and Having," in *Remembering the Phallic Mother: Psychoanalysis, Modernism, and the Fetish* (Ithaca, NY: Cornell University Press, 1993), pp. 38–39.

29. Terry Eagleton, "Capitalism, Modernism, Postmodernism," *Against the Grain: Essays 1975–1985* (London: Verso, 1986), p. 133. In this context (Warhol), it is useful to cite David Roberts: "Warhol's simulation of soup cans not only foregrounds the contingency of the work of art as commodity but also the appearance of the commodity as work of art" ("Profane Illuminations," in *Art and Enlightenment: Aesthetic Theory after Adorno* [Lincoln, NE: University of Nebraska Press, 1991], p. 204).

30. W. J. T. Mitchell, "The Rhetoric of Iconoclasm: Marxism, Ideology, and Fetishism," *Iconology: Image, Text, Ideology* (Chicago: University of Chicago Press, 1986), p. 188.

31. Ibid., p. 205.

32. W. F. Haug, *Critique of Commodity Aesthetics: Appearance, Sexuality and Advertising in Capitalist Society*, trans. Robert Buck (Minneapolis: University of Minnesota Press, 1986), p. 42. For a defense of Haug, see Andrew Goodwin, *Dancing in the Distraction Factory* (Minneapolis: University of Min-

nesota Press, 1992), pp. 46–48; for a critique, see Lowe, *The Body in Late-Capitalist USA*, pp. 72–73.

33. See, in general, Pierre Bourdieu, *Distinction*, trans. Richard Nice (Cambridge, MA: Harvard University Press, 1984).

34. John O'Neill, *Five Bodies: The Human Shape of Modern Society* (Ithaca, NY: Cornell University Press, 1985), p. 18.

35. Ibid., p. 18.

36. See, for example, the special issue of *differences* on "The Phallus" (Vol. 4, No. 1 [1992]). See also, in general, Peter Lehman, *Running Scared: Masculinity and the Representation of the Male Body* (Philadelphia, PA: Temple University Press, 1993).

37. As far as I can determine, no one has really studied Warhol's record covers in the context of his other work, from the period of *Electric Chairs*, *Lonesome Cowboys*, and *Screen Test* (with Gerard Malanga) to, say, *Pork*. For a comprehensive survey of Warhol's work since his death in 1987—a death that arguably marks a new moment in the discursive history of pop art—see *Andy Warhol: A Retrospective*, ed. Kynaston McShine (New York: Museum of Modern Art, 1989).

38. On the more general phenomenon of pop art, see *Modern Dreams: The Rise and Fall and Rise of Pop* (Cambridge, MA: MIT Press, 1988); *Pop Art: The Critical Dialogue*, ed. Carol Anne Mahsun (Ann Arbor: UMI Research Press, 1989); and *Post-Pop Art*, ed. Paul Taylor (Cambridge: MIT Press, 1989), in particular Mary Ann Staniszewski's "Capital Pictures," pp. 159–70. For a sense of the changing debate on the cultural left with respect to Warhol as well as pop in general, compare Donald Kuspit's early "Pop Art: A Reactionary Realism" (1976)—which leans hard on Marx-Adorno's sense of commodity fetishism—with the Staniszewski ("Pop art makes capital visible" [*Post-Pop Art*, pp. 159–60]). For what it's worth, I might add that one of the ironies of Haug's reading of Warhol is that pop art was not only a "resounding influence and success in Europe," in particular Germany, but that—as Paul Taylor notes—it was "perceived as a *criticism* of American capitalism" (*Post-Pop Art*, p. 17, emphasis mine).

39. For some sense of this moment (i.e., the Federal Republic in the late 1960s and early 1970s, in particular *Das Argument* and its *Project Ideologie*), see Haug's and Stuart Hall's introduction to the *Critique of Commodity Aesthetics*, pp. 1–4 and 5–9 respectively.

40. Lacan, "The Signification of the Phallus," *Écrits: A Selection*, trans. Alan Sheridan (New York: Norton, 1977), p. 288.

41. For an excellent historical overview of consumption-as-masturbation (as well as hysteria), see Roy Porter, "Baudrillard: History, Hysteria and Con-

sumption," in *Forget Baudrillard?*, ed. Chris Rojek and Bryan S. Turner (London: Routledge, 1993), p. 13.

42. See "100 Classic Album Covers" (#10), in *Rolling Stone* (November 14, 1991), p. 97. For this cover, see Velvet Underground and Nico, *The Velvet Underground* (MGM/Verve, 1969).

43. Bob Colacello reports: "Andy gave Glenn [O'Brien] a big thrill when he asked him to pose for the cover of the Rolling Stones' new album, *Sticky Fingers*. . . . [However,] Glenn wasn't the only one Andy photographed for this project. . . . When the album came out, Glenn was certain that . . . he [was] on the inside and Jay Johnson on the outside, but Andy would never say exactly whose crotch he had immortalized" ("Spring '71," *Holy Terror: Andy Warhol Close-Up* [New York: Harper Collins, 1990], p. 5). For a wonderful take on this "model" ambiguity, see the photograph of the Stones (where each member of the band is shown strategically posing with the *Sticky Fingers* cover), in David Bourdon's *Warhol* (New York: Abrams, 1989), p. 315.

44. Craig Braun, cited in "100 Classic Album Covers," *Rolling Stone*, p. 97. For a brief comparison of the cover of *Sticky Fingers* and Madonna's *Like a Prayer*, see Carla Freccero, "Our Lady of MTV," in *Feminism and Postmodernism*, ed. Margaret Ferguson and Jennifer Wicke (Durham, NC: Duke University Press, 1994), p. 189. On Warhol and rock, see Van M. Cagle, *Reconstructing Pop/ Subculture: Art, Rock, and Warhol* (Thousand Hills, CA: Sage, 1995).

45. For this citation as well as the production details of the *Sticky Fingers* cover (including the distribution problems that resulted from the inserted zipper), see the entry on *Sticky Fingers* (#4) in "100 Classic Album Covers," p. 93.

46. Richard Dyer, "Introduction," *Heavenly Bodies: Film Stars and Society* (New York: St. Martin's, 1986), p. 3.

47. See, in this context, *Pop Out: Queer Warhol*, ed. Jennifer Doyle, Jonathan Flatley, and José Esteban Muñoz (Durham, NC: Duke University Press, 1996).

48. Laura Mulvey, "Visual Pleasure and Narrative Cinema," *Visual and Other Pleasures* (Bloomington, IN: Indiana University Press, 1989), pp. 14–26. For an auto-critique, see Mulvey's "Afterthoughts on 'Visual Pleasure and Narrative Cinema' Inspired by King Vidor's *Duel in the Sun* (1946)," *Visual and Other Pleasures*, pp. 29–38.

49. On the commodity aestheticians—not only Haug but Hans Heinz Holz and Friedrich Tomberg—see Peter Uwe Hohendahl, "The Polarization of Aesthetic Theory," *Reappraisals: Shifting Alignments in Postwar Critical Theory* (Ithaca, NY: Cornell University Press, 1991), pp. 160–70.

50. In order to re-mark in this essay a revised sense of commodity fetishism, I have—where appropriate—placed it in quotations ("commodity

fetishism"). The standard discussion of the topic is G. A. Cohen's "Fetishism,"
in *Karl Marx's Theory of History: A Defense* (New York: Basic, 1982), pp. 115–
33. In addition to work cited elsewhere in this book, see Michael Taussig, *The
Devil and Commodity Fetishism in South America* (Chapel Hill, NC: University
of North Carolina Press, 1980); Thomas Keenan, "The Point Is to (Ex)Change
It: Reading *Capital*, Rhetorically," in *Fetishism as Cultural Discourse* (152–85);
Slavoj Žižek's provocative remarks on the topic in *The Sublime Object of
Ideology* (London: Routledge, 1989), pp. 23–27; Jacques Derrida, "*Apparition of
the Inapparent,*" *Specters of Marx: The State of Debt, the Work of Mourning, and
the New International*, trans. Peggy Kamuf (New York: Routledge, 1994), pp. 125–
76; Emily Apter, "Specularity and Reproduction: Marx, Freud, Baudrillard," in
Fetish (New York: Princeton Architectural Press, 1992), pp. 20–33; Mulvey, "Intro-
duction: Fetishisms," *Fetishism and Curiosity* (Bloomington, IN: Indiana University
Press, 1996), pp. 1–15; and Jon Stratton, "Commodity Fetishism and Cultural
Fetishism," *The Desirable Body: Cultural Fetishism and the Erotics of Consumption* (Manchester, UK: Manchester University Press, 1996). On the historical devel-
opment of commodity culture, see, most recently, Thomas Richards, *The Commodity
Culture of Victorian England: Advertising and Spectacle, 1851–1914* (Stanford,
CA: Stanford University Press, 1990).

51. So, for example, Lowe argues in "Consumption Practices" *à la* Kelvin
Lancaster that the "commodity in late capitalism . . . has become a package of
changing 'product characteristics' " (*The Body in Late-Capitalist USA*, p. 47).
For the Lancaster, see *Consumer Demand: A New Approach* (New York: Columbia University Press, 1971).

52. As I have suggested (see note 23 above), there are limits to this sort
of homology. Thus, where one might argue that the truth of fetishism revolves
around what I call the complex of (female) organs, the truth of commodity
fetishism is simply use-value (unless one would want to argue, according to
what I take to be a "bad" homologism, that the proletariat is something like
the repressed "body" of woman). On this last, though, see Lyotard's *outré*
reading of Marx as Little Girl Marx in "The Desire Named Marx," in *Libidinal
Economy*, pp. 95–154.

53. See Douglas Kellner, "Commodities, Needs, and Consumption in the
Consumer Society," *Jean Baudrillard: From Marxism to Postmodernism and
Beyond* (Stanford, CA: Stanford University Press, 1989), esp. pp. 37–38.

54. For a very basic introduction to the subject of consumption, see
Robert Bocock, *Consumption* (New York: Routledge, 1993); for an advanced
discussion, see—among the recent spate of books on the topic—Martyn J. Lee,
Consumer Culture Reborn: The Cultural Politics of Consumption (New York:
Routledge, 1993). In addition to Lee, who offers the most nuanced and thor-
ough Marxist discussion of consumption in terms of both Fordism and post-
Fordism, see Gary Cross, *Time and Money: The Making of Consumer Culture*
(New York: Routledge, 1993); *Lifestyle Shopping: The Subject of Consumption*,

ed. Rob Shields (New York: Routledge, 1993); *The Authority of the Consumer*, ed. Russell Keat, Nigel Whiteley, and Nicholas Abercrombie (New York: Routledge, 1994); *Consuming Modernity: Public Culture in a South Asian World*, ed. Carol Breckenridge (Minneapolis, MN: University of Minnesota Press, 1995); John Urry, *Consuming Places* (New York: Routledge, 1995); and Celia Lury, *Consumer Culture* (New Brunswick, NJ: Rutgers University Press, 1996). Consumption is also, of course, a prime philosopheme in Kant and Hegel (e.g., food for understanding). For a discussion of this economy of conservation where nothing is discounted, and even "distaste" is a kind of "taste" (*de-gout*), see Arkady Plotnitsky, "The Maze of Taste," in *Reconfigurations* (63–112).

55. See Scott Lash's "Postmodernism: Towards a Sociological Account," *Sociology of Postmodernism* (London: Routledge, 1990), esp. pp. 5–8.

56. For my use of these terms (i.e., "rhetoric of commodities" and "work of consumption"), see O'Neill, "Consumer Bodies," *Five Bodies*, pp. 99 and 102 respectively.

57. Jim McGuigan, *Cultural Populism* (New York: Routledge, 1992), p. 72.

58. On the new revisionists, see James Curran, "The 'New Revisionism' in Mass Communication Research," *European Journal of Communication 5*, Nos. 2–3 (June 1990), pp. 135–64.

59. Karl Marx, *The Grundrisse*, ed. and trans. David McLellan (New York: Harper, 1972), pp. 23–24. *Ökonomische Manuskripte* (1857–58), MEGA II/1.1 (Berlin: Dietz Verlag, 1976). I must bracket the whole question of "productive" versus "non-productive consumption." The relevant source here is the section in the second volume of *Capital*, "Exchange within Department II," where Marx divides the annual production of commodities into two sub-divisions: (1) articles of necessity (those commodities—including so-called consumer necessities like tobacco—consumed by the working class as well as a portion of the capitalist class), and (2) articles of luxury (those goods which "enter into the consumption of only the capitalist class and can therefore be exchanged only for spent surplus-value, which never falls to the share of the laborer"). See *Capital*, Vol. 2 (New York: International, 1968), p. 403.

60. For the most recent, detailed reading of Marx's position on consumption, see Ben Fine and Ellen Leopold, "Marx's Economics and Consumption," *The World of Consumption* (New York: Routledge, 1993), pp. 254–63.

61. Fine and Leopold, *The World of Consumption*, p. 262.

62. I am playing here on the word *Trieb* which can be translated as "desire" or, as in psychoanalysis, "drive." Though Lacan distinguishes between desire (*désir*) and drive (*pulsion*), I have strategically conflated Marx's and Lacan's understanding of *Trieb* in order to introduce an analytical distinction into Marx's relatively simple conception of consumption. For Baudrillard, of

course, consumption or what he calls consummativity mirrors production-as-productivity and, in the process, reduces need (*besoin*) to labor (*besogne*). On the notion of consummativity, see Baudrillard's "The Ideological Genesis of Needs," *For a Critique of the Political Economy of the Sign*, pp. 63–87. On the psychoanalytic sense of *Trieb*, see Jean Laplanche, "The Order of Life," in *Life and Death in Psychoanalysis*, trans. Jeffrey Mehlman (Baltimore, MD: Johns Hopkins University Press, 1976), pp. 8–18; and Lacan, "The Transference and the Drive," in *The Four Fundamental Concepts of Psycho-Analysis*, trans. Alan Sheridan (New York: Norton, 1978), esp. pp. 161–200.

63. Marx, echoing Ricardo, writes: "If the accumulation of capital were to cause a rise of wages and an increase in the laborer's consumption, unaccompanied by increase in the consumption of labor-power by capital, the additional capital would be consumed unproductively" (C 499).

64. On Lacan's triad—need/demand/desire—see, among other things, "The Signification of the Phallus": "that which is . . . alienated in needs constitutes an *Urverdrängung* (primal repression), an inability . . . to be articulated in demand, but it re-appears in something it gives rise to that presents itself in man as desire" (*Écrits*, p. 286). I should note that my play here on the word *demand*—economic demand as *demande*—is merely meant to underscore the complex "nature" of consumption.

65. I am alluding here to Brecht's notion of the culinary (*kulinarisch*), which—even given its debased status in his aesthetics (i.e., culinary vs. epic theatre)—nonetheless plays a critical role. Bluntly, "cooking" can be an art. For the Brecht, see, for example, his notes on *Mahagonny*, "The Modern Theatre Is the Epic Theatre" (1930), in *Brecht on Theatre*, trans. John Willet (New York: Hill & Wang, 1987), pp. 33–42.

66. For a similar argument about hunger (which is obviously indebted to Lacan), see Baudrillard, "The Ideological Genesis of Needs," *For a Critique of the Political Economy of the Sign*, p. 69, note 1. In this context, see also Anne Friedberg's discussion of commodity experiences: "In the age of mechanical reproduction, *services replace goods as commodities.* . . . These goods, with the mysterious qualities of the commodity's 'fetish character,' offer *commodity experiences* that satisfy, as Marx would have it, the imagination, not the stomach" (*Window Shopping: Cinema and the Postmodern* [Berkeley, CA: University of California Press, 1993], p. 55).

67. Susan Willis, *A Primer for Everyday Life* (New York: Routledge, 1991), p. 148.

68. Ibid., p. 21.

69. Ibid., p. 136. For my sense of "displeasure" here, see also Laura Kipnis, "(Male) Desire and (Female) Disgust: Reading *Hustler*," in *Ecstasy Unlimited: On Sex, Capital, Gender, and Aesthetics* (Minneapolis: University of Minnesota Press, 1993), pp. 219–41.

70. I am referring of course to Marcel Duchamp's readymade, the 1917 *Fountain*. For a history and analysis, see William Camfield, "Marcel Duchamp's *Fountain*: Aesthetic Object, Icon, or Anti-Art?" in *The Definitively Unfinished Marcel Duchamp*, ed. Thierry de Duve (Cambridge: MIT Press, 1991), pp. 133–84.

71. Arjun Appadurai, "Introduction: Commodities and the Politics of Value," in *The Social Life of Things: Commodities in Cultural Perspective*, ed. Appadurai (New York: Cambridge University Press, 1986), pp. 3–63.

72. According to William Pietz, this is where readers of Baudrillard should look for postmodern commodity fetishism, not in the "extreme development of the commercialization of social appearances" (as in Baudrillard) but in the "full development of financial fetishism" (*Fetishism as Cultural Discourse*, p. 149). I would only add that if the latter is the most important political-economic expression of postmodern fetishization, one must attend to the cultural-economic sphere of social appearances as well—with the obvious proviso that one should not do so at the expense of the financial. For a useful discussion of postmodern finance and fictitious capital, see David Harvey, in particular "Time-Space Compression and the Postmodern Condition," in *The Condition of Postmodernity* (Cambridge, MA: Blackwell, 1989), pp. 284–307.

73. Jean Baudrillard, *The Mirror of Production*, trans. Mark Poster (St. Louis: Telos Press, 1975), p. 127. The following passage is representative: "In opposition to the competitive system, the monopolistic system institutes *consumption* as control, as the arbiter of the contingency of demand, as planned socialization by the code" (p. 126).

74. This is how Baudrillard puts it in *The Mirror of Production*: "The real rupture is not between 'abstract' labor and 'concrete' labor, but between symbolic exchange and work (production, economics)" (p. 45). On symbolic exchange, see Mike Gane, "A General Theory," *Baudrillard: Critical and Fatal Theory* (New York: Routledge, 1991), pp. 83–85.

75. *Pace* Gane, I want to argue that a theoretical relation has in fact been established, if only implicitly, between symbolic exchange and use-value. See Gane, *Baudrillard*, p. 83. For an excellent discussion of these issues, albeit from a rather different, semiological perspective, what he calls—with real wit—bar games (*exercices à la barre*), see Gary Genosko, in particular "The Table of Conversions" where he takes up in detail the four logics of value in Baudrillard: *utility* (instrument), *equivalence* (commodity), *difference* (sign), and *ambivalence* (symbol) (*Baudrillard and Signs: Signification Ablaze* [New York: Routledge, 1994], pp. 6–17).

76. Baudrillard, *Mirror of Production*, p. 19. One might cite as well the following passage: "Need, use-value, and the referent 'do not exist.' They are only concepts produced and projected into a generic dimension by the development of the very system of exchange value" (MP 30). However, Baudrillard

notes that "this does not mean *that they have never existed*" (MP 30, note 11). Baudrillard's model is not, therefore, without its historical dimension, attenuated as it may be.

77. See Julian Pefanis, "Theories of the Third Order," *Heterology and the Postmodern: Bataille, Baudrillard, and Lyotard* (Durham, NC: Duke University Press, 1991), p. 64.

78. With respect to Figure 2.9, the arc from final consumption to need refers to what one might call the *loop of desire*. It is important to note that although this figure might seem to imply the existence of some sort of unmediated need which precedes the "moment" or process of production, the upper arc or loop is meant to problematize any such naturalism. Put another way: in the late twentieth century, it is virtually impossible—except, perhaps, in infants (hence Lacan's notion of *demande*, where the child is literally dependent on an external source for physical survival)—to distinguish between need and desire. (See note 92 below.) In fact, in the "first," post-Fordist world at least, it is pretty clear that desire drives need, and that sign-value in all its phantasmagoric play is, in this sense, all about desire. Rather more to the political point, while the loop of desire is, as it were, "loopy" (i.e., cannot be reduced to the calculus of restricted economics), this *annulus*, for all its annihilative character (*res nulla*), can also become a vicious circle of sorts—what one might call compulsive consumption.

79. For this distinction between the tactical and strategic, see Baudrillard: "use-value and the signified do not have the same weight as exchange-value and the signifier respectively. Let us say they have a tactical value—whereas exchange-value and the signifier have strategic value" (CPES 137). In this tactical context, I might add that a general (political) economy of "commodity fetishism" is *not*, *pace* Derrida, merely a "phase within the strategy of general economy" (*Writing and Difference*, p. 337, note 33). This is, as it were, the difference between Marxism or, more precisely, *post*-Marxism and deconstruction: although the former general (political) economy is not restricted to the classical conception of revolution (i.e., class revolution), it is rather less "sovereign" in its economics than deconstruction since it remains unapologetically *invested* in the question of the (re-) distribution of (surplus-) value.

80. I have italicized the word *process* in this sentence in order to re-mark the dynamic and historical character of the mode of production. As Raymond Williams reminds us: "It is only when we realize that 'the base,' to which it is habitual to refer variations, is itself a dynamic and internally contradictory process—the specific activities and modes of activity, over a range from association to antagonism, of real men and classes of men—that we can begin to free ourselves from the notion of an 'area' or a 'category' with fixed properties" ("From Base to Superstructure," *Marxism and Literature* [New York: Oxford University Press, 1977], p. 82).

81. Jean Baudrillard, "Consumer Society," trans. Jacques Mourrain, in *Selected Writings*, ed. Mark Poster (Stanford, CA: Stanford University Press, 1988), p. 38.

82. Ibid., p. 40.

83. See Mark Miller, "Towards a Theory of Consumption," *Material Culture and Mass Consumption* (Oxford, UK: Basil Blackwell, 1991), p. 180.

84. In this sense it is not enough, for example, to establish fair exchange rates (as neoclassical economics would have it), since such laissez-faire economic justice is a function of the "individual negotiation of exchange contracts" rather than, say, genuinely democratic access to the means of production (Susan Himmelweit, "Surplus Value," *A Dictionary of Marxist Thought*, ed. Tom Bottomore et al. [Cambridge, MA: Harvard University Press, 1983], p. 473).

85. Robert Heilbroner, *The Worldly Philosophers* (New York: Simon & Schuster, 1986), p. 68.

86. For a *précis* of this concept, see Roy Bhaskar's entry on "Contradiction," in *A Dictionary of Marxist Thought*, pp. 93–94.

87. However, for an excellent critique of reflexive and, all too frequently, moralizing theories of consumerism and cultural imperialism (which tend to displace the necessity for an *a priori* critique of our own culture of capitalism), see John Tomlinson, *Cultural Imperialism: An Introduction* (Baltimore, MD: Johns Hopkins University Press, 1991), esp. pp. 102–39. For a reading of consumption as cultural transvestism (Superbarrio, Chilean punk, etc.), see Celeste Olalquiaga, *Megalopolis: Contemporary Cultural Sensibilities* (Minneapolis, MN: University of Minnesota Press, 1992).

88. The realization problem refers to the "need to sell that output that is produced in order to convert surplus value from its labour form via its commodity form to profit, its money form" (Meghnad Desai, "Underconsumption," in *A Dictionary of Marxist Thought*, p. 495).

89. I am alluding here to the so-called "reproduction schema" developed in the second volume of *Capital*, where Marx distinguishes between the means of production (machine goods) and the means of consumption (wage goods). See, in general, "Simple Reproduction" and, in particular, the influential and still controversial section on "The Two Departments of Social Production," in *Capital* 2, pp. 392–488 and 395–98 respectively.

90. I would only cite Veblen here in order to suggest the difficulties of differentiating between true and false needs (which does not of course excuse us from the task of doing so). Two citations: "In the view of economic theory the expenditure in question is no more and no less legitimate than any other expenditure"; "It frequently happens that an element of the standard of living which set out being primarily wasteful, ends with becoming, in the apprehension of the consumer, a necessary of life; and it may in this way become as indispensable as any other item of the consumer's habitual expenditure." See "Conspicuous Consumption," *The Theory of the Leisure Class: An Economic Study of Institutions* (New York: Viking Press, 1965), pp. 97 and 99 respectively.

91. See Robert Goldman and Stephen Papson, "Green Marketing and the Commodity-Self," *Sign Wars: The Cluttered Landscape of Advertising* (New York: Guilford, 1996), pp. 187–215.

92. My sense of circulation here is not the restricted one that Marx employs in the *Grundrisse* or the second volume of *Capital*. Thus, in the latter text ("Time of Circulation"), Marx not only demarcates the sphere of production from the sphere of circulation but explains that the latter sphere is itself composed of two processes: (1) the transformation of capital "from the commodity form into that of money" (p. 124), and (2) "from the money form into that of commodities" (p. 124). My sense of circulation, then, refers less to that sphere of exchange in which commodities are bought and sold than to what Marx, in the subtitle to the third volume of *Capital*, calls "The Process of Capitalist Production as a Whole." On the former, see, however, chapter 3 in the first volume of *Capital* ("Money, or the Circulation of Commodities [C 81–126]); the whole of the second volume of *Capital*, which of course is subtitled "The Process of Circulation of Capital"; and, in the third volume of *Capital*, "Medium of Circulation and Capital," pp. 442–60. For the classic cultural studies restatement of Marx, see Stuart Hall, "Encoding, Decoding" (1980), in *The Cultural Studies Reader*, ed. Simon During (New York: Routledge, 1993), pp. 90–103; and Richard Johnson, "What Is Cultural Studies Anyway?" (1985–86), in *What Is Cultural Studies?*, ed. John Storey (New York: Arnold, 1996), pp. 75–114, especially his discussion of the Mini-Metro (82–86). For a discussion of the circulation of reflexive capital accumulation, see Scott Lash and John Urry, "After Organized Capitalism," *Economies of Signs and Space* (London: Sage, 1994), pp. 1–11. For an excellent examination of "social circulation" with respect to cultural production in general and academic institutions in particular, see Evan Watkins's *Work Time: English Departments and the Circulation of Cultural Value* (Stanford, CA: Stanford University Press, 1989).

93. Given the polemical focus in this essay on a general economy of consumption, it is clear that the issue of distribution—as my citation here of Marx is intended to stress—can hardly be ignored, especially today. As Jameson observes in "The Antinomies of Postmodernity": "The new developments of post-Fordism blur the distinction between the two other categories of the triad, distribution and consumption, in such a way that new modes of distribution (the fundamental trait of post-Fordism as a concept) can be parlayed into a rhetoric of consumption and of the market as an ideological value" (*The Seeds of Time* [New York: Columbia University Press, 1994], p. 41).

94. I am recollecting Spivak here ("putting 'under erasure' is as much an affirmative as a negative gesture" [OW 168]) as well as Foucault: "A whole history remains to be written of *spaces*— . . . from the great strategies of geopolitics to the little tactics of the habitat" ("The Eye of Power," *Power/Knowledge*, p. 149).

Part Three

1. Terry Eagleton, *Ideology: An Introduction* (London: Verso, 1991), p. 36.

2. Fredric Jameson, *Postmodernism, or, The Cultural Logic of Late Capitalism* (Durham, NC: Duke University Press, 1991), p. 162.

3. For my sense of this term, see John Thorton Caldwell, *Televisuality: Style, Crisis, and Authority in American Television* (New Brunswick, NJ: Rutgers University Press, 1993).

4. My recourse in this book to MTV is intended as a generic reference to music television, though it is clear that MTV is only one program service among others (M2, VH1, etc.).

5. For example, E. Ann Kaplan observes that "MTV functions like one continuous ad in that nearly all of its short segments are indeed ads of one kind or another" (*Rocking around the Clock: Music Television, Postmodernism, and Consumer Culture* [New York: Routledge, 1989], p. 12).

6. For a critique of this position, see Andrew Goodwin, *Dancing in the Distraction Factory* (Minneapolis, MN: University of Minnesota Press, 1993), esp. pp. 16–19, 149–55, and 180–88. Basically, Goodwin's argument is that MTV is by no means a paradigmatic instance of postmodernism since if its postmodern effects (e.g., editing) distinguish it from "regular TV," they do not represent a substantial difference with respect to "contemporary popular music" (182). About this local point (see also note 8 below), I would only observe that while it is true that much of the early literature on music television focused on its visual elements at the expense of its aural and pop-musical dimensions (hence the real use-value of Goodwin's book), MTV—to risk an ontological statement—ultimately remains more a visual than audio medium. The relevant question here is: How often do people listen to MTV without actually watching it?

7. *Simstim* is variously translated as "simulated" or "simulation stimulation." In "Literary MTV," George Slusser writes: "[On MTV] disembodied motifs are introduced in rapid, random, yet permutational fashion in order to create one-dimensional moods around what is an endlessly reiterated non-narrative.... Gibson has an apt term for this—'simstim'" (*Mississippi Review* 47/48 [1988], pp. 279–88). On Mona as Madonna wannabe, there is this in *Mona Lisa Overdrive*. After Mona has been surgically altered to make her look more like Angela Mitchell, she muses: "There were lots of girls got themselves worked over to look like [Angie], but they were mostly pathetic. Wannabes...." ([New York: Bantam, 1988], p. 176).

8. Daniel Harris, "Make My Rainy Day," *The Nation* (January 8, 1992), p. 790. I echo Robert Christgau here: "Madonna has rendered me a postmodernist in spite of myself, one of the burgeoning claque of marginal, generally left-leaning intellectuals for whom she has come to embody nothing less than mass

culture itself" ("Madonnathinking Madonnabout Madonnamusic" [1991], in *Desperately Seeking Madonna,* ed. Adam Sexton [New York: Delta, 1993], p. 201).

9. Harris, "Make My Rainy Day," p. 79.

10. John Fiske, "British Cultural Studies and Television," in *Channels of Discourse: Television and Contemporary Criticism,* ed. Robert C. Allen (Chapel Hill, NC: University of North Carolina Press, 1987), p. 284.

11. Fiske, *Television Culture* (New York: Routledge, 1990), p. 124.

12. For a diachronic account of Screen theory, see Antony Easthope's "The Trajectory of *Screen,* 1971–1979," in *The Politics of Theory,* ed. Francis Barker et al. (Colchester, UK: University of Essex, 1983), pp. 121–33; for a synchronic account, see his "Film Theory," in *British Post-Structuralism* (New York: Routledge, 1988), pp. 34–70. See also in general Rob Lapsley and Michael Westlake's *Film Theory: An Introduction* (New York: St. Martin's, 1987).

13. Fiske's critique of the radical text also focuses on Colin MacCabe's critique of cinematic realism ("Realism and Cinema: Notes on Brechtian Theses" [1981]) as well as MacCabe's participation in the *Days of Hope* debate in the late 1970s ("*Days of Hope,* A Response to Colin McArthur" [1981] and "Memory, Fantasy, Identity: *Days of Hope* and the Politics of the Past" [1981]).

14. I have italicized music videos to distinguish them from their aural counterparts; where relevant, I have also cited the director of the video in parentheses.

15. Needless to say, MTV is less absolutely defined by its music videos today, *circa* 1997, than when it first aired the Buggles' "Video Killed the Radio Star" on August 1, 1981.

16. Meaghan Morris, "Banality in Cultural Studies," in *Logics of Television: Essays in Cultural Criticism,* ed. Patricia Mellencamp (Bloomington, IN: Indiana University Press, 1990), p. 14.

17. Lisa Lewis, *Gender Politics and MTV: Voicing the Difference* (Philadelphia, PA: Temple University Press, 1990), p. 204.

18. For Lewis's understanding of "access" and "discovery signs," see "Female Address Video," in *Gender Politics and MTV,* pp. 109–10.

19. For a genealogy of these youth cultures, see, in general, Dick Hebdige's *Subculture: The Meaning of Style* (New York: Routledge, 1991).

20. On generational politics as well as the problematic relation between feminism and popular culture, see Shelagh Young, "Feminism and the Politics of Power: Whose Gaze Is It Anyway?" in *The Female Gaze: Women as Viewers of Popular Culture,* ed. Lorraine Gamman and Margaret Marshment (Seattle: Real Comet Press, 1989), pp. 173–88.

21. For a positive take on *Open Your Heart* (as well as *Express Yourself*), see Susan Douglas, "I'm Not a Feminist But . . . ," *Where the Girls Are: Growing Up Female with the Mass Media* (New York: Times Books, 1994), pp. 287–88. For another affirmative reading of *Open Your Heart*, one that explores the gay gaze—in particular, the relay of gazes among the boy, Madonna, and the mannequin sailors, see Stephen Drukman, "The Gay Gaze, or Why I Want My MTV," in *A Queer Romance: Lesbians, Gay Men, and Popular Culture*, ed. Paul Burston and Colin Richardson (London: Routledge, 1995), pp. 81–98.

22. The concept of consumption is arguably the leitmotif around which *Rocking around the Clock* as a whole is woven; to track this motif, which dominates the first third of the book, see pp. 4, 19, 28, 30, 32, 44, 47, 50, and 143.

23. Jim McGuigan, *Cultural Populism* (New York: Routledge, 1992), p. 70.

24. Ibid.

25. Cathy Schwichtenberg, ed., *The Madonna Connection: Representational Politics, Subcultural Identities, and Cultural Theory* (Boulder, CO: Westview Press, 1992). For an absolutely mainstream (and adamantly obtuse) review of *Sex* and *The Madonna Connection*, see Michiko Kakutani, "Madonna Writes; Academics Write about Her," *New York Times* (October 21, 1992), p. B2. On the academic appropriation of Madonna, see also Elizabeth Tippens's "Mastering Madonna," *Rolling Stone* (September 17, 1992), pp. 89, 111.

26. I am alluding here to Lacan's notion of *le point de capiton*; see, for instance, "The Agency of the Letter in the Unconscious or Reason since Freud," *Écrits*, p. 154. For an especially interesting discussion of this concept, see the work of Slavoj Žižek, in particular "The 'Quilting Point,' " in *For They Know Not What They Do: Enjoyment as a Political Factor* (London: Verso, 1991), pp. 16–21.

27. On the body/commodity/nationality, see Lauren Berlant's "National Brands/National Body: *Imitation of Life*," in *Comparative American Identities: Race, Sex, and Nationality in the Modern Text*, ed. Hortense Spillers (New York: Routledge, 1991), pp. 110–40.

28. See, for example, Susan McClary, "Living to Tell: Madonna's Resurrection of the Fleshly," in *Feminine Endings: Music, Gender, and Sexuality* (Minneapolis, MN: University of Minnesota Press, 1991), pp. 148–66, esp. 161–63.

29. On "butch girls," see Sonya Andermahr, "A Queer Love Affair?: Madonna and Lesbian and Gay Culture," in *The Good, the Bad, and the Gorgeous: Popular Culture's Romance with Lesbianism*, ed. Diana Hamer and Belinda Budge (London: Pandora, 1994), pp. 34–35.

30. See, for example, Butler's "Identity, Sex, and the Metaphysics of Substance" in *Gender Trouble* (New York: Routledge, 1990): "If . . . substances are nothing other than the coherences contingently created through the regulation of attributes, it would seem that the ontology of substance itself is not only an artificial effect, but essentially superfluous" (p. 24).

31. For a smart essay on the issue of appropriation, the conclusion of which collapses, alas, into cliche (*"Is she or isn't she?*, we wonder, as [Madonna] accumulates millions at the expense of our continued fascination" [p. 32]), see Amy Robinson, "Is She or Isn't She?: Madonna and the Erotics of Appropriation," in *Acting Out: Feminist Performances*, ed. Lynda Hart and Peggy Phelan (Ann Arbor, MI: University of Michigan Press, 1993), pp. 337–51. On *Vogue* in particular, see Dan Rubey, "Voguing at the Carnival: Desire and Pleasure on MTV," in *Present Tense: Rock and Roll Culture*, ed. Anthony De Curtis (Durham, NC: Duke University Press, 1992), pp. 235–70; and Jackie Goldsby, "Queens of Language: *Paris Is Burning*," in *Queer Looks: Perspectives on Lesbian and Gay Film and Video*, ed. Martha Gever, Pratibha Parmar, and John Greyson (New York: Routledge, 1993), pp. 108–15.

32. Lauren Berlant and Elizabeth Freeman, "Queer Nationality," *Boundary 2* 19, No. 1 (1992), pp. 149–80.

33. See also Peter Parisi, " 'Black Bart' Simpson: Appropriation and Revitalization," *Journal of Popular Culture* 27, No. 1 (Summer 1993), pp. 125–42.

34. Though the following essays leave something to be desired, both critically and rhetorically, see Thomas K. Nakayama and Lisa Peñaloza's "Madonna T/Races: Music Videos through the Prism of Color" and Ronald B. Scott's "Images of Race and Religion in Madonna's Video *Like a Prayer*," in *The Madonna Connection*, pp. 39–55 and 57–77 respectively. On the racial implications of *Justify My Love*, see Anna Marie Smith, " 'By Women, For Women and about Women' Rules OK?: The Impossibility of Visual Soliloquy," in *A Queer Romance*, pp. 207–9.

35. Greta Gaard, "The Laugh of Madonna: Censorship and Oppositional Discourse," *The Journal of the Midwest Modern Language Association* 25, No. 1 (Spring 1992), pp. 41–47. For another, "double" reading of Madonna's relation to lesbianism, see Deb Schwartz, "Madonna and Sandra: Like We Care," in *Desperately Seeking Madonna*, pp. 214–17. On the last (i.e., Madonna and Sandra), see also Jean Walton, "Sandra Bernhard: Lesbian Postmodern or Madonna Postlesbian?" in *The Lesbian Postmodern*, ed. Laura Doan (New York: Columbia University Press, 1994), esp. pp. 254–56; and Michael Musto, "Immaculate Connection," *Out in Culture: Gay, Lesbian, and Queer Essays on Popular Culture*, ed. Corey K. Creekmur and Alexander Doty (Durham: Duke University Press, 1995), pp. 434–35.

36. This is, of course, the first sentence of the last paragraph of *Gender Trouble* (p. 148).

37. Though it does not mention this ex post facto revelation about "Rock the Vote" (1990), see Roseann M. Mandziuk's "Feminist Politics and Postmodern Seductions," in *The Madonna Connection*, pp. 167–87, esp. 173–76.

38. Ann Cvetkovich puts it this way: "As part of the project of historicizing the body and identity, it might be important to ask who has historically had greater access to transformation" ("The Powers of Seeing and Being Seen: *Truth or Dare* and *Paris Is Burning*," in *Film Theory Goes to the Movies*, ed. Jim Collins, Hilary Radner, and Ava Preacher Collins [New York: Routledge, 1993], p. 160).

39. See Camille Paglia's "Madonna I: Animality and Artifice" and "Madonna II: Venus of the Radio Waves" in *Sex, Art, and American Culture* (New York: Vintage, 1992), pp. 3–5 and 6–13 respectively.

40. Barry King, "The Star and the Commodity: Notes toward a Performance Theory of Stardom," *Cultural Studies* 1, No. 2 (May 1987), pp. 145–59. For an excellent discussion, in the context of Madonna the commodity and star-text, see also Goodwin, "Rethinking the Commodified Text" and "Metanarratives of Stardom and Identity," in *Dancing in the Distraction Factory*, pp. 42–48 and 98–130 respectively.

41. See Barry King, "Articulating Stardom" (1985), in *Star Texts: Image and Performance in Film and Television*, ed. Jeremy G. Butler (Detroit, MI: Wayne State University Press, 1991), pp. 125–54; reprinted in *Stardom: Industry of Desire*, ed. Christine Gledhill (New York: Routledge, 1991), pp. 167–82. For the most recent and best discussion of actors' labor and subjectivity with respect to commodity fetishism (i.e., *star* commodity-body-sign), see Danae Clark, *Negotiating Hollywood: The Cultural Politics of Actors' Labor* (Minneapolis, MN: University of Minnesota Press, 1995).

42. For some sense of this issue, see Leslie Savan's reading of Madonna's "Make a Wish" commercial for Pepsi (which of course Pepsi cancelled as soon as they saw the "art" version, *Like a Prayer*), "Desperately Selling Soda," in *Sound and Vision*, ed. Simon Frith, Andrew Goodwin, and Lawrence Grossberg (London: Routledge, 1993), pp. 87–90. As Savan observes of this particular instance of global marketing (where the demographic target is the "global teen"): "If Madonna . . . could wish herself into stardom through the magic of video, a little cola consumer in Thailand or Paraguay can be like a star through the magic of advertising" (p. 89). For an excellent discussion of the "cola wars," see Leslie Sklair, "The Culture-Ideology of Consumerism in the Third World," *Sociology of the Global System* (Baltimore, MD: Johns Hopkins University Press, 1991), pp. 162–65.

43. Edgar Morin, *The Stars*, trans. Richard Howard (New York: Grove, 1961), p. 136.

44. Michael Goldberg, "Madonna to Sign $60 Million Deal," *Rolling Stone* (April 16, 1992), p. 628. Of course, Janet Jackson has since trumped

Madonna on this score, having signed a deal with Virgin Records in 1996 for $80 million.

45. "The Forbes 500s," *Forbes* 149, No. 9 (April 27, 1992), p. 316. With respect to Time Warner, Roy Shuker has noted that "Madonna is arguably Time Warner's most effective corporate symbol" (*Understandng Popular Music* [New York: Routledge, 1994], p. 134).

46. Fred Goodman, "Madonna and Oprah: The Companies They Keep," *Working Women* 16, No. 12 (December 1991), pp. 52–55, 84. See also Matthew Schifrin with Peter Newcomb, "A Brain for Sin and a Bod for Business," *Forbes* 146, No. 7 (October 1, 1990), pp. 162–66. Alanis Morrisette and her début album, *Jagged Little Pill* (Maverick/Reprise, 1994), has of course transformed Maverick from a "vanity label" into an "industry force" (though she was also preceded by the platinum-selling Candlebox). See Chris Williams, "The Quiet Riot Grrrl," *Entertainment Weekly* 318 (March 15, 1996), pp. 31–33.

47. McClary writes: "It may be that Madonna is best understood as head of a corporation that produces images of her self-representation, rather than as the spontaneous, 'authentic' artist of rock mythology" (*Feminine Endings*, p. 149).

48. While the commodity has arguably been an implicit topic of Madonna's work—from, say, *Material Girl* to *Open Your Heart* to *Body of Evidence* (1993)—it has generally been tied to the problem of sexuality and self-commodification, *affirmative* self-commodification. Certainly, this is the "moral" of *Open Your Heart*, where the protagonist's power derives from the way in which she exercises control over *her* commodity-body. At the same time, this "progressive" thematic receives a rather different twist in the later Madonna vehicle, *Body of Evidence* (1993). As art dealer and star witness, Madonna's character in *Body of Evidence* functions not only as a classic *femme fatale* but as a vampiress who feeds on the "old," patriarchal body of capital (see note 96 below). Yet the conclusion could not be more different from the happy ending of *Open Your Heart*; here, Madonna's character ends up rather worse off than Lucy Westenra—not only dead but guilty as accused. But however one reads this ending—whether as yet another, late Victorian illustration of the suppression of female sexuality or, more probably, as an ironic indictment of a system, capitalism, which condemns women for employing their bodies as commodities—*Body of Evidence* is ultimately less about capitalism as such than the "ethics" of accumulation.

49. See Mike Budd, Robert M. Entman, and Clay Steinman, "The Affirmative Character of U.S. Cultural Studies," which argues that American Cultural Studies has diluted the "critical" tradition in mass communication studies, the latter of which involved a "radical institutional analysis of multi-national media corporations," in particular the "political economy of capitalist media production of commodities" (*Critical Studies in Mass Communication* 7 [1990], pp. 169–84).

50. Pat Califia, "Sex and Madonna," in *Madonnarama*, ed. Lisa Frank and Paul Smith (Pittsburgh, PA: Cleis Press, 1993), p. 172.

51. Michele Ingrassia with Carol Hall, "Newsmakers," *Newsweek* (October 4, 1993), p. 91.

52. Ibid., p. 91.

53. Andrew Ferguson, "Bad Girls Don't Cry," *National Review* (May 30, 1994), p. 72. For a similar argument ("Unfortunately for the pop star, America had begun to develop a cultural immunity to the Madonna virus" [p. 145]), see Douglas Rushkoff, *Media Virus: Hidden Agendas in Popular Culture* (New York: Ballantine, 1994), pp. 141–46.

54. Ferguson, "Bad Girls Don't Cry," p. 72.

55. On Madonna's role in the sex/culture wars, see Nan D. Hunter, "Contextualizing the Sexuality Debates: A Chronology," which notes not only Reverend Donald Wildmon and the American Family Association's condemnation of *Like a Prayer* and Pepsi's consequent disavowal of "Make a Wish" (1989) but MTV's "it's-just-not-for-us" refusal to air *Justify My Love* (1990) (in *Sex Wars: Sexual Dissent and Political Culture*, ed. Lisa Duggan and Hunter [New York: Routledge, 1995], p. 27). See also Nadine Strossen's *Defending Pornography*, which notes that at the March 1993 conference on "Feminist Legal Perspectives on Pornography and Hate Propaganda" held at the Univesity of Chicago Law School, *Sex* was "ritually torn to shreds" (*Free Speech, Sex, and the Fight for Women's Rights* [New York: Scribner, 1995], pp. 88 and 235).

56. Jon Pareles, "Madonna's Return to Innocence," *New York Times* (October 23, 1994), Section 2, p. 38.

57. Fran Lloyd, "Introduction," *Deconstructing Madonna*, ed. Lloyd (London: B. T. Batsford, 1993), p. 14.

58. Frank and Smith, "Introduction: How to Use Your Madonna," *Madonnarama*, p. 13.

59. Madonna, quoted in "People," *Time* (October 3, 1994), p. 87.

60. Pareles, "Madonna's Return to Innocence," *New York Times*, p. 1. On the link between Madonna and Frida Kahlo, in particular Kahlo's *My Birth* (1932), see Janis Bergman-Carton, "Strike a Pose: The Framing of Madonna and Frida Kahlo," *Texas Studies in Literature and Language* 35, No. 4 (Winter 1993), pp. 440–52.

61. bell hooks, "Madonna: Plantation Mistress or Soul Sister?" in *Desperately Seeking Madonna*, pp. 218–26.

62. Kobena Mercer, "Reading Racial Fetishism," in *Fetishism as Cultural Discourse*, ed. Emily Apter and William Pietz (Ithaca, NY: Cornell University

Press, 1993), p. 320. See also the introduction to this book for my sense of Mercer's essay.

63. I use the term *aggressivity* as opposed to *aggression* in order to underscore this instinct's relation to desire.

64. On internalized racism, see hooks's "Back to Black: Ending Internalized Racism," *Outlaw Culture: Resisting Representations* (New York: Routledge, 1994), pp. 173–82.

65. Seduction is a motif of sorts in hooks's work; see, for instance, "Seductive Sexualities," in *Yearning: Race, Gender, and Cultural Politics* (Boston, MA: South End Press, 1990), pp. 193–202; and "Seduction and Betrayal: *The Crying Game* and *The Bodyguard*" and "Seduced by Violence No More," *Outlaw Culture*, pp. 53–62 and 109–14 respectively.

66. On the commodification of blackness see, in particular, hooks's "Spending Culture: Marketing the Black Underclass," in *Outlaw Culture*, pp. 145–54; reprinted in *Killing Rage: Ending Racism* (New York: Henry Holt, 1995), pp. 172–83.

67. Similarly, in the context of a discussion of Lee Atwater, hooks observes *à la* Madonna how easy it is to "appropriate and commodify an aspect of a people's culture without allowing any personal transformaton to take place" ("Moving Into and Beyond Feminism," *Outlaw Culture*, p. 220).

68. I am drawing here on Freud, in particular "Instincts and Their Vicissitudes" (1915), trans. Cecil M. Baines, in *General Psychological Theory*, ed. Philip Rieff (New York: Collier, 1978), pp. 83–103. In this important essay, Freud argues that an instinct can be submitted to the following four vicissitudes: (1) reversal into its opposite, (2) turning round upon the subject, (3) repression, and (4) sublimation. "Reversal into its opposite" can, in turn, be transformed into (a) reversal of the aim of the instinct—from, say, active to passive (as in sadomasochism or scopophilia-exhibitionism), or (b) reversal of content (e.g., "change of love into hate" [p. 91]).

69. For a lucid discussion of the complex relation between identification and desire, see Diana Fuss's *Identification Papers* (New York: Routledge, 1995), in particular "Identification and Desire" (pp. 67–72). For hooks's understanding of (dis)identification, see, in general, "The Oppositional Gaze," in *Black Looks: Race and Representation* (Boston: South End Press, 1992), pp. 115–32.

70. hooks, "Power to the Pussy: We Don't Wannabe Dicks in Drag," *Madonnarama*, pp. 65–80. Reprinted in *Outlaw Culture*, pp. 9–24.

71. For a similarly structured title and argument, see hooks, "Camille Paglia: 'Black Pagan' or White Colonizer?" in *Outlaw Culture*, pp. 83–90.

72. Thomas A. Kemple, "The Black Madonna," *Reading Marx Writing: Melodrama, the Market, and the "Grundrisse"* (Stanford, CA: Stanford University Press, 1995), p. 177.

73. In this context, see Cornel West's comments on the Age of Europe in "The New Cultural Politics of Difference," in *The Cultural Studies Reader*, ed. Simon During (New York: Routledge, 1993), pp. 203–17, esp. pp. 205–08. Glossing West, Stuart Hall writes in "What Is This Black in 'Black' Popular Culture?" that the "emergence [of the United States as a world power] is both a displacement of and a hegemonic shift in the *definition* of culture—a movement from high culture to American mainstream popular culture and its mass-cultural, image-mediated, technological forms" (*Black Popular Culture*, ed. Gina Dent [Seattle: Bay Press, 1992], pp. 21–22).

74. If, according to Freud in "Mourning and Melancholia" (1917), both mourning and melancholia reflect "ambivalence" and "loss of the object" (p. 179), hooks's "ecstasy" can be read as a manic reversal of melancholia, the latter of which is distinguished for Freud from mourning by the "regression of libido into the ego," or *the movement from desire to identification* (trans. Joan Rivere, *General Psychological Theory*, p. 179).

75. See Freud's "Mourning and Melancholia" where he defines mourning as, *inter alia*, the "loss of some abstraction" (e.g., "an ideal" [p. 164]).

76. *Coming to Power* (Boston: Alyson Publications, 1981) is, of course, the title of the well-known collection edited by the Samois Collective.

77. hooks returns to this issue—the academy as a place of repression and confinement—in "Moving Into and Beyond Feminism," *Outlaw Culture*, p. 232.

78. See also hooks's remarks on Madonna's "little-girl pornographic shoot" in "What's Passion Got to Do with It?" in *Outlaw Culture*, p. 49.

79. Emphasis mine. Part of my point here is that although these sorts of locutions—mass patriarchal gaze, heterosexist pornographic gaze (PP 68), patriarchal pornographic sexual hedonism (PP 72), etc.—clearly do some critical work, I'm not so sure the rhetorical gain isn't offset by a loss in analytical specificity.

80. For an excellent, because balanced, account of post-Fordism, see Martyn J. Lee, *Consumer Culture Reborn* (New York: Routledge, 1993), pp. 108–18.

81. The literature on pornography is extensive; for recent statements of the *pro* position, see, for example, *Dirty Looks: Women, Pornography, Power*, ed. Pamela Church Gibson and Roma Gibson (London: British Film Institute, 1993); *Bad Girls and Dirty Pictures: The Challenge to Reclaim Feminism*, ed. Alison Assiter and Avedon Carol (London: Pluto Press, 1993); Nadine Strossen, *Defending Pornography*; and Wendy McElroy, *XXX: A Woman's Right to Pornography* (New York: St. Martin's Press, 1995), which, happily enough, includes not only a list of *pro*-pornography organizations (e.g., Feminists for Free Expression) but a list of purveyors as well (199–201). On the topic of black

pornography in particular, see also Judith Wilson, "Getting Down to Get Over: Romare Bearden's Use of Pornography and the Problem of the Black Female Body in Afro-U.S. Art," in *Black Popular Culture*, pp. 112–22. On pornography in the context of fetishism, see Berkeley Kaite, *Pornography and Difference* (Bloomington, IN: Indiana University Press, 1995), in particular the part on "The Fetish" (91–134). On Madonna and pornography, see Brian McNair, "Putting the Porn into Pop," *Mediated Sex: Pornography and Postmodern Culture* (London: Arnold, 1996), pp. 156–66. McNair writes: "Madonna's *Sex*, in presenting the star as the object of the pornographer's gaze, did more than any other pop culture artifact of the time to validate pornography as a form" (p. 157).

82. This language of longing is explicit in "Power to the Pussy": e.g., "We longed to witness the material girl enter mature womanhood. . . . We longed for this, in part, to see serious radical female icons manifesting [their] feminist promise" (p. 67); "We long for female icons who show everyone that we can triumph despite fierce anti-feminism" (p. 67); etc.

83. Drawing on Cornel West, Gina Dent has elaborated on the distinction between pleasure and joy (*jouissance*), as in the phrase "black pleasure, black joy." For Dent (as for Lacan), "*Jouissance* is not the complement to sexual pleasure; it is its supplement. It is not only oppositional but alternative" ("Black Pleasure, Black Joy: An Introduction," *Black Popular Culture*, p. 10). The standard discussion of *jouissance* is Lacan's *Seminar XX* (1972–73); for a translation of the crucial chapter on "feminine *jouissance*," see Lacan, "God and the Jouissance of The Woman. A Love Letter," in *Feminine Sexuality*, ed. Juliet Mitchell and Jacqueline Rose and trans. Rose (New York: Pantheon, 1983), pp. 138–48. For hooks on popular culture, see, in particular, hooks's "Dialectically Down with the Critical Program," where she talks persuasively about the necessary dialecticity, at once negative and affirmative, of the "progressive critique" of black popular culture (*Black Popular Culture*, pp. 48–55). On popular culture and cultural studies, see also the introductions to *Yearning* and *Outlaw Culture*, "Liberation Scenes" and "The Heartbeat of Cultural Revolution," pp. 1–13 and 3–4 respectively.

84. The notion of cannibalism or what hooks calls, after British slang, "eating the other" is a prominent theme in her work; see, for example, "Eating the Other: Desire and Resistance," *Black Looks*, pp. 21–39. On this topic, see also Deborah Root, *Cannibal Culture: Art, Appropriation, and the Commodification of Difference* (Boulder, CO: Westview, 1996).

85. Carol A. Queen, "Talking about *Sex*," *Madonnarama*, p. 143.

86. Though the issue of camp hardly represents a sufficient critical response to the representation of, say, lesbians in *Sex*, it is nonetheless important to address this particular context or perspective. For a useful discussion of this issue with respect to post-1960s camp, see Pamela Robertson, "Does Feminist Camp Make a Difference?, or, What We Talk about When We Talk about Madonna," in *Guilty Pleasures: Feminist Camp from Mae West to Madonna*

(Durham, NC: Duke University Press, 1996), pp. 115–38. Writing about the prostitution scenario in *Sex*, Queen writes: "Here camp meets sex-radical feminist theory, though I couldn't find a single reviewer who so much as noticed" (M 149). At the same time, while John Champagne feels, *pace* hooks, that the *Vanity Fair* layout expresses a "camp sensibility," most of *Sex* lacks— according to him—the "spectacle-value of camp" (M 128). Speaking of camp, see the "MTV Raw" pastiche of Robert Aldrich's *Hush . . . Hush, Sweet Charlotte* (1965) with "Madonna" and "Courtney Love" as Bette Davis and Olivia de Havilland.

87. Madonna, *Sex* (New York: Warner Books, 1992). hooks's citation skips a couple of crucial sentences from Madonna's monologue about S/M: "Some people want to be punished. Some women want to be slapped around" (M 176). Madonna's remarks here about monied, educated women "digging" abuse are both "irresponsible" (as Madonna herself seems to recognize) and "dangerous" (hooks). hooks, however, adds: "By making them, Madonna uses *Sex* as a platform to express right-wing anti-feminist sentiments that, if uttered in another context, might have provoked public protest and outrage" (PP 74). The critical issue of context aside (assuming one can in fact put it aside), I would only add that while the above remarks by Madonna are clearly anti-feminist, I am not clear about what is gained by saying, as hooks does, that such remarks are "right-wing." Simply put, I do not think the Right has a monopoly on misogyny—far from it.

88. For this "economic" account of sadomasochism (which is predicated on an understanding of fastasy as the fantasmatic), see my "Lust, Fantasy, Male Hysteria: *Clint Eastwood* (Un-) Bound," *Minnesota Review* 43/44 (November 1995), pp. 150–63. For a provocative discussion of fantasy in the context of pornography, see especially Laura Kipnis's *Bound and Gagged: Pornography and the Politics of Fantasy in America* (New York: Grove Press, 1995).

89. For one, restricted-economic reading of this dynamic, see Lynn S. Chancer, "Employing Chains of Command: Sadomasochism and the Workplace," *Sadomasochism in Everyday Life* (New Brunswick, NJ: Rutgers University Press, 1992), pp. 93–124.

90. On the triple movement—"identification *of* the symptom," "traversal of the fantasy," and "identification *with* the symptom," see Slavoj Žižek, *The Sublime Object of Ideology* (New York: Verso, 1989), pp. 124–28.

91. On this point, see Lacan's "In You More Than You," where he comments that the "fundamental mainspring of the analytic operation is the maintenance of the distance between the I—identification—and the *a*" (*The Four Fundamental Concepts of Psycho-Analysis*, trans. Alan Sheridan [New York: Norton, 1978], p. 272).

92. On capitalism-as-prostitution, see my "Troping Prostitution: Two or Three Things about (Post-) Marxism/Feminism," *Genders* 12 (Winter 1991),

pp. 120–39. On the modernist recourse to the figure of the prostitute as a counter to commodity culture, see Laurie Teal, "The Hollow Women: Modernism, The Prostitute, and Commodity Aesthetics," *differences* 7, No. 3 (Fall 1995), pp. 80–108. As for the association of Madonna with both prostitution and sadomasochism, in particular the "explosion of demand for s/m prostitution services" in the wake of Madonna, see Catherine Waldby, "Destruction: Boundary Erotics and Refigurations of the Heterosexual Male Body," in *Sexy Bodies: The Strange Carnalities of Feminism*, ed. Elizabeth Grosz and Elspeth Probyn (New York: Routledge, 1995), p. 273.

93. Dita, Madonna's persona in *Sex*, appears to be an allusion—as Metzstein notes (DM 94)—to Dita Parlo, an actress featured in, among other things, Vigo's *L'Atalante* (1934).

94. I am of course alluding here to the illustrated *Caught Looking: Feminism, Pornography, and Censorship*, ed. Kate Ellis et al. (New York: Caught Looking, 1986).

95. For a cogent critique of a similar lachrymose scenario, see Laura Kipnis's take on Robin Morgan in "Disgust and Desire: *Hustler* Magazine," in *Bound and Gagged*, pp. 122–60, esp. 137–41.

96. On the representation of Madonna as a vampire, see Kirsten Marthe Lentz, "Chameleon, Vampire, Rich Slut" (M 165).

97. The classic passage from "The Culture Industry" reads: "The culture industry perpetually cheats its consumers of what it perpetually promises. The promissory note which, with its plots and staging, it draws on . . . is endlessly prolonged; the promise, which is actually all the spectacle consists of, is illusory: all it actually confirms is that the real point will never be reached, that the diner must be satisfied with the menu" (Adorno and Horkheimer, *Dialectic of Enlightenment*, trans. John Cumming [New York: Continuum, 1987], p. 139). See note 98 below.

98. Here is Metzstein the cultural moralist on Madonna: "The Queen of desire is selling desire which can never be fulfilled. This is the point of a product which slid into the world, symbiotically tied to the media which self-interestedly promoted both itself and this bastard child of the 'culture industry' " (DM 91).

99. Speaking of lesbian spectators, Lentz observes of the "All Access" photograph that "what's fun about the notion of 'all access' isn't only the 'access' we think we're being given. The fun also resides in the 'all' so seductively inscribed upon [Madonna's] body. The inclusiveness implied by the 'all' positions Madonna's female admirers in an openly sexual relationship, albeit in the form of a wish" (M 154). For a copious illustration of this sexual dream-wish at work, see Kay Turner, *I Dream of Madonna* (San Francisco: Collins, 1993). In this sexual context, I should note that the British title of *Truth or Dare* was, appropriately enough, *In Bed with Madonna*. On the last, see Jonathan Romney, "Access All Areas: The Real Space of Rock Documentary," in *Cellu-*

loid Jukebox: Popular Music and the Movies since the 50s, ed. Romney and Adrian Wootton (London: British Film Institute, 1995), pp. 82–92. As for the Meisel photograph, it may well owe something—like David Fincher's direction of *Vogue*—to the work of fashion photographer Horst P. Horst (e.g., *Mainbocher Corset, Paris*); on this subject, see Maria Demopoulos: "'Thieves Like Us': Directors under the Influence," *Film Comment* 32, No. 3 (May/June 1996), pp. 33–37.

100. For my democratic invocation here in the context of prostitution and pornography (where, of course, pornography itself can be said to be etymologically derived from prostitution [*porne graphein*]), see Lynn Hunt's introduction to *The Invention of Pornography: Obscenity and the Origins of Modernity, 1500–1800*, ed. Hunt (New York: Zone Books, 1993), pp. 9–45. As she writes *à la* Foucault: "pornography as a regulatory category was invented in response to the perceived menace of the democratization of culture" (p. 3).

101. Steve Allen, "Madonna," *Journal of Popular Culture* 27, No. 1 (Summer 1993), p. 11.

102. Ibid., p. 1.

103. For Madonna as Statue of Liberty, see Andrew Ross, "This Bridge Called My Pussy" (M 58). For a dissenting view (i.e., Madonna as Liberty Blonde, "the blonde as an advertisement for the virtues of renouncing one's origins, the siren message of Americanism and colonialism"), see Paul Coates, "Gentlemen and Blondeness," *Film at the Intersection of High and Mass Culture* (New York: Cambridge University Press, 1994), p. 113. On the related issue of French libertinism, see also Kathryn Norberg, "The Libertine Whore: Prostitution in French Pornography from Margot to Juliette," *The Invention of Pornography*, pp. 225–52.

104. Allen, "Madonna," *Journal of Popular Culture*, p. 11.

105. For my Warholian reading of Madonna, see Jonathan Flatley, "Warhol Gives Good Face: Publicity and the Politics of Prosopopoeia," in *Pop Out: Queer Warhol*, ed. Jennifer Doyle, Flatley, and José Esteban Muñoz (Durham, NC: Duke University Press, 1996), pp. 101–33.

106. John Champagne, "Stabat Madonna" (M 122). This strain of cultural studies—the consumption-as-resistance school—is, according to hooks, "especially true of the academic work produced about popular icons (Madonna, for example)" (*Outlaw Culture*, p. 4).

107. Champagne, "Stabat Madonna" (M 122). For a different take on this same issue—what Regina Austin calls the consumption-as-deviance position (or "aliention critique") vs. the consumption-as-resistance position—see "'A Nation of Thieves': Consumption, Commerce, and the Black Public Sphere," in *The Black Public Sphere*, ed. Black Public Sphere Collective (Chicago: University of Chicago Press, 1995), pp. 229–52.

108. Douglas Kellner, "Madonna, Fashion, and Image," in *Media Culture: Cultural Studies, Identity and Politics between the Modern and Postmodern* (New York: Routledge, 1995), pp. 263–96. On Kellner's understanding of the difference between cultural studies and critical theory (i.e., the Frankfurt School), see, for example, "Theory Wars and Cultural Studies," in *Media Culture*, pp. 15–54.

109. See in this context, Lynne Layton, "Who's That Girl?: A Case Study of Madonna," in *Women Creating Lives: Identities, Resilience, and Resistance*, ed. Carol E. Franz and Abigail J. Stewart (Boulder, CO: Westview Press, 1994), pp. 143–55.

110. Akbar S. Ahmed, "A Material Girl in a Material World," in *Postmodernism and Islam: Predicament and Promise* (New York: Routledge, 1992), pp. 216–19.

111. The Warholian invocation is Madonna's; on her conception of an "artistic think tank" that would combine the Bauhaus and the "factory," see the *New York Times* (April 20, 1992), p. B1.

112. On "Make a Wish" (March 2, 1989), see—in addition to the references listed above in note 42—Richard Morgan, "In Being a Good Corporate Citizen" (April 10, 1989), in *Deconstructing Madonna*, pp. 93–100; and Nancy J. Vickers, "Maternalism and the Material Girl," in *Embodied Voices: Representing Female Vocality in Western Culture*, ed. Leslie C. Dunn and Nancy A. Jones (New York: Cambridge University Press, 1994), pp. 230–46.

Coda

1. Gayatri Spivak, "Poststructuralism, Marginality," *Outside in the Teaching Machine* (New York: Routledge, 1993), pp. 75–76.

2. Ibid.

3. But see Henry Giroux's "Consuming Social Change: The United Colors of Benetton," which argues that if a "politics of difference is to be linked not merely to registering 'otherness' but to identifying the conditions through which others become critical agents, the ethic of consumerism must be challenged by exposing its limits" (*Disturbing Pleasures: Learning Popular Culture* [New York: Routledge, 1994], p. 23).

4. On the politics of disidentification (which problematizes any simple version of "identity politics" or "politics of difference"), see Judith Butler's "Phantasmatic Identification and the Assumption of Sex," *Bodies That Matter: On the Discursive Limits of "Sex"* (New York: Routledge, 1993), pp. 93–120.

5. In his essay on fetishism, Freud writes the following about a young man who has apparently "scotomized" the death of his father: "in every situ-

ation in life he oscillated between two assumptions—on the one his father was still alive and hindered him from action, on the other his father was dead and he had the right to regard himself as his successor" ("Fetishism," trans. Joan Riviere, in *Collected Papers*, Vol. 5 [London: Hogarth Press, 1953], pp. 202–03).

6. See Lentz, "Chameleon, Vampire, Rich Slut" (M 157).

7. I am thinking here of Benjamin's famous, Klee-inspired thesis about progress (*Angelus Novus*) and Stuart Hall's metaphor for theoretical work: "the metaphor of struggle, of wrestling with the angels." For the Benjamin, see "Theses on the Philosophy of History," in *Illuminations*, ed. Hannah Arendt and trans. Harry Zohn (New York: Schocken, 1969), pp. 257–58; for the Hall, see "Cultural Studies and Theoretical Legacies," in *Cultural Studies*, ed. Lawrence Grossberg, Cary Nelson, and Paula A. Treichler (New York: Routledge, 1992), p. 280.

8. As Martin Jay notes in "Adorno in America," Adorno frequently adopted the trope of chiasmus to describe not only the relation between nature and history ("history is nature, nature is history") but his complex, sometimes tortured relationship to America (*Permanent Exiles: Essays on the Intellectual Migration from Germany to America* [New York: Columbia University Press, 1986], pp. 136–37).

Selected Bibliography

Abercrombie, Nicholas, Russell Keat, and Nigel Whiteley, ed. *The Authority of the Consumer*. New York: Routledge, 1994.

Adorno, Theodor. "Culture Industry Reconsidered." Trans. Anson G. Rabinbach. *New German Critique* 6 (Fall 1975): 12–19.

———. *In Search of Wagner*. Trans. Rodney Livingstone. London: New Left Books, 1981.

———. *Introduction to the Sociology of Music*. Trans. E. B. Ashton. New York: Seabury Press, 1976.

———. "Letters to Walter Benjamin." Trans. Harry Zohn. *Aesthetics and Politics*. Trans. ed. Ronald Taylor. London: Verso, 1988. 110–33.

———. *Minima Moralia: Reflections from Damaged Life*. Trans. E. F. N. Jephcott. New York: Verso, 1987.

———. *Negative Dialectics*. Trans. E. B. Ashton. New York: Seabury Press, 1973.

———. *Negative Dialektik*. Frankfurt: Suhrkamp, 1975.

Adorno, Theodor, with the assistance of George Simpson. "On Popular Music." *On the Record*. Ed. Simon Frith and Andrew Goodwin. New York: Pantheon, 1990. 301–14.

———. "On the Fetish Character in Music and the Regression of Listening." *The Essential Frankfurt School Reader*. Ed. Andrew Arato and Eike Gebhardt. New York: Urizen Books, 1978. 270–95.

———. *Philosophy of Modern Music*. Trans. Anne G. Mitchell and Wesley V. Blomster. New York: Seabury Press, 1973.

———. *Prisms*. Trans. Samuel and Shierry Weber. Cambridge, MA: MIT Press, 1986.

Adorno, Theodor, and Max Horkheimer. *Dialectic of Enlightenment*. Trans. John Cumming. New York: Continuum, 1987.

Agger, Ben. *Cultural Studies and Critical Theory*. Washington, DC: Falmer Press, 1992.

Aglietta, Michel. *A Theory of Capitalist Regulation*. Trans. David Fernbach. London: New Left Books, 1979.

Ahmad, Aijaz. *In Theory: Classes, Nations, Literatures*. London: Verso, 1992.

Ahmed, Akbar S. *Postmodernism and Islam: Predicament and Promise*. New York: Routledge, 1992.

Allen, Steve. "Madonna." *Journal of Popular Culture* 27, No. 1 (Summer 1993): 1–9.

Amariglio, Jack, and Antonio Callari. "Marxian Value Theory and the Problem of the Subject: The Role of Commodity Fetishism." *Fetishism as Cultural Discourse*. Ed. Emily Apter and William Pietz. Ithaca, NY: Cornell University Press, 1993. 186–216.

Andermahr, Sonya. "A Queer Love Affair?: Madonna and Lesbian and Gay Culture." *The Good, the Bad, and the Gorgeous: Popular Culture's Romance with Lesbianism*. Ed. Diane Hamer and Belinda Budge. London: Pandora, 1994. 34–35.

Appadurai, Arjun. "Introduction: Commodities and the Politics of Value." *The Social Life of Things: Commodities in Cultural Perspective*. Ed. Appadurai. New York: Cambridge University Press, 1986. 3–63.

Apter, Emily. *Feminizing the Fetish: Psychoanalysis and Narrative Obsession in Turn-of-the-Century France*. Ithaca, NY: Cornell University Press, 1991.

———. "Specularity and Reproduction: Marx, Freud, Baudrillard." *Fetish*. New York: Princeton Architectural Press, 1992. 20–33.

Aronowitz, Stanley. "Tensions of Critical Theory: Is Negative Dialectics All There Is?" *Postmodernism and Social Theory*. Ed. Steven Seidman and David Wagner. Cambridge, MA: Blackwell, 1992. 289–321.

Aronson, Ronald. *After Marxism*. New York: Guilford Press, 1995.

Assiter, Alison, and Avedon Carol, ed. *Bad Girls and Dirty Pictures: The Challenge to Reclaim Feminism*. London: Pluto Press, 1993.

Austin, Regina. " 'A Nation of Thieves': Consumption, Commerce, and the Black Public Sphere." *The Black Public Sphere*. Ed. Black Public Sphere Collective. Chicago: University of Chicago Press, 1995. 229–52.

Bangs, Lester. *Psychotic Reactions and Carburetor Dung*. New York: Vintage, 1987.

Barthes, Roland. *Mythologies*. Trans. Annette Lavers. New York: Farrar, Straus & Giroux, 1990.

———. *The Pleasure of the Text*. Trans. Richard Miller. New York: Hill and Wang, 1975.

———. "Upon Leaving the Movie Theatre." *Cinematographic Apparatus: Selected Writings*. Ed. Theresa Hak Kyung Cha. New York: Tanem Press, 1980. 1–4.

Baudrillard, Jean. *Fatal Strategies*. Ed. Jim Fleming. Trans. Philip Beitchman and W. G. J. Niesluchowski. New York: Semiotext(e), 1990.

———. *For a Critique of the Political Economy of the Sign*. Trans. Charles Levin. St. Louis: Telos Press, 1981.

———. *The Mirror of Production*. Trans. Mark Poster. St. Louis: Telos Press, 1975.

———. *Pour une critique de l'économie politique du signe*. Paris: Gallimard, 1972.

———. *Selected Writings*. Ed. Mark Poster. Trans. Jacques Mourrain. Stanford, CA: Stanford University Press, 1988.

Benjamin, Walter. *Charles Baudelaire: A Lyric Poet in the Era of High Capitalism*. Trans. Harry Zohn. London: New Left Books, 1973.

———. *Illuminations*. Ed. Hannah Arendt. Trans. Harry Zohn. New York: Shocken, 1969.

———. "Reply." Trans. Harry Zohn. *Aesthetics and Politics*. Trans. ed. Ronald Taylor. London: Verso, 1988. 131–41.

Bergman-Carton, Janis. "Strike a Pose: The Framing of Madonna and Frida Kahlo." *Texas Studies in Literature and Language* 35, No. 4 (Winter 1993): 440–52.

Berlant, Lauren. "National Brands/National Body: *Imitation of Life*." *Comparative American Identities: Race, Sex, and Nationality in the Modern Text*. Ed. Hortense Spillers. New York: Routledge, 1991. 110–40.

Berlant, Lauren, and Elizabeth Freeman. "Queer Nationality." *Boundary 2* 19, No. 1 (1992): 149–80.

Bérubé, Michael. *Public Access: Literary Theory and American Cultural Politics*. New York: Verso, 1994.

Bhabha, Homi. *The Location of Culture*. New York: Routledge, 1994.

Bhaskar, Roy. "Contradiction." *A Dictionary of Marxist Thought*. Ed. Tom Bottomore. Cambridge, MA: Harvard University Press, 1983. 93–4.

———. *Dialectic: The Pulse of Freedom*. London: Verso, 1993.

Blackburn, Robin, ed. *After the Fall: The Failure of Communism and the Future of Socialism*. London: Verso, 1991.

Blake, Andrew. "Madonna the Musician." *Deconstructing Madonna*. Ed. Fran Lloyd. London: B. T. Batsford, 1993. 17–28.

Bocock, Robert. *Consumption*. New York: Routledge, 1993.

Bogue, Ronald. *Deleuze and Guattari*. London: Routledge, 1989.

Bourdieu, Pierre. *Distinction*. Trans. Richard Nice. Cambridge, MA: Harvard University Press, 1984.

Bourdon, David. *Warhol*. New York: Abrams, 1989.

Braidotti, Rosi. *Patterns of Dissonance: A Study of Women in Contemporary Philosophy*. Trans. Elizabeth Guild. New York: Routledge, 1991.

Brantlinger, Patrick, and James Naremore. "Introduction: Six Artistic Cultures." *Modernity and Mass Culture*. Ed. Brantlinger and Naremore. Bloomington, IN: Indiana University Press, 1991.

Braudy, Leo. *The Frenzy of Renown: Fame and Its History*. New York: Oxford University Press, 1986.

Brecht, Bertolt. *Brecht on Theatre*. Trans. John Willet. New York: Hill and Wang, 1987.

Breckenridge, Carol, ed. *Consuming Modernity: Public Culture in a South Asian World*. Minneapolis, MN: University of Minnesota Press, 1995.

Buck-Morss, Susan. *The Origin of Negative Dialectics: Theodor W. Adorno, Walter Benjamin, and the Frankfurt Institute*. New York: Macmillan Free Press, 1977.

Budd, Mike, Robert M. Entman, and Clay Steinman. "The Affirmative Character of U.S. Cultural Studies." *Critical Studies in Mass Communication* 7 (1990): 169–84.

Burger, Christa. "Modernity as Postmodernity." *Modernity and Identity*. Ed. Scott Lash and Jonathan Friedman. Cambridge, MA: Blackwell, 1992.

Butler, Judith. *Bodies That Matter: On the Discursive Limits of "Sex"*. New York: Routledge, 1993.

———. *Gender Trouble: Feminism and the Subversion of Identity*. New York: Routledge, 1990.

———. *Subjects of Desire: Reflections on Twentieth-Century France*. New York: Columbia University Press, 1987.

Cagle, Van M. *Reconstructing Pop/Subculture: Art, Rock, and Warhol*. Thousand Hills, CA: Sage, 1995.

Caldwell, John Thornton. *Televisuality: Style, Crisis, and Authority in American Television*. New Brunswick, NJ: Rutgers University Press, 1993.

Califia, Pat. "*Sex* and Madonna." *Madonnarama*. Ed. Lisa Frank and Paul Smith. Pittsburgh, PA: Cleis Press, 1993. 169–84.

Camfield, William. "Marcel Duchamp's *Fountain*: Aesthetic Object, Icon, or Anti-Art?" *The Definitively Unfinished Marcel Duchamp*. Ed. Thierry de Duve. Cambridge, MA: MIT Press, 1991. 133–84.

Chambers, Iain. *Urban Rhythms: Pop Music and Popular Culture*. New York: St. Martin's, 1983.

Champagne, John. "Stabat Madonna." *Madonnarama*. Ed. Lisa Frank and Paul Smith. Pittsburgh, PA: Cleis Press, 1993. 111–38.

Chancer, Lynn S. *Sadomasochism in Everyday Life*. New Brunswick, NJ: Rutgers University Press, 1992.

Chow, Rey. "Ethics after Idealism." *Diacritics* 23, No. 1 (Spring 1993): 3–22.

Christgau, Robert. "Madonnathinking Madonnabout Madonnamusic." *Desperately Seeking Madonna*. Ed. Adam Sexton. New York: Delta, 1993. 201–07.

Clark, Danae. *Negotiating Hollywood: The Cultural Politics of Actors' Labor*. Minneapolis, MN: University of Minnesota Press, 1995.

Coates, Paul. *Film at the Intersection of High and Mass Culture*. New York: Cambridge University Press, 1994.

Cohen, G. A. *Karl Marx's Theory of History: A Defense*. New York: Basic, 1982.

Cohen, Margaret. *Profane Illuminations: Walter Benjamin and the Paris of Surrealist Revolution*. Berkeley, CA: University of California Press, 1993.

Colacello, Bob. *Holy Terror: Andy Warhol Close-Up*. New York: Harper Collins, 1990.

Colletti, Lucio. *Marxism and Hegel*. Trans. Lawrence Garner. London: New Left Books, 1973.

Collins, Jim. *Uncommon Cultures: Popular Culture and Postmodernism*. New York: Routledge, 1989.

Cross, Gary. *Time and Money: The Making of Consumer Culture*. New York: Routledge, 1993.

Curran, James. "The 'New Revisionism' in Mass Communications Research." *European Journal of Communication* 5, Nos. 2–3 (June 1990): 135–64.

Cvetkovich, Ann. "The Powers of Seeing and Being Seen: *Truth or Dare* and *Paris Is Burning*." *Film Theory Goes to the Movies*. Ed. Jim Collins, Hilary Radner, and Ava Preacher Collins. New York: Routledge, 1993. 155–69.

D'Amico, Robert. *Marx and Philosophy of Culture*. Gainesville, FL: University Presses of Florida, 1981.

Debord, Guy. *The Society of the Spectacle*. Detroit, MI: Black and Red, 1983.

Deleuze, Gilles. *Nietzsche and Philosophy*. Trans. Hugh Tomlinson. Minneapolis, MN: University of Minnesota Press, 1983.

———. *Nietzsche et la philosophie*. Paris: Presses Universitaires de France, 1973.

———. *Spinoza: Practical Philosophy*. Trans. Robert Hurley. San Francisco: City Lights, 1988.

Deleuz, Gilles, and Félix Guattari. *Anti-Oedipus: Capitalism and Schizophrenia*. Trans. Robert Hurley, Mark Seem, and Helen R. Lane. Minneapolis, MN: University of Minnesota Press, 1988.

———. *Thousand Plateaus*. Trans. Brian Massumi. Minneapolis, MN: University of Minnesota Press, 1987.

Deleuz, Gilles, and Claire Parnet. *Dialogues*. Trans. Hugh Tomlinson and Barbara Habberjam. New York: Columbia University Press, 1987.

Demopoulos, Maria. " 'Thieves Like Us': Directors under the Influence." *Film Comment* 32, No. 3 (May/June 1996): 33–37.

Dent, Gina. "Black Pleasure, Black Joy: An Introduction." *Black Popular Culture*. Ed. Dent. Seattle: Bay Press, 1992. 1–19.

Derrida, Jacques. "Jacques Derrida." Interviewed by Imre Salusinsky. *Criticism in Society*. New York: Methuen, 1987. 18–25.

———. *Positions*. Trans. Alan Bass. Chicago: University of Chicago Press, 1982.

———. *Specters of Marx: The State of Debt, the Work of Mourning, and the New International*. Trans. Peggy Kamuf. New York: Routledge, 1994.

———. *Writing and Difference*. Trans. Alan Bass. Chicago: University of Chicago Press, 1978.

Desai, Meghnad. "Underconsumption." *A Dictionary of Marxist Thought*. Ed. Tom Bottomore. Cambridge, MA: Harvard University Press, 1983. 495–98.

Desmond, William, ed. *Hegel and His Critics*. Albany, NY: SUNY Press, 1989.

Dews, Peter. "Adorno, Poststructuralism, and the Critique of Identity." *The Problem of Modernity: Adorno and Benjamin*. Ed. Andrew Benjamin. London: Routledge, 1989. 1–22.

———. *Logics of Disintegration: Post-Structuralist Thought and the Claims of Critical Theory*. New York: Verso, 1989.

Dollimore, Jonathan. *Sexual Dissidence: Augustine to Wilde, Freud to Foucault.* Oxford, UK: Oxford University Press, 1991.

Douglas, Susan. *Where the Girls Are: Growing Up Female with the Mass Media.* New York: Times Books, 1994.

Doyle, Jennifer, Jonathan Flatley, and José Esteban Muñoz, ed. *Pop Out: Queer Warhol.* Durham, NC: Duke University Press, 1988.

Drukman, Stephen. "The Gay Gaze, or Why I Want My MTV." *A Queer Romance: Lesbians, Gay Men, and Popular Culture.* Ed. Paul Burston and Colin Richardson. London: Routledge, 1995. 81–98.

Dyer, Richard. *Heavenly Bodies: Film Stars and Society.* New York: St. Martin's, 1986.

Eagleton, Terry. *Against the Grain: Essays 1975–1985.* London: Verso, 1986.

———. *Ideology: An Introduction.* London: Verso, 1991.

Easthope, Antony. *British Post-Structuralism.* New York: Routledge, 1988.

———. "The Trajectory of *Screen,* 1971–1979." *The Politics of Theory.* Ed. Francis Barker et al. Colchester, UK: University of Essex Press, 1983. 121–33.

Ellis, Kate, Beth Jaker, Nan D. Hunter, Barbara O'Dair, and Abby Tallmer, ed. *Caught Looking: Feminism, Pornography, and Censorship.* East Haven, CT: LongRiver Books, 1986.

Engh, Barbara. "Adorno and the Sirens: Tele-Phono-Graphic Bodies." *Embodied Voices: Representing Female Vocality in Western Culture.* Ed. Leslie Dunn and Nancy A. Jones. Cambridge, UK: Cambridge University Press, 1994. 120–35.

Ferguson, Andrew. "Bad Girls Don't Cry." *National Review* (May 30, 1994): 72.

Fine, Ben, and Ellen Leopold. *The World of Consumption.* New York: Routledge, 1993.

Fiske, John. "British Cultural Studies and Television." *Channels of Discourse: Television and Contemporary Criticism.* Ed. Robert C. Allen. Chapel Hill, NC: University of North Carolina Press, 1987. 254–89.

———. *Media Matters: Everyday Culture and Political Change.* Minneapolis, MN: University of Minnesota Press, 1994.

———. *Reading the Popular.* Boston, MA: Unwin Hyman, 1989.

———. *Television Culture.* New York: Routledge, 1990.

Flatley, Jonathan. "Warhol Gives Good Face: Publicity and the Prose of Prosopopoeia." *Pop Out: Queer Warhol.* Ed. Jennifer Doyle, Flatley, and José Esteban Muñoz. Durham, NC: Duke University Press, 1996. 101–33.

"The Forbes 500s." *Forbes* 149, No. 9 (April 27, 1992): 190–396.

Foster, Hal. "The Art of Fetishism: Notes on Dutch Still Life." *Fetishism as Cultural Discourse*. Ed. Emily Apter and William Pietz. Ithaca, NY: Cornell University Press, 1993. 251–65.

Foucault, Michel. *Discipline and Punish: The Birth of the Prison*. Trans. Alan Sheridan. New York: Vintage, 1979.

———. *The History of Sexuality*. Vol. 1. Trans. Robert Hurley. New York: Vintage, 1980.

———. *Language, Counter-Memory, Practice*. Trans. Donald F. Bouchard. Ithaca, NY: Cornell University Press, 1977.

———. "Preface." *Anti-Oedipus: Capitalism and Schizophrenia* by Gilles Deleuze and Félix Guattari. Trans. Robert Hurley et al. Minneapolis, MN: University of Minnesota Press, 1988. xi–xxiv.

———. *Power/Knowledge: Selected Interviews and Other Writings 1972–1977*. Ed. Colin Gordon. Trans. Gordon, Leo Marshall, John Mepham, and Kate Soper. New York: Pantheon, 1980.

Frank, Lisa, and Paul Smith. "Introduction: How to Use Your Madonna." *Madonnarama*. Ed. Frank and Smith. Pittsburgh, PA: Cleis Press, 1993. 7–19.

Freccero, Carla. "Our Lady of MTV." *Feminism and Postmodernism*. Ed. Margaret Ferguson and Jennifer Wicke. Durham, NC: Duke University Press, 1994. 179–99.

Freud, Sigmund. "Fetischismus." *Psychologie des Unbewußten*. In *Studienausgabe* 3. Frankfurt am Main: S. Fischer Verlag, 1975. 377–88.

———. "Fetishism." Trans. Joan Riviere. *Collected Papers*. Vol. 5. Ed. James Strachey. London: The Hogarth Press, 1953. 198–204.

———. "Instincts and Their Vicissitudes." Trans. Cecil M. Baines. *General Psychological Theory*. Ed. Philip Rieff. New York: Collier, 1978. 83–103.

———. "Mourning and Melancholia." Trans. Joan Riviere. *General Psychological Theory*. Ed. Philip Rieff. New York: Collier, 1978. 164–79.

———. *Three Essays on the Theory of Sexuality*. Trans. James Strachey. London: The Hogarth Press, 1962.

Friedberg, Anne. "A Denial of Difference: Theories of Cinematic Identification." *Psychoanalysis and Cinema*. Ed. E. Ann Kaplan. New York: Routledge, 1990. 36–45.

————. *Window Shopping: Cinema and the Postmodern*. Berkeley, CA: University of California Press, 1993.

Frith, Simon. "The Cultural Study of Popular Music." *Cultural Studies*. Ed. Lawrence Grossberg, Cary Nelson, and Paula A. Treichler. New York: Routledge, 1992. 174–82.

————. "The Sound of *Erotica*: Pain, Power, and Pop." *Madonnarama*. Ed. Lisa Frank and Paul Smith. Pittsburgh, PA: Cleis Press, 1993. 87–92.

Frow, John. *Cultural Studies and Cultural Value*. Oxford, UK: Clarendon Press, 1995.

Fuss, Diana. *Identification Papers*. New York: Routledge, 1995.

Gaar, Gillian G. *She's a Rebel: The History of Women in Rock & Roll*. Seattle: Seal Press, 1992.

Gaard, Greta. "The Laugh of Madonna: Censorship and Oppositional Discourse." *The Journal of the Midwest Modern Language Association* 25, No. 1 (Spring 1992): 41–47.

Gamman, Lorraine, and Merja Makinen. *Female Fetishism*. New York: New York University Press, 1994.

Gane, Mike. *Baudrillard: Critical and Fatal Theory*. New York: Routledge, 1991.

Gasché, Rodolphe. "Objective Diversions: On Some Kantian Themes in Benjamin's 'The Work of Art in the Age of Mechanical Reproduction.' " *Walter Benjamin's Philosophy: Destruction and Experience*. Ed. Andrew Benjamin and Peter Osborne. New York: Routledge, 1994. 183–204.

Gendron, Bernard. "Theodor Adorno Meets the Cadillacs." *Studies in Entertainment: Critical Approaches to Mass Culture*. Ed. Tania Modleski. Bloomington, IN: Indiana University Press, 1986. 18–36.

Genosko, Gary. *Baudrillard and Signs: Signification Ablaze*. New York: Routledge, 1994.

Gibson, Pamela Church, and Roma Gibson, ed. *Dirty Looks: Women, Pornography, Power*. London: British Film Institute, 1993.

Gibson, William. *Mona Lisa Overdrive*. New York: Bantam, 1988.

Giroux, Henry. *Disturbing Pleasures: Learning Popular Culture*. New York: Routledge, 1994.

Goldberg, Michael. "Madonna to Sign $60 Million Deal." *Rolling Stone* (April 16, 1992): 628.

Goldman, Robert. *Reading Ads Socially*. New York: Routledge, 1992.

Goldman, Robert, and Stephen Papson. *Sign Wars: The Cluttered Landscape of Advertising.* New York: Guilford, 1996.

Goldsby, Jackie. "Queens of Language: *Paris Is Burning.*" *Queer Looks: Perspectives on Lesbian and Gay Film and Video.* Ed. Martha Gever, Pratibha Parmar, and John Greyson. New York: Routledge, 1993. 108–15.

Goodman, Fred. "Madonna and Oprah: The Companies They Keep." *Working Women* 16, No. 12 (December 1991): 52–55, 84.

Goodwin, Andrew. *Dancing in the Distraction Factory: Music Television and Popular Culture.* Minneapolis, MN: University of Minnesota Press, 1992.

Goux, Jean-Joseph. *Symbolic Economies: After Marx and Freud.* Trans. Jennifer Curtiss Gage. Ithaca, NY: Cornell University Press, 1990.

Gripsrud, Jostein. *The Dynasty Years: Hollywood Television and Critical Media Studies.* New York: Routledge, 1995.

Grossberg, Lawrence. *We Gotta Get Out of This Place: Popular Conservatism and Postmodern Culture.* New York: Routledge, 1992.

Grosz, Elizabeth. "Labors of Love: Analyzing Perverse Desire." *Space, Time, and Perversion: Essays on the Politics of Bodies.* New York: Routledge, 1995. 155–71.

———. "Lesbian Fetishism." *differences* 3, No. 2 (Summer 1991): 39–44.

———. *Volatile Bodies: Toward a Corporeal Feminism.* Bloomington, IN: Indiana University Press, 1994.

Habermas, Jürgen. *Autonomy and Solidarity: Interviews.* Ed. Peter Dews. London: Verso, 1986.

———. *The Philosophical Discourse of Modernity.* Cambridge, MA: MIT Press, 1990.

Hall, Stuart. "Cultural Studies and Theoretical Legacies." *Cultural Studies.* Ed. Lawrence Grossberg, Cary Nelson, and Paula A. Treichler. New York: Routledge, 1992. 277–86.

———. "Encoding, Decoding." *The Cultural Studies Reader.* Ed. Simon During. New York: Routledge, 1993. 90–103.

———. *The Hard Road to Renewal: Thatcherism and the Crisis of the Left.* London: Verso, 1988.

———. "Introduction." *Critique of Commodity Aesthetics: Appearance, Sexuality and Advertising in Capitalist Society* by W. F. Haug. Trans. Robert Buck. Minneapolis, MN: University of Minnesota Press, 1986. 1–4.

———. "What Is This Black in 'Black' Popular Culture?" *Black Popular Culture*. Ed. Gina Dent. Seattle: Bay Press, 1992. 21–33.

Harding, James M. "Adorno, Ellison, and the Critique of Jazz." *Cultural Critique* 31 (Fall 1995): 129–58.

Harris, Daniel. "Make My Rainy Day." *The Nation* (January 8, 1992): 790.

Harris, Kenneth Mark. *The Film Fetish*. New York: Peter Lang, 1992.

Harvey, David. *The Condition of Postmodernity*. Cambridge, MA: Blackwell, 1989.

Haug, W. F. *Critique of Commodity Aesthetics: Appearance, Sexuality and Advertising in Capitalist Society*. Trans. Robert Buck. Minneapolis, MN: University of Minnesota Press, 1986.

Hebdige, Dick. *Subculture: The Meaning of Style*. New York: Routledge, 1991.

Hegel, G. W. F. *Hegel: Texts and Commentary*. Ed. and trans. Walter Kaufmann. Notre Dame: University of Notre Dame Press, 1986.

———. *Lectures on the Philosophy of History*. Trans. J. Sibree. London: George Bell, 1900.

———. *Science of Logic*. Trans. A. V. Miller. New York: Humanities Press, 1976.

———. *Wissenschaft der Logik*. Ed. George Lasson. Hamburg: Felix Meiner, 1963.

Heilbroner, Robert. *The Worldly Philosophers*. New York: Simon and Schuster, 1986.

Himmelweit, Susan. "Surplus Value." *A Dictionary of Marxist Thought*. Ed. Tom Bottomore. Cambridge, MA: Harvard University Press, 1983. 472–75.

Hodge, Joanna. "Feminism and Postmodernism: Misleading Divisions Imposed by the Opposition between Modernism and Postmodernism." *The Problems of Modernity: Adorno and Benjamin*. Ed. Andrew Benjamin. London: Routledge, 1989. 86–111.

Hohendahl, Peter Uwe. *Prismatic Thought: Theodor W. Adorno*. Lincoln, NE: University of Nebraska Press, 1995.

———. *Reappraisals: Shifting Alignments in Postwar Critical Theory*. Ithaca, NY: Cornell University Press, 1991.

hooks, bell. *Black Looks: Race and Representation*. Boston, MA: South End Press, 1992.

———. *Killing Rage: Ending Racism*. New York: Henry Holt, 1995.

———. "Madonna: Plantation Mistress or Soul Sister?" *Desperately Seeking Madonna.* Ed. Adam Sexton. New York: Delta, 1993. 218–26.

———. *Outlaw Culture: Resisting Representations.* New York: Routledge, 1994.

———. "Power to the Pussy: We Don't Wannabe Dicks in Drag." *Madonnarama.* Ed. Lisa Frank and Paul Smith. Pittsburgh, PA: Cleis Press, 1993. 65–80.

———. *Yearning: Race, Gender, and Cultural Politics.* Boston, MA: South End Press, 1990.

Hunt, Lynn. "Introduction." *The Invention of Pornography: Obscenity and the Origins of Modernity, 1500–1800.* Ed. Hunt. New York: Zone Books, 1993. 9–45.

Hunter, Nan D. "Contextualizing the Sexuality Debates: A Chronology." *Sex Wars: Sexual Dissent and Political Culture.* Ed. Lisa Duggan and Hunter. New York: Routledge, 1995. 16–29.

Huyssen, Andreas. *After the Great Divide: Modernism, Mass Culture, Postmodernism.* Bloomington, IN: Indiana University Press, 1986.

———. "Introduction to Adorno." *New German Critique* 6 (Fall 1975): 2–11.

———. "Mass Culture as Woman: Modernism's Other." *Studies in Entertainment.* Ed. Tania Modleski. Bloomington, IN: Indiana University Press, 1986. 188–207.

Ian, Marcia. *Remembering the Phallic Mother: Psychoanalysis, Modernism, and the Fetish.* Ithaca, NY: Cornell University Press, 1993.

Inglis, Fred. *Cultural Studies.* Cambridge, MA: Blackwell, 1993.

Ingrassia, Michele, with Carol Hall. "Newsmakers." *Newsweek* (October 4, 1993): 91.

Jameson, Fredric. *The Ideologies of Theory: Syntax of History.* Vol. 2. Minneapolis, MN: University of Minnesota Press, 1988.

———. *Late Marxism: Adorno, or, The Persistence of the Dialectic.* New York: Verso, 1990.

———. *Postmodernism, or, The Cultural Logic of Late Capitalism.* Durham: Duke University Press, 1991.

———. *The Seeds of Time.* New York: Columbia University Press, 1994.

Jardine, Alice. *Gynesis: Configurations of Women and Modernity.* Ithaca, NY: Cornell University Press, 1985.

Jay, Martin. *Adorno.* Cambridge, MA: Harvard University Press, 1984.

———. "Adorno in America." *Permanent Exiles: Essays on the Intellectual Migration from Germany to America.* New York: Columbia University Press, 1986. 120–37.

Johnson, Richard. "What Is Cultural Studies Anyway?" *What Is Cultural Studies?* Ed. John Storey. New York: Arnold, 1996. 75–114.

Kaite, Berkeley. *Pornography and Difference.* Bloomington, IN: Indiana University Press, 1995.

Kakutani, Michiko. "Madonna Writes; Academics Write about Her." *New York Times* (October 21, 1992): B2.

Kaplan, E. Ann. *Rocking around the Clock: Music Television, Postmodernism, and Consumer Culture.* New York: Routledge, 1989.

Keenan, Thomas. "The Point Is to (Ex)Change It: Reading *Capital*, Rhetorically." *Fetishism as Cultural Discourse.* Ed. Emily Apter and William Pietz. Ithaca, NY: Cornell University Press, 1993. 152–85.

Kellner, Douglas. *Herbert Marcuse and the Crisis of Marxism.* Berkeley, CA: University of California Press, 1984.

———. *Jean Baudrillard: From Marxism to Postmodernism and Beyond.* Stanford, CA: Stanford University Press, 1989.

———. *Media Culture: Cultural Studies, Identity, and Politics between the Modern and the Postmodern.* New York: Routledge, 1995.

Kemple, Thomas. *Reading Marx Writing: Melodrama, the Market, and the "Grundrisse."* Stanford, CA: Stanford University Press, 1995.

Kenney, William Howland. "Historical Context and the Definition of Jazz." *Jazz among the Discourses.* Ed. Krin Gabbard. Durham, NC: Duke University Press, 1995. 110–16.

Kinder, Marsha. *Playing with Power in Movies, Television, and Video Games: From Muppet Babies to Mutant Ninja Turtles.* Berkeley, CA: University of California Press, 1991.

King, Barry. "Articulating Stardom." *Stardom: Industry of Desire.* Ed. Christine Gledhill. New York: Routledge, 1991. 167–82.

———. "Articulating Stardom." *Star Texts: Image and Performance in Film and Television.* Ed. Jeremy G. Butler. Detroit: Wayne State University Press, 1991. 125–54.

———. "The Star and the Commodity: Notes toward a Performance Theory of Stardom." *Cultural Studies* 1, No. 2 (May 1987): 145–59.

Kipnis, Laura. *Bound and Gagged: Pornography and the Politics of Fantasy in America.* New York: Grove Press, 1995.

———. *Ecstasy Unlimited: On Sex, Capital, Gender, and Aesthetics.* Minneapolis, MN: University of Minnesota Press, 1993.

Kuspit, Donald. "Pop Art: A Reactionary Realism." *Pop Art: The Critical Dialogue.* Ed. Carol Anne Mahsun. Ann Arbor, MI: UMI Research Press, 1989. 203–16.

Lacan, Jacques. *Écrits: A Selection*. Trans. Alan Sheridan. New York: Norton, 1977.

———. *The Four Fundamental Concepts of Psycho-Analysis*. Trans. Alan Sheridan. New York: Norton, 1978.

———. "God and the Jouissance of ~~The~~ Woman. A Love Letter." *Feminine Sexuality*. Ed. Juliet Mitchell and Jacqueline Rose. Trans. Rose. New York: Pantheon, 1983. 138–48.

Lancaster, Kelvin. *Consumer Demand: A New Approach*. New York: Columbia University Press, 1971.

Laplanche, Jean. *Life and Death in Psychoanalysis*. Trans. Jeffrey Mehlman. Baltimore, MD: Johns Hopkins University Press, 1976.

Lapsley, Rob, and Michael Westlake. *Film Theory: An Introduction*. New York: St. Martin's, 1987.

Larsen, Neil. *Modernism and Hegemony*. Minneapolis, MN: University of Minnesota Press, 1990.

Lash, Scott. *Sociology of Postmodernism*. London: Routledge, 1990.

Lash, Scott, and John Urry. *Economies of Signs and Space*. London: Sage, 1994.

Layton, Lynne. "Who's That Girl?: A Case Study of Madonna." *Women Creating Lives: Identities, Resilience, and Resistance*. Ed. Carol E. Franz and Abigail J. Stewart. Boulder, CO: Westview Press, 1994. 143–55.

Lee, Martyn J. *Consumer Culture Reborn: The Cultural Politics of Consumption*. New York: Routledge, 1993.

Lehman, Peter. *Running Scared: Masculinity and the Representation of the Male Body*. Philadelphia: Temple University Press, 1993.

Lentz, Kirsten Marthe. "Chameleon, Vampire, Rich Slut." *Madonnarama*. Ed. Lisa Frank and Paul Smith. Pittsburgh, PA: Cleis Press, 1993. 153–68.

Lewis, Lisa. *Gender Politics and MTV: Voicing the Difference*. Philadelphia: Temple University Press. 1990.

Lipietz, Alain. *Mirages and Miracles: The Crises of Global Fordism*. Trans. David Macey. London: Verso, 1987.

Lloyd, Fran. "Introduction." *Deconstructing Madonna*. Ed. Lloyd. London: B. T. Batsford, 1993. 9–15.

Low, Gail Ching-Liang. *White Skin/Black Masks: Representations of Colonialism*. New York: Routledge, 1996.

Lowe, Donald. *The Body in Late-Capitalist USA*. Durham, NC: Duke University Press, 1995.

Lukács, Georg. *History and Class Consciousness: Studies in Marxist Dialectics.* Trans. Rodney Livingstone. Cambridge, MA: MIT Press, 1988.

Lunn, Eugene. "The Frankfurt School in the Development of the Mass Culture Debate." *The Aesthetics of the Critical Theorists.* Ed. Ronald Roblin. Lewiston, NY: Edwin Mellen Press, 1990. 26–84.

———. *Marxism and Modernism: An Historical Study of Lukács, Brecht, Benjamin, and Adorno.* Berkeley, CA: University of California Press, 1982.

Lury, Celia. *Consumer Culture.* New Brunswick, NJ: Rutgers University Press, 1996.

Lyotard, François. *Libidinal Economy.* Trans. Iain Hamilton Grant. Bloomington, IN: Indiana University Press, 1993.

Macdonald, Dwight. *Against the American Grain.* New York: Random House, 1962.

Madonna. *Sex.* New York: Warner Books, 1992.

Magnus, Bernd, and Stephen Cullenberg. "Introduction." *Whither Marxism?: Global Crises in International Perspective.* Ed. Magnus and Cullenberg. New York: Routledge, 1995. vii–xxiii.

Mahsun, Carol Anne, ed. *Pop Art: The Critical Dialogue.* Ann Arbor, MI: UMI Research Press, 1989.

Mandziuk, Roseann M. "Feminist Politics and Postmodern Seductions." *The Madonna Connection: Representational Politics, Subcultural Identities, and Cultural Theory.* Ed. Cathy Schwichtenberg. Boulder, CO: Westview Press, 1993. 167–87.

Manuel, Frank E. *A Requiem for Karl Marx.* Cambridge, MA: Harvard University Press, 1995.

Marcus, Greil. *Lipstick Traces: A Secret History of the 20th Century.* Cambridge, MA: Harvard University Press, 1989.

Marcuse, Herbert. *An Essay on Liberation.* Boston: Beacon Press, 1969.

———. *Negations: Essays in Critical Theory.* Trans. Jeremy J. Shapiro. Boston: Beacon Press, 1968.

Marx, Karl. *Capital: A Critique of Political Economy.* 3 Vols. Ed. Friedrich Engels. Trans. Samuel Moore and Edward Aveling. New York: International, 1967.

———. *Das Kapital. Kritik der Politischen Ökonomie.* 1883. Vol. 1. In Marx and Friedrich Engels, *Gesamtausgabe.* MEGA II/8. Berlin: Dietz Verlag, 1989.

————. *The Grundrisse*. Ed. and trans. David McLellan. New York: Harper, 1972.

————. *Ökonomische Manuskripte*. 1857–58. MEGA II/1.1. Berlin: Dietz Verlag, 1976.

————. *The Poverty of Philosophy*. Trans. anon. New York: International, 1963.

Massumi, Brian. *A User's Guide to Capitalism and Schizophrenia*. Cambridge, MA: MIT Press, 1992.

May, Todd. "Difference and Unity in Gilles Deleuze." *Gilles Deleuze and the Theatre of Philosophy*. Ed. Constantin V. Boundas and Dorothea Olkowski. New York: Routledge, 1994. 33–50.

McCallum, E. L. "How to Do Things with Fetishism." *differences* 7, No. 3 (Fall 1995): 24–59.

McClary, Susan. *Feminine Endings: Music, Gender, and Sexuality*. Minneapolis, MN: University of Minnesota Press, 1991.

McClintock, Anne. "Maid to Order: Commercial S/M and Gender Power." *Dirty Looks: Women, Pornography, Power*. Ed. Pamela Church Gibson and Roma Gibson. London: British Film Institute, 1993. 207–31.

McElroy, Wendy. *XXX: A Woman's Right to Pornography*. New York: St. Martin's, 1995.

McGuigan, Jim. *Cultural Populism*. New York: Routledge, 1992.

McHugh, Patrick. "Ecstasy and Exile: Cultural Theory between Heidegger and Adorno." *Cultural Critique* 25 (Fall 1993): 121–52.

McNair, Brian. *Mediated Sex: Pornography and Postmodern Culture*. London: Arnold, 1996.

McShine, Kynaston, ed. *Andy Warhol: A Retrospective*. New York: Museum of Modern Art, 1989.

Mercer, Kobena. "Reading Racial Fetishism: The Photographs of Robert Mapplethorpe." *Fetishism as Cultural Discourse*. Ed. Emily Apter and William Pietz. Ithaca, NY: Cornell University Press, 1993. 307–29.

————. *Welcome to the Jungle: New Positions in Black Cultural Studies*. New York: Routledge, 1994.

Metz, Christian. *The Imaginary Signifier*. Trans. Celia Britton, Annwyl Williams, Ben Brewster, and Alfred Guzzetti. Bloomington, IN: Indiana University Press, 1982.

Metzstein, Margery. "*Sex*: Signed, Sealed, and Delivered." *Deconstructing Madonna*. Ed. Fran Lloyd. London: B. T. Batsford, 1993. 91–98.

Miklitsch, Robert. " 'Going through the Fantasy': Screening Slavoj Žižek." *South Atlantic Quarterly* (forthcoming: Spring 1998).

———."Lust, Fantasy, Male Hysteria: *Clint Eastwood* (Un-) Bound." *Minnesota Review* 43/44 (November 1995): 150–63.

———. "Punk Pedagogy, or Performing Contradiction: The Risks and Rewards of (Anti-) Transference." *The Review of Education/Pedagogy/Cultural Studies* 16, No. 1 (1994): 57–67. Reprinted in *Education and Cultural Studies: Toward a Performative Practice*. Ed. Henry Giroux and Patrick Shannon. New York: Routledge, 1997. 259–70.

———. "Troping Prostitution: Two or Three Things About (Post-) Marxism/ Feminism." *Genders* 12 (Winter 1991): 120–39.

Miller, Mark. *Material Culture and Mass Consumption*. Oxford: Basil Blackwell, 1991.

Mitchell, W. J. T. *Iconology: Image, Text, Ideology*. Chicago: University of Chicago Press, 1986.

Modleski, Tania. *Feminism without Women: Culture and Criticism in a "Postfeminist" Age*. New York: Routledge, 1991.

Morgan, Richard. "In Being a Good Corporate Citizen." *Desperately Seeking Madonna*. Ed. Adam Sexton. New York: Delta, 1993. 93–95.

Morin, Edgar. *The Stars*. Trans. Richard Howard. New York: Grove, 1961.

Morris, Meaghan. "Banality in Cultural Studies." *Logics of Television: Essays in Cultural Criticism*. Ed. Patricia Mellencamp. Bloomington, IN: Indiana University Press, 1990. 14–43.

Mort, Frank. *Cultures of Consumption: Masculinities and Social Space in Late Twentieth-Century Britain*. New York: Routledge, 1996.

———. "The Politics of Consumption." *New Times: The Changing Face of Politics in the 1990s*. Ed. Stuart Hall and Martin Jacques. London: Lawrence and Wishart, 1989. 160–72.

Morton, Donald, and Mas'ud Zavarzadeh. *Theory, (Post)Modernity, Opposition: An "Other" Introduction to Literary and Cultural Studies*. Washington, DC: Maisonneuve Press, 1991.

Mulvey, Laura. "Introduction: Fetishisms." *Fetishism and Curiosity*. Bloomington, IN: Indiana University Press, 1996. 1–15.

———. *Visual and Other Pleasures*. Bloomington, IN: Indiana University Press, 1989.

Musto, Michael. "Immaculate Connection." *Out in Culture: Gay, Lesbian, and Queer Essays on Popular Culture*. Ed. Corey K. Creekmur and Alexander Doty. Durham, NC: Duke University Press, 1995. 427–36.

Nägele, Rainer. "The Scene of the Other: Theodor W. Adorno's Negative Dialectic in the Context of Poststructuralism." *Postmodernism and Politics*. Ed. Jonathan Arac. Minneapolis, MN: University of Minnesota Press, 1986. 91–111.

Nakayama, Thomas K., and Lisa Peñaloza. "Madonna T/Races: Music Videos through the Prism of Color." *The Madonna Connection: Representational Politics, Subcultural Identities, and Cultural Theory*. Ed. Cathy Schwichtenberg. Boulder, CO: Westview Press, 1993. 39–55.

Nehring, Neil. *Flowers in the Dustbin: Culture, Anarchy, and Postwar England*. Ann Arbor, MI: University of Michigan Press, 1993.

Nietzsche, Friedrich. *Ecce Homo*. Trans. Walter Kaufmann. New York: Vintage, 1969.

Norberg, Kathryn. "The Libertine Whore: Prostitution in French Pornography from Margot to Juliette." *The Invention of Pornography*. Ed. Lynn Hunt. New York: Zone Books, 1993. 225–52.

Olalquiaga, Celeste. *Megalopolis: Contemporary Cultural Sensibilities*. Minneapolis, MN: University of Minnesota Press, 1992.

"100 Classic Album Covers." *Rolling Stone* (November 14, 1991): 97.

O'Neill, John. *Five Bodies: The Human Shape of Modern Society*. Ithaca, NY: Cornell University Press, 1985.

Paglia, Camille. *Sex, Art, and American Culture*. New York: Vintage, 1992.

Pareles, Jon. "Madonna's Return to Innocence." *New York Times* (October 23, 1994): Section 2, 1, 38.

Parisi, Peter. " 'Black Bart' Simpson: Appropriation and Revitalization." *Journal of Popular Culture* 27, No. 1 (Summer 1993): 125–42.

Patton, Cindy. "Embodying Subaltern Memory." *The Madonna Connection: Representational Politics, Subcultural Identities, and Cultural Theory*. Ed. Cathy Schwichtenberg. Boulder, CO: Westview Press, 1993. 81–105.

Patton, Paul. "Marxism and Beyond: Strategies of Reterritorialization." *Marxism and the Interpretation of Culture*. Ed. Cary Nelson and Lawrence Grossberg. Urbana, IL: University of Illinois Press, 1988. 123–39.

Pefanis, Julian. *Heterology and the Postmodern: Bataille, Baudrillard, and Lyotard*. Durham, NC: Duke University Press, 1991.

Petro, Patrice. "Modernity and Mass Culture in Weimar: Contours of a Discourse on Sexuality in Early Theories of Perception and Reception." *New German Critique* 40 (Spring 1987): 115–46.

"The Phallus." Special issue of *differences* 4, No. 1 (1992).

Pietz, William. "Fetishism and Materialism: The Limits of Theory in Marx." *Fetishism and Cultural Discourse*. Ed. Emily Apter and Pietz. Ithaca, NY: Cornell University Press, 1993. 119–51.

———. "The Problem of the Fetish, I." *Res* 9 (Spring 1985): 5–17.

———. "The Problem of the Fetish, II." *Res* 13 (Spring 1987): 23–45.

Plotnitsky, Arkady. *In the Shadow of Hegel: Complementarity, History, and the Unconscious*. Gainesville, FL: University Press of Florida, 1993.

———. *Reconfigurations: Critical Theory and General Economy*. Gainesville, FL: University Press of Florida, 1993.

Porter, Roy. "Baudrillard: History, Hysteria, and Consumption." *Forget Baudrillard?* Ed. Chris Rojek and Bryan S. Turner. London: Routledge, 1993. 1–21.

Press, Joy, and Simon Reynolds. *The Sex Revolts: Gender, Rebellion, and Rock 'n' Roll*. Cambridge, MA: Harvard University Press, 1995.

Queen, Carol A. "Talking about *Sex*." *Madonnarama*. Ed. Lisa Frank and Paul Smith. Pittsburgh, PA: Cleis Press, 1993. 139–52.

Richards, Thomas. *The Commodity Culture of Victorian England: Advertising and Spectacle, 1851–1914*. Stanford, CA: Stanford University Press, 1990.

Roberts, David. *Art and Enlightenment: Aesthetic Theory after Adorno*. Lincoln, NE: University of Nebraska Press, 1991.

Robertson, Pamela. "Does Feminist Camp Make a Difference?, or, What We Talk about When We Talk about Madonna." *Guilty Pleasures: Feminist Camp from Mae West to Madonna*. Durham, NC: Duke University Press, 1996. 115–38.

Robinson, Amy. "Is She or Isn't She?: Madonna and the Erotics of Appropriation." *Acting Out: Feminist Performances*. Ed. Lynda Hart and Peggy Phelan. Ann Arbor, MI: University of Michigan Press, 1993. 337–61.

Romney, Jonathan. "Access All Areas: The Real Space of the Rock Documentary." *Celluloid Jukebox: Popular Music and the Movies since the 50s*. Ed. Romney and Adrian Wootton. London: British Film Institute, 1995. 82–92.

Root, Deborah. *Cannibal Culture: Art, Appropriation, and the Commodification of Difference*. Boulder, CO: Westview, 1996.

Rose, Gillian. *The Melancholy Science: An Introduction to the Thought of Theodor W. Adorno*. New York: Columbia University Press, 1978.

Rose, Tricia. *Black Noise: Rap Music and Black Culture in Contemporary America*. Hanover, NH: University Press of New England, 1994.

Rose, Tricia, Manthia Diawara, Alexander Doty, Wahneema Lubiano, Andrew Ross, Ella Shohat, Lynn Spigel, Robert Stam, and Michelle Wallace. "A Symposium on Popular Culture and Political Correctness." *Social Text* 36 (Fall 1993): 16–22.

Ross, Andrew. *No Respect: Intellectuals and Popular Culture*. New York: Routledge, 1989.

———. "This Bridge Called My Pussy." *Madonnarama*. Ed. Lisa Frank and Paul Smith. Pittsburgh, PA: Cleis Press, 1993. 47–64.

Rubey, Dan. "Voguing at the Carnival: Desire and Pleasure on MTV." *Present Tense: Rock and Roll Culture*. Ed. Anthony De Curtis. Durham, NC: Duke University Press, 1992. 235–70.

Rushkoff, Douglas. *Media Virus: Hidden Agendas in Popular Culture*. New York: Ballantine, 1994.

Rylance, Rick. *Roland Barthes*. Hemel Hempstead, U.K.: Harvester Wheatsheaf, 1994.

Samois Collective, ed. *Coming to Power: Writings and Graphics on Lesbian S/M*. Boston: Alyson Publications, 1981.

Savage, Jon. *England's Dreaming: Anarchy, Sex Pistols, Punk Music, and Beyond*. New York: St. Martin's, 1992.

Savan, Leslie. "Desperately Selling Soda." *Sound and Vision*. Ed. Simon Frith, Andrew Goodwin, and Lawrence Grossberg. London: Routledge, 1993. 87–90.

Schifrin, Matthew, with Peter Newcomb. "A Brain for Sin and a Bod for Business." *Forbes* 146, No. 7 (October 1990): 162–66.

Schwartz, Deb. "Madonna and Sandra: Like We Care." *Desperately Seeking Madonna*. Ed. Adam Sexton. New York: Delta, 1993. 214–17.

Schwichtenberg, Cathy, ed. *The Madonna Connection: Representational Politics, Subcultural Identities, and Cultural Theory*. Boulder, CO: Westview Press, 1992.

Scott, Ronald B. "Images of Race and Religion in Madonna's Video *Like a Prayer*." *The Madonna Connection: Representational Politics, Subcultural Identities, and Cultural Theory*. Ed. Cathy Schwichtenberg. Boulder, CO: Westview Press, 1993. 57–77.

Shields, Rob, ed. *Lifestyle Shopping: The Subject of Consumption*. New York: Routledge, 1993.

Shuker, Roy. *Understanding Popular Music*. New York: Routledge, 1994.

Silverman, Kaja. *The Acoustic Mirror: The Female Voice in Psychoanalysis and Cinema*. Bloomington, IN: Indiana University Press, 1988.

Sklair, Leslie. *Sociology of the Global System*. Baltimore, MD: Johns Hopkins University Press, 1991.

Slusser, George. "Literary MTV." *Mississippi Review* 47/48 (1988): 279–88.

Smith, Anna Marie. " 'By Women, For Women and about Women' Rules OK?: The Impossibility of Visual Soliloquy." *A Queer Romance: Lesbians, Gay Men, and Popular Culture*. Ed. Paul Burston and Colin Richardson. London: Routledge, 1995. 199–215.

Smith, Paul. *Clint Eastwood: A Cultural Production*. Minneapolis, MN: University of Minnesota Press, 1994.

Spivak, Gayatri. "Can the Subaltern Speak?" *Marxism and the Interpretation of Culture*. Ed. Cary Nelson and Lawrence Grossberg. Urbana, IL: University of Illinois Press, 1988. 271–313.

———. *In Other Worlds*. New York: Methuen, 1987.

———. *Outside in the Teaching Machine*. New York: Routledge, 1993.

Staniszewski, Mary Ann. "Capital Pictures." *Post-Pop Art*. Ed. Paul Taylor. Cambridge, MA: MIT Press, 1989. 159–70.

Steele, Valerie. *Fetish: Fashion, Sex, and Power*. New York: Oxford University Press, 1996.

Stratton, Jon. *The Desirable Body: Cultural Fetishism and the Erotics of Consumption*. Manchester, UK: Manchester University Press, 1996.

Strinati, Dominic. *An Introduction to Theories of Popular Culture*. New York: Routledge, 1995.

Strossen, Nadine. *Defending Pornography: Free Speech, Sex, and the Fight for Women's Rights*. New York: Scribner's, 1995.

Studlar, Gaylyn. *In the Realm of Pleasure: Von Sternberg, Dietrich, and the Masochistic Aesthetic*. Urbana, IL: University of Illinois Press, 1988.

Subotnik, Rose Rosengard. *Developing Variations: Style and Ideology in Western Music*. Minneapolis, MN: University of Minnesota Press, 1991.

Taussig, Michael. *The Devil and Commodity Fetishism in South America*. Chapel Hill, NC: University of North Carolina Press, 1980.

Taylor, Paul, ed. *Post-Pop Art*. Cambridge, MA: MIT Press, 1989.

Teal, Laura. "The Hollow Women: Modernism, The Prostitute, and Commodity Aesthetics." *differences* 7, No. 3 (Fall 1995): 80–108.

Tester, Keith. *Media, Culture, and Morality*. New York: Routledge, 1994.

Thornton, Sarah. *Club Cultures: Music, Media, and Subcultural Capital.* Hanover, NH: University Press of New England, 1996.

Tippens, Elizabeth. "Mastering Madonna." *Rolling Stone* (September 17, 1992): 89, 111.

Tomlinson, John. *Cultural Imperialism: An Introduction.* Baltimore, MD: Johns Hopkins University Press, 1991.

Turner, Kay. *I Dream of Madonna.* San Francisco: Collins, 1993.

Urry, John. *Consuming Places.* New York: Routledge, 1995.

Varadharajan, Asha. *Exotic Parodies: Subjectivity in Adorno, Spivak, and Said.* Minneapolis, MN: University of Minnesota Press, 1995.

Veblen, Thorstein. *The Theory of the Leisure Class: An Economic Study of Institutions.* New York: Viking Press, 1965.

Vickers, Nancy J. "Maternalism and the Material Girl." *Embodied Voices: Representing Female Vocality in Western Culture.* Ed. Leslie C. Dunn and Nancy A. Jones. New York: Cambridge University Press, 1994. 230–46.

Viegener, Matias. " 'The Only Haircut That Makes Sense Anymore': Queer Subculture and Gay Resistance." *Queer Looks.* Ed. Martha Gever, et al. NY: Routledge, 1993. 116–33.

Waldby, Catherine. "Destruction: Boundary Erotics and Refigurations of the Heterosexual Male Body." *Sexy Bodies: The Strange Carnalities of Feminism.* Ed. Elizabeth Grosz and Elspeth Probyn. New York: Routledge, 1995. 266–77.

Walton, Jean. "Sandra Bernhard: Lesbian Postmodern or Madonna Postlesbian?" *The Lesbian Postmodern.* Ed. Laura Doan. New York: Columbia University Press, 1994. 244–61.

Warner, Michael. "Introduction." *Fear of a Queer Planet: Queer Politics and Social Theory.* Ed. Warner. Minneapolis, MN: University of Minnesota Press, 1993. vii–xxxi.

Watkins, Evan. *Work Time: English Departments and the Circulation of Cultural Value.* Stanford, CA: Stanford University Press, 1989.

West, Cornel. "Interview with Cornel West." Interviewed by Anders Stephanson. *Universal Abandon?: The Politics of Postmodernism.* Ed. Andrew Ross. Minneapolis, MN: University of Minnesota Press, 1988. 269–86.

———. "The New Cultural Politics of Difference." *The Cultural Studies Reader.* Ed. Simon During. New York: Routledge, 1993. 203–17.

Whitebook, Joel. *Perversion and Utopia: A Study in Psychoanalysis and Theory.* Cambridge, MA: MIT Press, 1995.

Wilke, Sabine. " 'Torn Halves of an Integral Freedom': Adorno's and Benjamin's Readings of Mass Culture." *The Aesthetics of the Critical Theorists.* Ed. Ronald Roblin. Lewiston, NY: Edwin Mellen Press, 1990. 124–46.

Williams, Chris. "The Quiet Riot Grrrl." *Entertainment Weekly* 318 (March 15, 1996): 31–33.

Williams, Linda. *Hard Core: Power, Pleasure, and the "Frenzy of the Visible".* Berkeley, CA: University of California Press, 1989.

Williams, Raymond. *Marxism and Literature.* New York: Oxford University Press, 1977.

Willis, Susan. *A Primer for Everyday Life.* New York: Routledge, 1991.

Wilson, Judith. "Getting Down to Get Over: Romare Bearden's Use of Pornography and the Problem of the Black Female Body in Afro-U.S. Art." *Black Popular Culture.* Ed. Gina Dent. Seattle: Bay Press, 1992. 112–22.

Wolin, Richard. *The Terms of Cultural Criticism.* New York: Columbia University Press, 1992.

Wood, Beatrice. *I Shock Myself: The Autobiography of Beatrice Wood.* San Francisco: Chronicle Books, 1988.

Young, Robert C. *Colonial Desire: Hybridity in Theory, Culture, and Race.* New York: Routledge, 1995.

———. "Decolonizing the Map." *The Post-Colonial Reader.* Ed. Bill Ashcroft, Gareth Griffiths, and Helen Tiffin. London: Routledge, 1995. 407–11.

Young, Shelagh. "Feminism and the Politics of Power: Whose Gaze Is It Anyway?" *The Female Gaze: Women as Viewers of Popular Culture.* Ed. Lorraine Gamman and Margaret Marshment. Seattle: Real Comet Press, 1989. 173–88.

Žižek, Slavoj. *For They Know Not What They Do.* London: Verso, 1991.

———. *Looking Awry: An Introduction to Jacques Lacan through Popular Culture.* Cambridge, MA: MIT Press, 1994.

———. *The Sublime Object of Ideology.* London: Verso, 1989.

———. *Tarrying with the Negative: Kant, Hegel, and the Critique of Ideology.* Durham: Duke University Press, 1993.

Zuidervaart, Lambert. *Adorno's Aesthetic Theory: The Redemption of Illusion.* Cambridge, MA: MIT Press, 1991.

Index

213